**London Borough of Hounslow**

Hounslow Library Services

Hounslow Library
CentreSpace
Treaty Centre
TW3 1ES
0845 456 2800

P10·L·2106

This item should be returned or renewed by the latest date shown. If it is not required by another reader, you may renew it in person or by telephone (twice only). Please quote your library card number. A charge will be made for items returned or renewed after the date due.

OM

8/10 MF				AIS
02				

IN PURSUIT OF STARDOM

LES NOMADES DU VELO ANGLAIS

Tony Hewson

In Pursuit of Stardom

First published in 2006 by:
Mousehold Press
Victoria Cottage
Constitution Opening
Norwich NR3 4BD

www.mousehold-press.co,uk

Reprinted 2006
Reprinted 2010

ISBN 978 1 874739 41 8

Printed by CLE Print, St Ives

In memory of
John Andrews,
Vic Sutton,
And my brother, John

Author's acknowledgements:
I would like to express my thanks for the help they have
given me to: Nev Barrett, Richard Bartrop, Ray Chandler,
Jean-Luc Desnos, Pascal Helion, Alan Huntington, Henri
Lumineau, Tom Mayfield, Peter McFarlane, Ray Minovi,
Dave Orford, Howard Peel, Norman Purdy, Peter Ryalls,
Shirley Sutton, Mick Ward, Ted Wren, Richard Yates.
And to Katie, whose patience has been tried.

'We live our lives forwards, but understand them backwards. So, in roving mind, may we be nomadic to the very end and, perhaps, who knows, beyond. Let nothing be lost, Sweet Self.'

PROLOGUE

I woke with a start and turned over in my bunk. I was frozen stiff. The February wind was blowing snowflakes through the open windows of the ambulance. I staggered up and slammed them shut. 'Idiots! Do you want us to freeze to death?' But the other snoring figures paid no heed to my words. It was cold. We were in Flanders. It was ice cold.

The story really begins a month before this in January 1958. Vic Sutton, Jock Andrews and I, Tony Hewson, three young men with little money and less experience but with one burning purpose, to seek adventure, to escape the humdrum life of the office or factory, to earn a living by bike racing on the Continent –
('Ice Cold in Flanders' – *Cycling and Mopeds*, March 18, 1959)

For aspiring roadmen, the 1950s were the best of times – and the worst. The Continent was an alluring blank page virtually unexplored by British racing cyclists, and those few that took the plunge enjoyed a rarity and curiosity value and often a warm welcome in the post-war afterglow of liberation from Nazi tyranny and before the gold rush of later decades. Yet it was by no means plain sailing. This largely forgotten tale is one of unremitting struggle to succeed against the odds, of hopes raised and dashed, triumphs mingled with farce.

Founded in 1942, the dynamic British League of Racing Cyclists had brought continental-style road racing to Britain in the face of virulent opposition from the cycling establishment whose Jeremiahs forecasted disaster. The Home Office would not tolerate racing on open roads, they said. There would follow a clampdown on all cyclists, not just the BLRC. But inside a decade they were proved wrong. By the 1950s, the gamble had paid off. Ian Steel's victory in the communist showcase Warsaw–Berlin–Prague brought both political and sporting prestige to the nation, and the commercially astute Lord Beaverbrook, no less, decided to use his *Daily Express* newspaper to promote a Tour of Britain. Soon Hercules Cycles were tilting at the Continent with a professional team based on the Riviera to contest the Tour de France, the Vuelta and the Classics. At home a full racing calendar grew up around the new category of semi-professionals known as independents. The trend seemed unstoppable. Suddenly, after fifty years of self-imposed semi-isolation, cycling here had come of age and was grabbing the headlines in a way it had never done before (and may never do again). Prime Minister Macmillan asserted, 'You've never had it so good!' He was speaking of the nation's growing prosperity and the end of wartime privations, but his words also rang true for cycling. Those were the days, my friend, those heady post-war optimistic days when anything seemed possible. Just wait, we would beat those continentals at their own game and then the great British public would elevate cycling beside football into the pantheon of sports.

Alas though, it was not to be. As the 'upstart' BLRC and the conservative National Cyclists Union and Road Times Trial Council wrangled on, newspaper tycoon Beaverbrook lost patience and pulled the plug on the British Tour, whilst financially-stretched Hercules abandoned their European adventure. Suddenly, it was back to the doldrums for our incipient professional class. We had hoped for a career debut in Britain, but it was now checked, and so we turned our gaze across the Channel to where the sport was, as ever, thriving.

But where to begin and how? There was no route map for us to follow. The only guiding light was French-based Brian Robinson, his success acquired on the back of the Hercules venture, salaried, all expenses paid. No other cycle manufacturer was now in a rush to repeat that costly failed experiment and French clubs had no tradition for welcoming guest-riders *d'Outre-Manche*. We were on our own. To penetrate the charmed ring of the professional road-racing circus abroad, we had to start from the bottom up, a tough DIY trail-blazing exercise.

So there we were, three youngsters, talented and ambitious but without backup – no equivalent to the present-day World Class Performance Plan or Dave Rayner Fund, no contract, salary, agent or cash sponsor, no doctor, soigneur, masseur, mechanic, coach (or even sports psychologist!) and at first living out of a converted ex-WD ambulance – entirely reliant upon ourselves and ignorant of how best to proceed other than by suck-it-and-see. Our palmarés, – I was a former Tour of Britain winner and national champion – counted for little abroad and our subsistence-level living would be grafted primarily from prize money. It was to be no holiday jaunt. Committed for the long term, we gambled on dogged perseverance providing the breakthrough: we would race and learn and one fine day catch the eye of some top *directeur sportif* – perhaps of Mercier, Peugeot or Helyett-Leroux – and like Robinson and Irishman Shay Elliott be offered professional contracts, the first rung on the ladder to financial security and possibly stardom. That was our dream. The attraction lay partly in its exciting unpredictability.

And what of our preferred destination, France? Despite being our ally in two world wars, France, to the average Briton, remained a mysterious and deeply foreign country to be approached with caution. Today's mass urge to holiday and settle there was far off in the future. Go beyond wartime associations with Dunkirk, Picardy and the Somme or the louchness of 'gay Paris', mention *la France profonde* of the Dordogne, Ardeche, Correze, Luberon or Charente, the stuff now of TV's 'A Place in the Sun', and jaws would drop. Might as well talk of Timbuctoo. In the staid Britain of the 1950s, a reputation for dodgy plumbing, risqué sex and chronic political instability, not to mention food and wine foppishness, all fomented this image of our 'queer neighbour over the water'. The extreme French passion verging on mental disorder for bike racing, by comparison a relatively insignificant cloth-cap sport in John Bull's island, simply added to the queerness that, apparently, infected most aspects of French life. Why would any sane Briton go to live there, for whatever reason? France was a total mess. Before my departure, non-cycling neighbours would half jest, 'That ambulance – trust you've got the men with white coats and straight jackets to go with it?'

Abroad our ambitions were also met with raised eyebrows. Eventual success focussed attention on our itinerant life-style, best expressed in *Miroir Sprint*'s headline '*Les Nomades du Velo Anglais*', and our peculiar desire to become racing cyclists in the French mode – puzzlingly deviant for many cognescenti convinced that the funereal time trial at dawn, however comically perverse and Corinthian hair-shirtish, was surely our true cup of eccentric British tea. Our perceived national characteristics of stiff upper lip, sang-froid and low cunning, perfectly suited the dull and devious game of cricket, but hardly the passionate hurly-burly of the professional bike race. So what were we up to, they mused, *ces Anglais*, defying convention by travelling in this rather squalid old ambulance, living like gypsies and yet challenging in a sport that defined the very art of being French? They hardly knew what to make of us.

Following its wartime defeat and Nazi occupation, and further humiliation in 1954 by the Vietnam People's Liberation Army at Dien Bien Phu, France lay under a post-war cloud. It was in slow, bloody retreat from Algeria. We caught it on the cusp of change, just as its primary role in the formation of the EU and abandonment of pretensions to Empire would begin to turn it into a confident forward-looking nation at the heart of Europe. Post-war impoverished France was starting on the long road to modernisation, but its cycling superstars still enjoyed that god-like image of former years, unsullied by later drugs scandals and the merciless intimacy of TV journalism. It was velo sport's Golden Age of Innocence.

And so we prospected the trail for Simpson and subsequent generations of British cyclists who have since sought careers abroad. What we lacked in material resources we made up for in self-belief, determination, the optimism of youth and a yearning for adventure. It was an undertaking of life-transforming dimensions, and for me as much a journey of mind and spirit as of body, a quest for the self. Like France, I would undergo radical transformation. Alongside this story of cycling exploits runs a parallel tale of growing up and growing beyond.

1

'They're very versatile are these ambulances.'

On the sprawling Sheffield council estate where I was raised in the 1930s and 40s, car owners were as rare as hens' teeth. Motoring was purely the preserve of the posh. Ordinary folk like me travelled by public transport, biked or walked. Then in the 1950s, as rationing ended and wage packets swelled, people began to aspire towards the convenience, speed and personal space of motor vehicle ownership. That glossy new showroom model was as yet beyond their means, but there were old bangers aplenty that had survived the war, with leaky mis-timed engines and dodgy brakes, and to meet demand, secondhand car dealers began popping up al fresco like willowherb, on wasteland and gappy bombsites all over the city. In December 1957 I visited each in turn in my search for our ideal mobile home. But it proved harder than I had imagined. Size mattered. Indeed, was crucial. There were lots of furniture vans, cavernous petrol-gobbling wastes of space, and many small delivery vans with little or no headroom. But the ideal in-betweens were in short supply, and I had almost given up hope when a fresh newspaper advertisement caught my eye: 'Ex-army ambulances in tip-top condition, regularly serviced, ideal for conversion.' Ideal for conversion, eh? They were sited at a breaker's yard near Chesterfield. I caught the next bus out.

Side-stepping rainbow-streaked potholes and piled-up wrecks, I approach this ramshackle cabin of an office. A malodorous whiff of toasting tyres assaults my nostrils. The smoke puts me in mind of a battlefield, and as the association of army ambulances with blood and guts is best forgotten, I try to focus on the homelier prospects of my mission – comfy bunks, space just enough to swing a cat, and a compact little kitchen smelling of new-baked bread and piping hot stew. Ah, Bisto! That vision of ordered domesticity that all we bike racers yearn to return to from battling the road.

A duffel-coated arm is wiping condensation from the office window and beckoning me inside. Ambulances? While the dealer makes an impressive show of thumbing through his scabby grease-stained ledger I take stock of surroundings. Weird! Occupying a whole wall is a shelf of battered pith helmets above a crudely painted shield, crossed plywood spears and, for good measure, an old framed lithograph of fixed-bayonet redcoats drawn up in battle square. Underneath, the legend reads: 'Square Deal from Kitchener'. Ha, ha!

He offers me a helmet to try on. I politely decline. So he pops it onto his own head and folds up his fatty hound's face into a grinning explanation. Of course, it's just a gimmick. Good one though and just the ticket for an aspiring businessman. His has real provenance too. Victorian parents christened him Kitchener after the noble Lord K who wopped the fuzzy-wuzzies at the Battle of Omdurman, 1891. Kitchener. Desert. Pith helmets. Get it?

'Anyway,' he laughs conducting me outside and pointing up at the overcast sky, 'stops me from catching sunstroke.' I wonder is he taking the pith? All this crackpot absurdity puts me on guard. What next – a slap on the back with Gordon of Khartoum's fly swat?

The four identical battle-grey ambulances are backed up to a leaning fence. Job lot, he says, much too good to scrap. At first view I can see no signs of the rust Jock has warned me against. Jock, our hands-on motoring expert, services his dad's car and by rights should be here doing the buying, but he resides far off in South London, where, so he asserts, 'car dealers are all crooks'. We'll buy cheaper and better 'up North', he reckons, *chez moi*, even though I'm a mechanical ignoramus who's only just passed his driving test.

Kitchener leaps up high onto a bonnet and with his toe-rag of a sleeve wipes the accumulated grime off a rectangular box above the windscreen. The word AMBULANCE appears in large red capitals through the glass. He jumps down and, by way of further inspiring my confidence, flicks the headlights on and off.

'Good solid vehicles. They make wonderful mobile retail outlets. Are you in the groceries line by any chance?'

'No, bicycles.'

'Well, yes, even bicycles, retail or wholesale. They're very versatile are these ambulances.'

Should I mention our plan to convert one into a mobile home and drive it round the Continent? The film 'Ice Cold in Alex' with John Mills, featuring an ambulance escaping Rommel's *Wermacht* in the Western Desert, is trailing in the cinemas. It possesses an aura of improbable romance. Given his penchant for theatrical dressing up, he might cash in with some tall yarn about this being its twin and advancing with Monty through Egypt, Libya and into Europe on D Day, joke about it already knowing its way through France. I decide not to give him the chance.

Instead I demonstrate my own expertise by going round kicking tyres, all sixteen, and trying to bounce the springs. He ripostes by starting up an engine. The cab shakes and his helmet tips ludicrously over his eyes. He takes it off and smooths his thinning hair. 'Any test,' he offers, tapping the speedometer. 'See, low mileage.' It never occurs to me to think it might be 'clocked'.

I walk around the back and open up the double doors. There's a pull-down step. I clamber in and splay my feet against the shuddering. A solid partition with a small window and an overhead light separates me from the cab. The internal space looks ideal for our purpose, about nine feet by five, enough for four bunks and a fold-up table. The long roof would accept a big rack for all our bikes and spares.

He is behind me, watching. 'Ninety quid,' he shouts, 'and you can take your pick.'

This is the most important purchase of my young life. I face up to the ranked vehicles and dither. Eeny-meeny-miny-mo – I opt for the one I first inspected, though by now he has all four engines running and all doors flung open.

'Sixty!' I yell over the throbbing of a hundred and twenty-four horsepower. Five months of working on the knocker as a door-to-door salesman has given me a brassy edge. He looks somewhat hurt and staring into the middle distance replaces his helmet as if advancing enemy hordes threaten his prosperity.

'Blimey, is it Christmas already? Go on, mate, eighty quid. It's a gift.'

Suddenly he's slipped into an accent that's nearer Watford than Derby. Jock hasn't allowed for a Southerner masquerading up here in sheep's clothing.

'Seventy!'

'Seventy five!'

Done. We shake hands.

Two days later I'm back with insurance documents and a fistful of readies to clinch the deal.

'I assume you're acquainted with the crash gearbox, squire?'

The what gearbox? Jock didn't mention any crash gearbox and I haven't a clue what he's talking about.

He takes me for a demonstration drive on the cinder path past the stacked wrecks. Every time he changes gear, there's a pause for thought before he rams the stick home. Sometimes his left foot does a little jig on the clutch. But I can't hear any crashing.

He stops and jumps down. I slide over into the driving seat.

'There you are. Nothing to it, like falling off a log.' It occurs to me that falling off a log can be unpredictable and painful. Is that what he means?

'Just remember it's not synchromesh and you'll be fine. Listen to those engine revs and give it space to change. Oh, and be careful how you exit.' He waves me off.

Exit? That sounds doubly ominous. Quivering slightly, I pull away in first gear and attempt to change up. But the gear-stick won't budge beyond neutral and there's an ear-splitting noise like some hellish collision of planets. My hand vibrates as if I'm strapped into the electric chair. The vehicle rolls to a halt. Through the mirror I observe Kitchener in rapid retreat to his cabin. Suddenly I panic as I realise I'm on my own with a beast I can't control, and only male pride stops me shouting, 'Lend us one of yer 'elmets, mate!'

Yes, I've passed my test all right, but in the driving school's sweet little Baby Austin with its hand-glide synchromesh gearbox. This is different. Commercial vehicles have this non-synchro or aptly named 'crash' gearbox, and fumbling a gear change is like trying to force a chisel into the jaws of a high-speed lathe. The mental image is of flying shrapnel. I wince and duck a slow passage down the main road with an ever-lengthening queue of frustrated drivers behind close to ramming me. At every crunch, pedestrians quake with shock and dogs run for cover. I'm dreading crowded Sheffield city centre traffic, but somehow I get through. By listening to the engine revolutions, as Kitchener advised, I gradually acquire the knack of smooth propulsion, which is to match engine speed to wheel/gearbox speed. Going up, you pause for the engine to slow; coming down, you have to double declutch and rev up to the speed of the lower gear – all guess-work until practice makes perfect – rather like learning to ride a bicycle.

'Jock, I've got us one of those ambulances.' I was speaking from a call box. Jock's parents were posh – they possessed a home phone.

As we chatted, I was aware of a buzz of excitement in our voices. This was the first practical step towards making a dream come true. Purchasing that vehicle was a commitment each to each, and everything we did from now on would make it harder to pull out.

'Do you reckon Vic can really do the carpentry bit?'

'I've got his word for it. He tells me he used to be a boat-builder.'

'Boat builder, eh? Noah Sutton? Well, he's got six weeks to build us an ark. Then we're off to the sunny Côte d'Azur. And for me to make those mattresses, I'll need the exact dimensions of the bunks. Pronto. So tell him to get his finger out.'

Jock was a bit sniffy about Vic. Jock and I were old cronies, Vic an unknown quantity. All we knew was he held a first-category racing licence, had done well in a couple of good local races and had a reputation as a climber, surprisingly, since he lived in pancake-flat Thorne. He had contacted Jock at a race the previous summer, asking to be included in our enterprise. We consulted and decided the more the merrier to keep costs low. But how would he fare abroad, racing against the world's best? We both knew from experience what a tough cut-throat school that was, a far cry from slower-paced Britain.

'This ambulance, it's got a crash gearbox,' I remarked casually.

'No problem. I learned to drive on army trucks.'

So that was our team: boat-builder Vic, upholsterer and car buff Jock, cack-hand me. Costly screwdrivers and honed chisels alike – in my hands they were all implements for a good bashing with a club hammer. As for spanners – well, I was known as Pliars-Fix-It Hewson. But I had my uses. I pushed a good Civil Service pen and was appointed clerk of works, liaison officer, route-planner, ferry-booker. My job also entailed keeping a beady eye on accounts – we were on a tight budget and couldn't afford to overspend. Into the bargain, I was interpreter, the only one of us to speak good French.

At the first opportunity I drove the ambulance north, to where Vic resided on a council estate in Thorne. We'd only been in contact by correspondence and my first impression was of a small, lightly built, blond-haired guy that a strong puff of wind might blow away. He seemed nervous, a bit cagey. This reticence evaporated as we studied his sketch plan inspired by the contents of my letter. He proposed to plywood the interior to improve insulation and prevent condensation, something I would never have thought of. I was even more impressed as he enthused about folding bunk beds that would double as banquettes, a collapsible space-saving gate-leg table and a compartment kitchenette. It looked like a marvellously economic allocation of our incredibly meagre space. He might not be Chippendale, I thought, but he certainly knows his trade.

'Cost?'

'Around fifteen quid for materials.'

'How long will it take?' I knew he was still in full-time work, saving up for the trip.

He did a swift calculation.

'Three bunks, a table, panelling, a kitchenette – five to six weekends and the odd evening. I can't promise miracles, though.'

'Four bunks,' I said, 'not three. Didn't Jock tell you we've got this guy from Brighton coming along for the ride, name of Derek Cover? He was in the South of France with Jock and me last year. He's a good bloke.'

Vic looked uncertain. Maybe he was offended at not being consulted, or thinking three egos in such narrow confines would be touch and go, but four impossible.

'He really is OK, a good laugh. He doesn't race over there, just poodles around and laps up the sun. He's one of those people with an ideal job, something to do with contract work on power stations. He picks it up and lets it go, free and easy.' I was trying to sound reassuring.

We had tea and Vic conducted me outside. Now it was my turn to need reassurance. Over-weight and grossly unfit, I had hardly touched my bike in six months and had a thirty-mile ride in the dark ahead of me. Testing my flabby muscles against all those bronzed aces racing early season on the Côte d'Azur suddenly seemed foolhardy.

As Vic waved me off, I realised I still knew next to nothing about him. Unlike my buddy Jock, he was a mystery man. I'd never even witnessed him astride a crossbar, much less turning a pedal in anger. He was terrifyingly inexperienced and I gave him two months. It remained to be seen how we would all get on together, when the going got tough.

2

'Of course, you realise this is a serious and irredeemable step.'

Jock *was* my buddy; we already had history. Over the years our respect for one another had grown, and the ambulance venture wasn't our first stab at continental racing. We had already gone through one baptism of fire on the Continent during the spring of 1957, and the idea of the ambulance had grown out of the lessons of that experience.

As I cycled home across featureless Thorne Waste on that night in December 1957, I reviewed the events that had brought us together, rewinding the clock back more than two years to the 1955 Tour of Britain and four weeks previous to that, the BLRC National Road Race Championship. The Tour made our reputations, he as a stage winner and I as the overall victor. In the breakaway on the long 157 miles stage from Sheffield to Phwelli, during which I assumed race leadership, I pipped him to a Welsh mountain prime – by inches. Ordinarily, the better sprinter, he should have won, but desperation for the time bonus helped me to take him on the line. I possessed stamina and guile; he was someone who, on his day, could run 'Iron Man' Bedwell close in the sprint, not to mention, as we later discovered, the best sprinter-roadmen in Europe.

He possessed outstanding qualities as a roadman, but I confess I had never even heard the name Andrews until that Championship of August 1955 on the notorious Handleys circuit. Middle and Nether Handley were hamlets in the foothills of the Derbyshire Peaks and around them ran this tough figure of eight course. We were to cover twelve laps, 110 miles in all, with each lap two stiff climbs – Springwell 1-in-12 and Troway 1-in-6. The Handleys was a favourite racing venue and I knew it well, since it was here in 1951, against all odds, that I out-sprinted the favourites, Derby's Arnold Parr, and Tynesider Don Sanderson, from a six-strong group to become BLRC National Junior Champion. Today was the senior title and I fancied my chances again – or rather our chances. Falcon Road Club team-mate Dick Bartrop and I were working together to bring the title to Sheffield and our confidence was high. We were both approaching peak fitness out of the recently completed seven-stage Amateur Circuit of Britain and looking towards the Tour of Britain, where we would dominate over Hercules and the other trade teams.

It was a hot August day of melting tarmac when the soon-to-be-famous Jimmy 'The Duke' Savile, commentating, set us on our way. When two riders attacked early, with 90 miles to go, it seemed a bold act of lunacy and we gave them no hope. One was probably the best amateur in Britain, Des Robinson, brother of Brian and recent overall winner of that Circuit of Britain, the other an unknown sucked-in cheeks southerner, who we thought was in for a big shock – the heat, incessant hills and fiery Robinson would soon shake him back into the peloton. Then we would hang Robbo out to dry and pick him off at our leisure.

That was the theory. But Dick and I were the shocked ones. Nothing went to plan. By halfway the duo's lead was three minutes and they showed no sign of cracking. We attacked together and we attacked singly, all in vain: the increasingly exhausted bunch sat on our wheels and refused to help. We had badly miscalculated the combined strength and determination of these two. The hilly circuit of tall-hedged lanes doubled and twisted, keeping them from view, their invisibility putting us at a profound psychological disadvantage.

Eventually, Gil Taylor, the Birmingham Premier star, broke clear and a lap or two later I managed to follow. That was how it ended: Robinson winning the sprint on the cinders at Staveley track, Gil third, with me fourth and Dick fifth.

I approached the gaunt figure stretched out on the grass, sipping his bottle. 'I'm sorry,' I said, 'but I don't know your name.'

'John Andrews,' he said. 'They call me Jock, God knows why!' We shook hands. He looked utterly exhausted, his eyes pinched from five hours staring at the bright landscape, flecks of dried salt around his lips and chin.

'I counted all those bloomin' hills – twenty four up and twenty four down. We were zigzagging towards the end. I didn't intend to break that early, but I'm glad now I did.'

That was typical of Jock, to chance his luck and see what happened. He would never be fazed by the strength of any opposition.

*Tour of Britain, 1955: for once outsprinting Jock Andrews for a prime
in the Welsh mountains.*

After the TOB, Jock and I often competed together and began staying
at each other's homes for a change of scenery. Our backgrounds
were chalk and cheese. I lived with my parents in a spartan Sheffield
council house and had been a scholarship boy at the local Catholic
grammar school. Jock's parents were house-owners in affluent
Tolworth, South London; they were a two-income family – his father
a manager for a grocery chain and mother working in the rag trade
– and he had been educated privately. They had possessions I could
only dream about: wall-to-wall carpets, a telephone, refrigerator,
motor car. After a long training ride over the Epsom Downs and
Bluebell Hill, we would stretch out in their comfortable lounge with
copies of *But et Club* and *Le Miroir Sprint* and background music
from the record player: Billie Holiday, Miles Davis, Charlie Mingus,
Lester Young, the MJQ, Peggy Lee and Frank Sinatra. In common
with many BLRC riders, we were jazz and blues sophisticates. The
music was uplifting, but discussion of the cycling scene only plunged
us into gloom. We felt we were stuck in a sort of no-man's land with
little hope of progress.

We were both strong elite riders and ambitious to test ourselves to
the limit, but how could we progress? The 1955 Tour, sponsored one-

off by Butlins Holiday Camps, had been the BLRC's last desperate throw to keep the flagship race afloat after the *Daily Express* pulled out. Now the home professional class was in free-fall. It would take the enterprising Dave Orford to come to the rescue by introducing *extra-sportif* team sponsors (most famously Ovaltine and the Milk Marketing Board) and a pro-Independent Riders Association. But all through 1956 we felt we were treading water. Sometimes we were forced to travel to the far ends of the country for a half-decent race. We were getting nowhere fast. At twenty-two, each year wasted was another year out of a traditionally short career in a sport where you were considered to have peaked at twenty-eight. Only six years left! Like Brian Robinson, we wanted to be a part of the real action, not stuck in timewarp Britain. But how? There was no Hercules to give us a leg up.

Then we had a stroke of luck. The elite, a circus of maybe sixty top independents and amateurs, regularly met up at races across the country. Chatting at one of these venues with Gil Taylor, Jock and I learned he was planning an early season training trip to the Côte d'Azur, prompted by the previous year's experience of a roving Brighton bikie called Derek Cover. Though winter training camps in the sun are now commonplace, such ventures were unheard of in 1950s Britain. For Gil and Derek, it was a chance to avoid the worst of winter, pile up some training miles and observe the continental aces at close hand, an extended holiday. But for Jock and me it meant much more. We saw it as a chance to use the promising contacts Derek had made with Nice cycle manufacturer *Urago Frères* to escape the British impasse and make our entrée into French professional cycling. We would gamble on giving up our jobs and establishing ourselves over there – permanently, as we hoped.

For me that wasn't a snap decision. Jobs then tended to be for life and I thought hard before abandoning mine for a shot in the dark. In any case, it wasn't a job, but a 'career'. I had joined the Civil Service at 17, straight from school, precisely because it sounded like the sort of undemanding, ambitionless sit-down occupation that would allow me free reign in my spare time to pursue my real ambition of becoming an amateur cycling star. It was a safe move my parents approved: they didn't trust the post-war boom to last, fearing a return to the dole queues and poverty of the 1930s when there was nothing more secure than being in government employ. My ill-paid post with the National Assistance Board (now DSS) was acquired by passing thirteenth from thousands in a competitive nationwide examination at almost A Level standard, and what had been acquired with such great effort wasn't to be thoughtlessly tossed aside. Once out, there was no way back. Moreover, it was an interesting job: I wasn't office-bound, but roamed the city and its environs dispensing state benefits to a wide variety of intriguing people – lonely pensioners with stories to tell, penniless former aristocrats, crooks just out of gaol, tramps in greasy Dickensian doss houses. Even for a working class youngster, it was a fascinating eye-opener to the seamy side of life.

I dithered over abandoning this safe refuge for a gamble on bike racing, and, strangely, it was a colleague at work in the end who helped me make up my mind. They were mostly in the stuffy older age bracket, my colleagues, committed to families and mortgages, and we shared little in common. But young Jack, a temporary clerk, fresh out of the merchant navy with a free spirit and roving eye, was different. We occasionally met up of an evening in the city's dance halls and pubs and he would mercilessly satirise the staid denizens of the office. But he also had a serious side, and it was Jack who re-introduced me to books and reading.

As a sickly child, reading was my supreme pleasure. From an early age my mother would read me bedtime stories from *Grimm's Fairy Tales* of witches and monsters, poor lost children and wicked stepmothers – as a virtual orphan herself she knew all about those. At the very first opportunity, aged seven, she subscribed me to Sheffield Junior Library and launched me out to read alone. It was my birthday and a most wonderful gift, an 'Open Sesame' in the pre-television era to far-flung worlds of the imagination. I devoured books – not just stories, but history, nature and real-life adventure. I soon associated reading with happiness and, because of my mother's influence, ultimate comfort and love. However, a stifling blinkered, academic education at grammar school and my teenage passion for sport all but squeezed everything else out and I hadn't read seriously for years – that is until I met Jack.

Jack's favourite authors were men's men with a zest for adventure, travel and living life on the edge: Steinbeck, Hemingway and Negley Farson. 'You should read them,' he said. 'They're inspirational.' He was right. One book especially, *Danger My Ally* by the explorer F.A. Mitchell-Hedge, so gripped my imagination, summarising what I thought should be my own red-blooded attitude to life, that I copied an extract and saved it in my wallet, where it remained for years, like a compass to guide me on the true path, as I then believed.

When you are young and strong and full of hope, sit down one day and think about the world. Decide what you would like to do above all else – and then go and do it. Follow your star to the bitter end, no matter what the hazards or the perils: no matter even if the star proves to be a false guide and you die in the attempt. You will have lived life to the full. You will have enjoyed yourself and, even if you leave behind no material treasure, you will leave riches in the hearts of those who have known strength from your strength and who will cherish your memory until their day is done.

Shades of our derring-do Empire! Well, wasn't I young and strong and full of hope? Maybe I couldn't round the Horn in a windjammer or slash my way through Amazonian jungles, but I could throw my hat into the ring of professional cycling. What was the alternative: remain in Britain and stagnate? I decided to hand in my resignation and follow my star to see where it led.

With Falcon Road Club member Dave Midgley, I cycled to Gil's home in Birmingham to make our final arrangements. Gil, his club-mate Graham, and Derek Cover would form an advance party to arrange accommodation and reconnoitre Nice. Dave and I would follow a week later, and later still, Jock, who needed more time to work and raise funds.

As Christmas approached, it only remained to give my employer the statutory four weeks' notice. I felt apprehensive. I had discussed my intentions with no one at the office, not even Jack, and it would come as a shock to all concerned. Civil servants rarely resigned; they died biro in hand. I slipped a note into the boss's in-tray, hoping to pass it all off with as little fuss as possible, but within the hour I was summoned upstairs. He sat behind his ordered desk, crowned with photographs of himself in Baden Powell regalia – he was some sort of high official in the Boy Scouts movement. Baldpate gleaming in a sunbeam, he was reading my letter with the concentration one might accord to a message in code. He was visibly put out: 'Of course, you realise this is a serious and irredeemable step. Once you have resigned, the Service can never re-admit you. You will

22

have burned your boats. I trust you have given the matter mature consideration?'

I nodded.

'Very well. I shall keep this letter for three days before submitting it to Head Office. If you change your mind, let me know at once.'

I think he was genuinely saddened. No doubt he had taken vicarious pleasure from his association with my cycling exploits. He had had me write about my trip behind the Iron Curtain to the Peace Race and my victory in the Tour of Britain for a Civil Service magazine. All managers burnished the office image to impress the powers on high. It must have been like parting with a trophy from his display case.

Those three days ticked by without a change of mind. Then I received a curt official acknowledgment of my resignation, and a reminder that I had signed the Official Secrets Act. I was ordered to return, amongst other things, my rubberised waterproof visiting-officer's raincoat and standard issue ballpoint pen. I had, indeed, burned my boats.

Winning the National Junior Championships at Chesterfield, 22nd July 1951 from Arnie Parr (Derby Halcyon) and Tynesider Don Sanderson.

3

'As for this,' tapping his suitcase, 'no room for my suit because it's stuffed with your blooming Shreddies.'

For Dave and me, it was our first time in France and all new and exciting from the moment our precious bikes were craned unceremoniously aboard the Dover ferry within a net of trunks and suitcases clattering down into the hold. From Paris Gare de Lyon, on the overnight train to Nice, our packed compartment of uniformed servicemen and habited nuns smelled authentically French – Gitanes, eau de cologne, wine, cheese and garlicky belches. We dozed fitfully as the electric engine whisked us south through the night into a dawn of red cliffs, pine trees and lapis lazuli sea. Oh, the purity of light far from smog-bound England! Fire flashed on the water from a sun peeping up beside snow-capped mountains, its splendour dispelling any secretly harboured doubts from my mind. The Alps and Côte d'Azur, just as I had dreamed! But this was only the start. Now it was up to me.

Gil, Graham and Derek had rented a small one-room apartment near the city centre, with shared bathroom ('Bathing only by arrangement with the establishment, giving 24 hours' notice!'). As we had two double beds for five bodies, it seemed sleeping was likewise by arrangement only. When I suggested to Gil that, bed-wise, his maths didn't add up, he countered with a reversal of that old Jewish tailor's joke: 'Never mind the width, look at the quality.' But the quality wasn't impressive either: the mattresses sagged to the centre.

'It'll bring us all to a closer understanding,' Gil joked. There was no homosexual undertone then when men routinely shared a bed and thought nothing of it. But from the start a zany sense of humour informed our companionship.

Nice was an ideal winter training venue. Sheltered from the Mistral by mountains, it enjoyed a sunny temperate climate. There was a choice of the flat, coastal highway towards Cannes, the three Corniches towards Italy, or the mountain passes, which elevated you, gasping, to the snow line. Traffic was light, even on the coast, and you could cycle comfortably two or three abreast. We saw many groups of plus-foured professionals out training, sleek in sunglasses and caps, zipping through the ozone haze. Some even condescended to glance our way, puzzled at our profoundly non-chic attire of bargain-basement windcheaters and slacks strapped up below the knee. Any acknowledgment of brotherhood had us in raptures. These were the real thing, real French *coureurs*. This was the Côte d'Azur, *the* place to be, and we were there.

Our favourite rides were via the Corniches. The undulating Petite Corniche, near sea-level, was the easy option, the Moyenne middling difficult. But the Grande Corniche, steepling to over 1,700 feet, really brought your breakfast up. It had been hacked from the mountainside by Napoleon's engineers, superfluously, I concluded, since the two lower routes were already more than adequate for the *Grande Armee* to practise pincer movements into Italy. Here we fantasised, dancing on the pedals like Dotto, or dropping nose-to-tyre, like Gem, swooping into Monaco where decorous white-gloved traffic cops, perched on their tiny concrete islands, waved us through the junctions like royalty.

Unlike my companions, I wasn't here on holiday. I needed to race and earn some cash. For once, I was in good health and determined to make the most of it. Derek's contact, *Urago Frères,* owned a cycle shop and small factory on Boulevard de Riquier and exported their frames into 50s Britain. Anglophile Madamoiselle Urago proved invaluable in providing me with information and entering me for races.

I knew I was in for a tough apprenticeship. The 1956 Warsaw–Berlin–Prague had given me some insight into racing inside a big fast-moving peloton, but now I was amongst the professionals and feeling even more like a new boy at school. Two races in particular exercised my concentration. The 125-mile Genoa–Nice was a mini Milan–San Remo, covering part of the same course, hugging the coastline. Thanks to the Uragos, Dave and I secured hotel and rail expenses to join the vast bunch that poured out of Genoa on March 2nd. I never even came close to seeing the front as this frenzied mob of two-wheeled humanity swept onwards and over the border into Menton. Ahead lay a big prime prize in Monaco and the slopes of La Turbie on the Grande Corniche, where, up front, the real battle would be joined.

The pace intensified until I was twirling in top gear, when suddenly the rider ahead switched. My wheel thwacked something solid and I became airborne, plunging with an almighty spoke-twanging crash. Somehow I clung to the handlebars. I'd impacted one of those small bowl-shaped concrete traffic podiums, normally policed but today vacant. No policeman with half a brain would risk exposing himself to cycling's version of the Pamplona bull-run. There was rolling road closure, but, for the rest, racers were expected to look out for themselves. With my race over, I bumped to Nice to finish 80th on a flattened front rim and learn that Bobet had won in the sprint from Anquetil. Bobet and Anquetil! Heavens above, I really was in amongst the aces.

Next day came the classic Nice–Mont Agel hill climb. The roll of honour included Henri Pelissier and Vietto from the 1920s and 30s and more recently Bahamontes and Dotto. This hill climb was no sprint up a short steep hill, but a rolling massed start out of Nice, with fourteen miles of scrapping for position along the Petite Corniche. In Monaco, a narrow orange-roofed back street squeezed the bunch onto the pavement before tilting us heavenwards to Mont Agel, cue for diminutive Spanish climber Gil, already two-times winner, to thrust his elfin arse from the saddle and storm out of sight up innumerable steep *lacets* en route to his hat trick.

Slogging up this minor col in 21st position through clapping onlookers, I caught up with him at the summit – already track-suited and chatting to journalists, looking mildly refreshed by his exertions. Awaiting Dave's arrival, I sought protection from the Mistral's icy blast behind the windmill-shaped observatory. At over 3,000 feet, a stunning panorama stretched ahead across the shimmering Mediterranean towards Corsica and behind to the snowy Alps. There was no baggage van and we had no helpers with extra clothing, making the descent a worse ordeal than the climb. The wind ripped through our sweat-soaked racing jerseys, and despite doing bit and bit back to Nice we shook with cold.

Gil and his party returned to England, and Derek and I set about finding a cheaper apartment outside of Nice. It was a long way outside, 15 miles northwest in the tiny hamlet of Peymeinade, near Grasse, and primitive – just a two-room concrete-floored cell with sticks of rickety furniture, shagged-out mattresses and dodgy, unearthed metal switches, which on damp evenings provided flickering light and buzzed menacingly. After suffering a shock that knocked me to the floor, we poked them on and off with a garden stick. Cold water was through a plastic pipe from an outside tap, and there was no heating stove. Fortunately for our health, the weather was warm by day, whilst at night we were to bed early. On the plus side, the rent was a fraction of those in fashionable Nice, and we saved on bus fares by cycling to our new residence carrying our suitcases on the handlebars.

Derek wasn't interested in racing and I could hardly wait for Jock's arrival. We had kept in touch by letter, and the day came when Derek and I rode out towards Cannes station to meet him. A distant figure appeared bobbing uphill towards us, grasping a bulky suitcase flat to the handlebars. But what on earth! He was wearing an outfit purchased for his sister's wedding: formal grey pin-stripe suit, polished black leather shoes, white shirt with collar and tie. Swarthy vest-clad peasants everywhere were tilling the rich red earth, whilst this apparition of an etiolated, office-garbed City gent looked as if it had just emerged from the rush-hour Tube on a stripped-down racing bicycle. It was Daliesque.

'What are you lot laughing at?' he demanded, mopping his brow with an immaculately pressed polka-dot handkerchief from the breast pocket. 'You said to bring something decent to wear, so I did. As for this,' tapping his suitcase, 'no room for my suit because it's stuffed with your bloomin' Shreddies.'

True, I had a penchant for these wee breakfast munchies, unobtainable in cereal-free France and, with my supply exhausted, he'd promised to replenish me. But six packets, a whole ship load? I was flabbergasted as back at the hovel he tipped them all out onto the table. Lugging that lot from London – here was friendship and no mistake.

Welcome to France, Jock.

4

'She's left her fingers in his mouth and he's biting them ever so gently – and she's smiling.'

Springtime, balmy sun-kissed days and everywhere the sap visibly rising. In places the high grasslands were bejewelled with blue and gold crocuses, wild narcissi, cowslips and scarlet anenome. Accompanied by Jock I plunged back into the regime of rigorous training with renewed vigour, leaving Derek to go his own gentler way, an arrangement that suited us all. Climbing the snaking hairpins to the *'villages perches'*, the huddled mountainside 'eagles' nests' of Tourette sur Loup, Gourdon, Eze, Cabris or Vence, we breathed the dizzying aromatic air of pine forests and freedom. Somewhere, shoved to the back of our consciousness, was that bad dream of gloomy winter-bound England, the monotonous daily grind of work and a racing scene fraught with political strife.

'Isn't this bloody marvellous?' Jock remarked.

We had paused at a village fountain, splashing our faces in the icy gush. Far below stretched a painter's landscape of green fields, red earth and orange Roman-tiled roofs, all the way to the dazzling white hotels on palm-lined Boulevard de la Croisette at Cannes and beyond to the crested splendour of the Mediterranean.

'It's like heaven!' He lofted his sunglasses for a sharper view. It wasn't just the panorama he was talking about; it was the two of us being there and being free.

We sniffed the breeze. Rising up from the grand perfumeries of Grasse came a potpourri of scents – jasmine, violets, rosemary, lavender – hinting at another world of languid luxury, a world I imagined cycling stardom might one day open to us. Those aces, I reckoned, were triply honoured. They enjoyed the masculine physical outdoor life, the drama of sport and the cream of good things wealth provided: smart clothes, fast cars and a ready supply of attractive star-struck girls.

I grinned at Jock. 'So you reckon heaven'll smell like a tart's boudoir, do you?'

'You bet!' he snorted. 'Trust you to put a damper on it. In paradise they've got a thousand dancing virgins with perfumes to knock you cold. It's in the Koran. An old Arab told me that when I was in Egypt with the army.'

Laughing, we resumed the road.

His form was amazing. I had 3,000 miles of training in my legs, including 600 racing, whereas Jock, working right up to the last minute to finance himself, had had his cycling restricted to evenings and weekends. Yet I could sense from how he attacked the hills and stayed distances of 90 miles or more that he was riding with strength and conviction. The proof soon came in the form of the Tour Cycliste du Var. This was a two-day, three-stage race for professionals and independents, organised by *Le Provençal*, a regional newspaper based in Draguignan. The ever-helpful Mademoiselle Urago had negotiated our entries and we were looking forward to the enormous perk of two nights' furlough from our hovel – soft hotel beds, good food and waiter service, all at the organiser's expense.

The starting line-up included the Swiss climbers Moresi and De Gasperi, the Spaniard Gil and the Frenchmen Dotto, Lerda, Bianchi and Lauredi. It was a good field, but smaller and less intimidating than others I'd encountered.

The hotel at Draguignan was given over exclusively to the race. That evening we felt ill at ease dining amidst the French riders' lively cross-table banter. It was like being privy to a comedians' convention. I listened intently, but most of their quick-fire argot went over my head.

'Are they taking the piss out of us?' Jock asked.

'No, each other, I think.'

We were allocated a corner table and no one had given us a second glance. I doubted whether they even realised we were fellow competitors. It was odd to see these faces, many familiar from magazine photographs, now in the flesh and sitting close enough to touch.

Next morning, as we signed on at the *permanence*, the atmosphere amongst them was more business-like, a case of quick handshakes and let's get on. The first stage was 125 miles by a meandering route to the coastal town of Frejus, and with no hills tough enough to split the field, Bianchi won a big bunch sprint. The real action was expected next day when the climbers would be turned loose on the ten-mile ascent of the cols Tallude and Le Babaou in the Massif des Maures.

The Draguinan hotel was the sort of moderate-priced family-run affair France excelled in, but the Frejus hotel was a whole galaxy superior. Our twin bedded room had an iron balcony overlooking the bay, and, most unusually, an en-suite with gold-plated fittings and monogrammed towels. The smart foyer, with its potted palms and alert smiling receptionist, exuded an atmosphere of discreet luxury. In the season I imagined a uniformed doorman posted in the entrance to salute well-heeled tourists and assist with their luggage.

It was a hotel for the rich and famous and, as poverty-stricken unknowns, we felt uneasily out of place: our shabby casual wear – scruffy jumpers, crumpled shirts, stained trousers (out of concern for me, Jock had left his pin-stripes behind) – clashed with the posh decor. We would have preferred the other riders' company, but they were billeted elsewhere. That evening the large dining room with harbour views was deserted, apart from a young couple holding hands across a table. Tiptoeing, we allowed them space to canoodle and seated ourselves beside a window overlooking the bay, its quivering luminescence and pale outline of tethered yachts the perfect romantic setting for our two lovebirds.

The table, draped with crisp white linen, silver napkin holders and finger bowls with lemon slices, had a tiny vase of scented freesias at its centre, a world apart from our cement-floor cell in Peymeinade. The wine waiter lit our candle and proffered his list. I supposed we were free to choose whatever we liked within reason, but we opted for a modest carafe of house Rose de Provence and a bottle of Evian.

This became my first experience of classic *cuisine française*, six perfect dishes presented with an eye as much for appearance as taste. We tried not to appear intimidated, though it was far from the standard Lyons Coffee House fare we had grown up with in Britain. We deduced from the impressive array of cutlery that we must work our way from the outside in. The soup and first platter of hors d'oeuvres presented no problems, but then the waiter produced something resembling a spineless cactus with fleshy leaves. It was on a platter dressed with lemon slices.

'*Qu'est ce que c'est, monsieur?*' I enquired.

'*Mais c'est un artichaut tout simple,*' he replied, as if it were the most obvious everyday thing in the world. And he was gone.

Artichoke? Jock and I conferred. What exactly was an artichoke?

The name was familiar, but not the thing itself. How on earth were we supposed to eat this *artichaut tout simple*? We had only knives, forks and dessertspoons left, none of which seemed appropriate to consume this strange vegetable dish. Should we saw or stab it? The wine waiter stood erect at his station, observing from a discreet distance and probably hoping we would make complete arseholes of ourselves to relieve his boredom.

'What are our young lovers doing with theirs?' I whispered to Jock– I had my back to them.

'They're tearing the leaves off with their fingers.'

'What!'

'Tearing the leaves. He's dipped one in some oil with a squeeze of lemon. And…'

'And what?' Jock had paused with a peculiar half smile on his face.

'Blimey! He's feeding her. She's opened her mouth and he's slipped one in between her teeth and now she's pulling back on it, stripping the flesh. Now it's her turn. She's slipped one into his mouth and…'

'Well go on then!'

'She's left her fingers there…'

Jock's whispered commentary grew in excitement.

'She's left her fingers in his mouth and he's biting them – ever so gently – and she's smiling. They're looking into each other's eyes and they're both smiling. She's pushed the candle and flowers to one side and now she's leaning across and putting her head close to his and I think they're going to kiss. No, they're not – she's waggling her tongue at him. She's licked a run of oil from his chin. They're kissing now though. I think she's stuck her tongue into his mouth. The wine waiter, he's watching them, but they don't seem to give a toss. They'll be at it in a minute across the table.'

'What's happened to the fingers?'

'Can't see. But I think they're still in there somewhere with the tongue. I'm getting horny!'

So was I.

Clearly, we had much more to learn about French cuisine. Yet it was lucky for us the couple's bedroom was well down the corridor out of voyeuristic sight and sound of ours, or their groans of pleasure over the main course might well have kept us awake all night.

Next morning some of the hotel staff appeared amongst the

crowd at the start of the race. The sommelier caught my eye and gave a friendly wave.

'*Bonne chance!*' he called.

The hills came soon enough and Dotto and his fellow mountaineers bounded off. Up the Col de Tallude the field split, but regrouped on the descent. The attacks intensified on the Col du Babaou and at the summit I was in the second group about a minute back. I'd ridden my heart and lungs out just to remain in contact and could only gasp at Jock's progress with the best climbers. He was at the rear, clinging on as they hopped and danced the way climbers do, accelerating, slowing and accelerating again, playing arhythmic nasty and nice to dislodge one another. If only they could stay clear to Hyeres, he would have a good chance in the sprint. But descending through a gritty hairpin, I met him dismounted at the roadside. He was holding aloft his front wheel. The tyre was in shreds and looked like it had exploded. His jersey was ripped and blood was running down his arm and leg. I slowed, but he waved me past. 'It's OK. I'm waiting for the sag-wagon.' Reassured he was still alive, there was nothing else I could do to help.

The field regrouped after a furious chase through the valley and a diminished bunch contested the sprint, won by Jean Milesi. The average speed had been 25 mph. No wonder I hadn't been able to hang on with the leaders on Babaou.

'Just my bloody luck!' Jock cursed over lunch, inspecting his wounds, blood seeping through the bandages. 'And I nearly collided with a tree too.' To me that 'nearly' sounded lucky, but in the circumstances it seemed tactful not to comment. 'I was flying. I reckon I'd have done all right in that sprint.'

It was not to be. Both of us knew cycling was a cruel mistress. It was not enough to be strong and in form. The gods had to be smiling on you.

There were 85 miles remaining to the finish in Draguignan. So far I'd conserved my energy and yet was still in overall contention. I suspected the morning's rapid stage would have left some legs more tired than mine, and I decided to look for an opportunity. It presented itself on the outskirts of Brignoles. Ahead, the Marseille rider Truc was out alone and, with Emmanuel Busto and Rene Genin, I launched an attack in his wake. We relayed each other hard, caught and dropped Truc, and soon had a lead of two minutes. Together with the time-check, the race information board warned us that

Tour de France stars Lerda, Lauredi (triple winner of the Dauphiné Libéré) and Dotto were leading the chase and we knew we couldn't afford to slacken off.

To me, Busto, managed by Pierre Molineris, and Genin were unknown quantities, though I learned later they were first-year professionals with Paris-Nice in their legs (Busto was 8th on the Manosque-Nice stage) and using this race as a warm-up for Paris–Roubaix.

As our proximity to Draguignan appeared on the signposts, I felt more and more confident. We were extending our lead and I knew this augured well for me on general classification. With press and newsreel motorbikes hovering, it felt wonderful to be the centre of attention for the first time in France. 'Who is this mysterious Englishman?' they might well be asking. Flattered, I was inspired to do harder and longer turns at the front to justify my presence and over-awe my companions.

It was a mistake. With twelve miles to go, I was punished by the beginnings of that feeling of profound weightlessness in the upper body that prefigures a biophysical descent to the gravity-free planet of Bonk. Suddenly the landscape shuddered and splintered like glass before my eyes. My energy reserves were running on empty and the hangman 'Exhaustion' started pulling his black bag over my head.

My turns at the front became shorter and weaker. Finally, I could do nothing but cling on at the back and wave my companions through. They were furious – perfidious Albion saving himself for the sprint – and they began shouting and gesticulating, which made me feel even worse. On the last hill, three miles from Draguinan, my resistance collapsed altogether and they simply rode away, dragging the press cars with them.

Now it was survival time. I was in the outskirts of the town. Alone and dead on the bike, I rocked and rolled in top gear, trying to squeeze out energy that wasn't there and desperate to avoid the calamity of being swallowed up by the bunch.

Knots of spectators slowly shook out into a solid line. At last the *Arrivée* banner appeared at the end of a long straight. The crowds were leaning out and shrieking, whether for me, or the fast approaching bunch, I neither knew nor cared. I crossed the line just seconds ahead of Bianchi, Anglade and Dotto, who led home the sprint. Genin had won the stage, but Busto was overall victor.

I stopped and sagged over the handlebars, sweat-soaked, trembling, barely conscious, red lights pulsing in and out of my vision. This is what it meant to give your all. Then someone was slapping me on the back. It was Jock and Derek: they had heard over the PA that I was in the breakaway.

'Brilliant ride! Well done! You were third.'

I smiled a wan thank you, though at heart I was deeply disappointed at losing a sure top three position on GC. Later I realised they were right, of course. It was a good-class professional race and to finish third on the half-stage and 7th on general classification was something to be proud of, whilst the prize money, the first of my continental career, was a much-needed psychological as well as financial boost. Above all, Jock and I had both made our marks. Next day's extensive coverage in *Le Provençal* praised us for our roles in animating the race and described me as '*l'étonnant anglais Hewson*'. It went on to say: '*The Tour du Var nous a fait découvrir avec les Anglais Andrews et Hewson de solides compagnes pour Robinson...*' [The Tour du Var revealed the Englishmen Andrews and Hewson as sturdy companions for Robinson...]. A front-page photograph featured me alongside Genin and Busto in the break. The organiser's gratitude extended to paying for another night's hotel accommodation in Draguignan, sparing injured Jock the pain of cycling back after the race.

At each call-over, officials had mangled the pronunciation of our names, duplicated next day in *L'Équipe*, where they posted me as *Hepwsol*. Soon, I vowed, when we became better known, they would have to learn to spell better in English.

Tour du Var, 1957, the winning break: Busto, Genin and Hewson.

34

5

'Coureurs cyclistes, eh?' He looked profoundly sceptical. 'Vous êtes anglais et vous êtes coureurs cyclistes!' His disbelieving tone said, 'Pull the other one!'

Now those two celebrated Ukrainians, Andrev and Hepwsol, were faced with a dilemma: where next to go in pursuit of their careers? The weather was hotting up, the short Côted'Azur racing season almost ended. Soon the sun-worshipping tourists would be back and rents would triple. Much as we had grown to love the region, there was no point in hanging on and we must move elsewhere. But where exactly was elsewhere? It was a question to which we had no certain answer. Meanwhile there was still one last race to be raced, the Grand Prix Sigrand.

Sigrand was a chain of department stores centred on Nice and Jock and I were amongst the 80 starters on a breezy Promenade Des Anglais, preparing to tackle a demanding 87 miles of mountainous terrain. The switchback nature of the course soon took its toll and by the time we reached the foot of La Roquette, the last col, only six coureurs remained in serious contention. The climber Gratton (winner of the 1958 Nice-Mont Agel) was already out on his own. Feeling strong and confident from the Tour du Var, I launched myself in pursuit. Only Milesi, former champion of Provence, could hold my wheel as I upped my gear from 48x24 to 48x21. Wooden stakes at measured intervals marked the road for travellers in times of snow. At the barren, wind-swept summit, I had cut Gratton's lead from six stakes to three, about 30 seconds, or so I guessed. Here Milesi suddenly came to life. After sucking my wheel every metre of the ascent, he now stormed past, crying, 'We can catch him!'

We rode our luck, braking at the last second on a succession of dangerous hairpins overlooking dizzy drops – I followed the more experienced rider's line – and caught Gratton in the suburbs of Nice. Two police motorcyclists klaxoned our passage to the promenade finish, as the pace slowed and the game of cat and mouse began. I gambled all on jumping first, a tactic too naïve to beat Milesi, one of France's best sprinter-roadmen. He chose his moment to power past and win by a length from Gratton. Again I had to be content with third. Two and a half minutes later, Jock, still suffering from his crash, finished fifth, well ahead of what remained of the peloton, torn apart in the mountains by a high average speed of 23 mph.

Once more the press heaped us with praise. *Nice Matin* wrote that the race had been distinguished *'par l'excellent exhibition des jeunes anglais Hewson et Andrews'*. We were delighted – even our names were spelled correctly.

Now it really was time to pack up and go. Derek's cash had run out and he was heading straight back to England. Jock and I each had a single lead to follow up, his the preferred option, mine the fallback. We had neither time nor money to research other possibilities.

Through his friend, London cycle dealer Fred Dean, Jock had a contact in Paris with a Monsieur Rensch. The significance of this was that Rensch claimed to have the ear of the president of the ACBB (*Association Cycliste de Boulogne-Bilancourt*), the most powerful and influential cycling club in France, and had offered to put in a good word on our behalf. It was the ACBB that had promoted the career of Irish star Shay Elliot after performing well in the 1956 amateur Route de France and spending time at the Simplex training camp on the Côted'Azur. ACBB man Micky Wiegant, *directeur-sportif* of Helyett-Leroux, then groomed him in Paris, where he enjoyed a successful career as an amateur before turning professional.

'If the ACBB can do all that for Shay, why not for us too?' Jock demanded.

I saw at once that circumstances were different. Wiegant had witnessed Shay's performances with his own eyes, whilst ours were merely reported. We were the promising anonymous, still needing to do much more to gain recognition and acceptance.

'I suppose it's worth a try,' I said, unconvinced.

We booked our rail tickets for Paris, and, the day after Grand Prix Sigrand, cycled to Grasse and boarded a bus to the station in Cannes. Our bikes were slung up on the huge bus-length roof rack alongside wire cages of squawking chickens, sacks of potatoes, boxes of flowers and other market paraphernalia. Seated awkwardly amidst prune-faced peasant women in black widow's weeds and hearty Caporal-puffing men, all gabbling in their strongly accented Provençal dialect, we in our very English shirts and slacks must have made an extraordinary apparition.

Halfway to Cannes came a roadblock. The bus halted. Two gendarmes clambered aboard and began checking papers. On sight of my passport, they suddenly grew agitated and ordered us off with our luggage, one going so far as to unbutton his revolver holster.

'*Qu'est-ce-qu'y a?*' I demanded, protesting we had a train to catch to Paris. The very mention of Paris and they seized our arms.

Apprehensive, we watched the bus depart with our bikes still on the roof. A peasant couple with noses pressed to the back window must have been congratulating their astute officers for apprehending three foreign felons on mission to raid Monsieur Blanc's chicken roost.

But it was no joke. Bundled into the back of a car and driven off to HQ in a nearby village, we were contained under armed guard in a passageway whilst our luggage was whisked away through a door marked *Inspecteur*. What on earth, I wondered, could have inspired our arrest?

The roadblocks were easy to understand. France was a troubled country. The FLN's war of independence being fought in Algeria would, in twelve months, lead to the collapse of the Fourth Republic and the return of General de Gaulle to power, amidst fears of civil strife. Acts of terrorism in France and its Algerian colony were creating an atmosphere of paranoia in official circles. De Gaulle, subject of a bundled coup d'etat in 1962, himself narrowly escaped assassination on many occasions. In Algeria, human rights were in short supply, massacre and torture commonplace. I guessed we were not under suspicion for theft, but of being foreigners with possible terrorist links.

At last we were hustled into the presence of *Monsieur l'Inspecteur*, who sat behind his large desk with our passports laid before him like a hand of patience. Our cases had been turned out and our belongings scattered on the floor. He surveyed us one by one with a cold stare. He had an ascetic face and wore steel-rimmed spectacles, which made him look uncomfortably like Himmler.

Of me he demanded, '*C'est vous qui parlez français?*' I nodded. '*Alors, dites moi, que faites vous ici en France?*'

I explained that we were racing cyclists and in Provence for the season.

'*Ils ont les bicyclettes,*' confirmed one of the gendarmes from the roadblock, silenced by a flicker of the inspector's fingers.

'*Coureurs cyclistes, eh?*' He looked profoundly sceptical. '*Vous êtes*

Anglais et vous êtes coureurs cyclistes!' His disbelieving tone said, 'Pull the other one!' He had obviously never heard of Englishmen racing bicycles in France. It was just too far-fetched for credence. Now he turned his icy stare onto Derek. *'Votre camarade, est-il aussi Anglais?'* His eyes flicked between Derek and his passport photograph. Derek was very dark-skinned with black wiry hair and I suddenly realised that Himmler might suspect he was of North African origin, which alone could explain our arrest.

'He says are you English, Derek?'

'Tell him 'course I bloody well am.' His grumpy response required no translation, and the two gendarmes stiffened to see how their superior would react to such palpable insolence.

He did so by tossing Derek's passport down and delivering me a lecture. Passports, we must understand, were unreliable identification. They could easily be forged or stolen, bought and sold. Passport photographs could be faked. And weren't we en route to Paris. Why? It wasn't the tourist season. You could see the way his razor-sharp mind was working. We were clearly suspicious characters, up to no good, but his ingenuity would foil whatever dastardly plot we might be planning.

Now he played his trump card. Taking up my passport, he opened it at a page marked by a strip of paper and jabbed at it triumphantly. A visa! He turned the pages. *'Et encore – et encore!'* Three visas on which the ink was barely dry, all from Iron Curtain countries – Poland, East Germany, and Czechoslovakia – all with incriminating hammer and sickle stamps. Surely I knew the communists supported Mohammed Ben Bella and the FLN, secretly supplying them with arms and explosives to destabilise France? It was common knowledge that only diplomats and communist sympathisers were allowed behind the Iron Curtain. So how could I explain my presence there? He studied my shabby appearance and then with a sneering half smile stuck in the knife.

'Assurement vous n'êtes pas diplomate!'

The visas? I could explain those. They were from my participation in the Peace Race.

'La Course de la Paix?'

He and his men looked blank and I could see they weren't knowledgeable on cycling matters. But their assumption that we were FLN supporters was beginning to look shaky. Undeterred, however, the inspector started to say we would be kept in custody until the British consulate confirmed our identities, when Jock suddenly jogged my elbow and thrust something into my hand. It was his crumpled copy of *Nice Matin*, purchased that morning in Grasse. I passed it over to the inspector. There on the front page was my photo alongside Milesi and Gratton with a glowing account of how the Englishmen Andrews and Hewson had imposed their authority on the Grand Prix Sigrand.

There was no denying what was there in black and white. Our story was corroborated and they had no more reason to detain us. There followed an embarrassed shaking of hands, but no apology. After re-packing our cases, we were given a lift to the bus station in Cannes, where, miraculously, our bikes still remained at the spot the bus driver had dumped them two hours previously. Our train to Paris, though, was long gone.

'You know,' said our chauffeur gendarme, 'you must not think too badly of our inspector. If they were all like him, we would have no problem with terrorist infiltrators.'

Probably not, I thought, but Carry on Up the Khyber like that and they might have a problem with *l'entente cordiale*.

Years later I saw Peter Sellars in the film 'The Pink Panther'. Now wasn't there just something about that bungling Inspector Clouseau...?

...though by 1958 we had grown much closer to 'les flics'.

6

This was the future, all our futures. Already the seismic Swinging Sixties were heaving up from under the dance floors of Ghent.

Did Rensch really have influence with one of France's most powerful clubs, the ACBB? Could he give us a shove up the ladder towards a professional career? We were about to find out.

After our arrest and detention in Cannes we reached Paris almost a day late, weary and unshaven. Derek returned to England, whilst Jock and I dumped our cases and bikes at left luggage and set out to find Rensch at his impressive bourgeois dwelling in the well-to-do suburb of Plessis-Trevise. He was out on a brief errand, but his wife, the classic French hypochondriac, entertained us with coffee and an encyclopaedic description of the *mal au coeur,* which by her account was blighting her life. We were on tenterhooks for matters to progress, but feigned polite interest until her man put in his appearance.

Ah yes, he remembered – but there was something less than joyous in his reception of us bleary-eyed Englishmen with our begging bowl. Maybe he now regretted that open-ended offer of help and was eager to shuffle us off. He made a swift phone call and gave us directions to find ACBB headquarters at the *Mairie de Boulogne-Bilancourt.* En route, Jock was his usual perky self, talking up our chances. Hadn't we just demonstrated we were riders of great promise and determination? Surely this would be our big breakthrough. Secretly, I remained sceptical.

At a side entrance bearing the brass nameplate of the ACBB, I rang the bell and a stocky, thickset man appeared, filling the doorframe. Apart from a perfunctory handshake, there was no introduction, begging the question was this the great president himself or just some minor club official? It mattered little anyway, because the doorstep interview was brusque and uncompromisingly negative. No, the ACBB could not assist us at present. Our performances certainly showed promise, but their sponsorship programme was fully committed. Shay Elliott? Of course he knew Shay. He was a top rider. With a shrug, which might or might not have expressed regret, he shut the door and shot home the bolt. It was *le brush-off par excellence*, a bucket of icy water sloshed in the face. Clearly, Rensch had over-estimated his influence. It had all come to nothing.

For a time we paced up and down outside, Jock scarcely able to believe what had happened. He had followed most of the conversation, but nevertheless insisted on debriefing me in case he'd missed some loophole or word of encouragement. There was none. After all, the ACBB must receive mountains of pleas for help from their home riders, and with testimonials more persuasive than Rensch's, why should they give preference to two unknown Englishmen? It wasn't as if they owed us personally for the 1944 liberation of Paris.

It was late afternoon by now and beginning to drizzle. We found a cheap hotel for the night near the Gare de L'Est. In a drab third floor room, with a depressing panorama over wet rooftops and scruffy backyards, we sat on the bed and gloomily discussed my fallback option. It was just a short trip across the border to Belgium, the land of the perpetual kermesse, of cobbles, dirt paths and endless fields of spinach. The bone-chilling winds of Flanders – it was a hard pill to swallow after our golden days in Provence. But what choice did we have? It was either that or to return to England and admit failure.

Unlike Jock, I wasn't entirely new to Belgium. It was just coming into favour with British cyclists as the venue for a holiday with a theme: the continental circuit race experience. Races were plentiful, with cash prizes down to thirtieth position, and entering them on a British licence was easy. Indeed the Belgians welcomed all comers, none more so than Madame Beurick, who ran a café and boarding house on Dendermonde Steenweg in Ghent. Her young adipose son, Albert, an anglophile and bike-racing aficionado, promoted the Café den Engel as a Mecca for British bikies. His business card grandly proclaimed himself as 'manager and agent of British racing cyclists'. Later, to show equal favour to our antipodean cousins, he interposed 'and Australian'. But at this time of political conflict, he was astute enough to have two separate cards printed with different headings – 'National Cyclists Union' or 'British League of Racing Cyclists' – dispensed according to whose side he judged you were on.

In September1956 Falcon Road Club members Tom Mayfield, Dick Bartrop, Ted Wren, Peter (Spanky) McFarlane and I spent a fortnight with hearty rosy-cheeked Albert, who took us in hand and introduced us to racing the Belgian way. For the novice it was an unforgettable and humbling experience.

Most races were associated with local fêtes (*'kermesses'*) and each year there were literally hundreds, catering for all categories and abilities of competitor. The mood was carnival, with bunting-decked streets resounding to the noise of festivity. At one venue a gaudy fancy-dress parade of ostrich-plumed instrument-swinging accordion players strutted in pantomime display. Umpah-pahing fairground rides belted out ear-busting slushy songs: 'Oh Johnny, spare a kiss for me alone' or 'The windmill's turning, my heart is yearning to be with you beside the Zuider Zee...', whilst the latest American jukeboxes from inside bars and cafes added to the cacophony. Perambulating peanut and soft drinks vendors yodelled their wares, *frites* stalls dangled bandoliers of sausages and salty dried fish, the colour and taste of rotting seaweed. 'Mmm! Very good!' Albert remarked in his glottal-stopped English, biting into a chunk of this beach detritus. 'Here, you try.'

Ugh! My God!

As the time for the race approached, there was an air of barely suppressed excitement and people took up vantage points, leaning from geranium-hung balconies, or squatting outside at cafe tables, drinking strong *Pils* 'Export' ale. Short circuits with multiple passages provided plenty of opportunity to applaud the frenzied ebb and flow of action. Here was a scene for Toulouse Lautrec, full of animation, ardour, vibrancy and colour, a sort of hybrid cross between 1970's Notting Hill Carnival and bike race. Pages of press coverage – previews and reports – extolled the stars, and spectators would point them out and rush for autographs. Yet despite this festive beer-swilling atmosphere, there was no drunken loutishness or brawling. It was the BLRC's dream of cycling, perfectly integrated with society.

Flanders' pavé-rich roads were amongst the worst in Europe, though Poland excelled in the monster *casse-pattes* (leg-smashers). The official racing calendar gave warning of what to expect. Races rated *'goeds'* might have surfaces consisting of a mix of pavé and concrete. But watch out for *'slechts wegs'*, which translated into medieval cobblestones, potholes to detrack a troop-carrier, grit-flinging cinder paths and slippery tram lines, which combined with greasy pavé were as lethal as jumping Beecher's Brook on a three-legged camel. Unsurprisingly, Belgium was the only country where the racing crash helmet was obligatory. The home riders were talented bike-handlers, well used to these conditions, but even they sometimes fell off. Imagine, then, how intimidating it was for a foreigner competing here for the first time, brought up on smooth roads and small, well-mannered bunches.

There was so much to learn. On the start-line the first question was how hard to inflate your tyres. This was crucial knowledge: too hard and you'd be shaken to pieces on the pavé and your wheels would lack grip on greasy corners; too soft and you'd suffer rim-flats and impact punctures. The Belgians knew the right pressure for every occasion, and you had to swallow your pride and ask permission to thumb their tyres, which immediately singled you out as an alien novice, a dangerous 'cowboy' to be avoided at all costs.

Then there were the cinder paths that offered escape from the shattering pavé. Negotiating these had to be learned from bitter practical experience. The races went flat-out from the flag and it was as much as you could do just to follow a wheel head down. Then suddenly, without warning, this wheel would flick off to right or left onto a path that had just materialised via a break in the verge or a farm entrance. By the time your brain had engaged, you were left stranded on the pavé, doing an idiot solo time trial, whilst the rest cycled smoothly past on the cinders in two Indian files, one advancing, one falling back, as the lead was shared.

Simple, you might think, just force a way back in. Try it! First you must find the right place, not easy in a race. Attempting to jump the high grass verge to smash and grab a position in the line was the sure recipe for a nasty crash or elbow in the face. You had to be patient and await another suitable entry point presenting itself. Even then you needed someone with a big heart to slow down and leave you a gap. How many big-hearted Belgian racers have you met? Not for nothing did they acquire nicknames like The Cannibal and The Bulldog of Flanders.

No, you ended up at the back amongst the deadbeats, until, under pressure of attack, the line ahead snapped, leaving you chasing, *hors de combat*.

For you, Tommy, ze war is over!

The only place to be, you learned, was in amongst the first dozen riders. The shorter the circuit, the more important this became. Short circuits meant frequent corners with frequent braking into them and frequent sprinting out. The further back you were in the bunch, the more exaggerated this became until at the very back your race was entirely stopping and starting, energy-wasting braking and energy-sapping sprinting. You had no hope of seeing the front, never mind attaining it. Even strong riders couldn't endure such punishment for long, before being spun off by centrifugal force. It was like the House of Fun at Blackpool Pleasure Beach with that polished slithery disc set into the floor where you squatted gripping by your fingernails as it spun faster and faster before flinging you aside. The only place to be was at its centre. The Belgian criterium was just such another slippery spinning disc and its 'centre', paradoxically, was the front.

OK, so get yourself to the front. Easy? Just try it! The struggle for the front began even before the race itself. On the start line, riders would push and shove their way forward, with guttural cries of 'Ho! Hey!' treading on your toes, scraping your shins, entangling their pedals with your rear mechanism, or advancing with their bikes lofted for use as battering rams, anything to force a passage. Some would start on the pavement, amongst the crowd, receiving a shove-off from a supporter. The flag fell, heralding an almighty sprint for the first bend, with more elbowing and guttural yelling. From then on, the pace never faltered.

Even to engage your shoe in the toe-clip was an art. Shuddering over cobbles, sometimes half a lap would pass and you'd still be beavering away at this seemingly simple task. Flick the pedal down and slide the shoe home. Kerthump! Damn! Lost it again!

Belgium was the toughest school of racing on the planet. The courses could be described in modern parlance as 'technical', a slight understatement. They were technical in the sense that crossing Niagra on a tightrope in a force twelve gale is technical. Outside of Belgium, the techniques were redundant, except for Paris-Roubaix and during the cyclo-cross season.

Chapeau then to those odd Brits who chose to bike-race there the year round: Basil Reeves and Dave Ricketts, resident for four years in Ghent, doing the kermesses and track for a living; Ian Greenfield, Les Scales and Dave Bedwell, parked up in a caravan near Loveral; Ken Mitchell and Bernard Pusey, staying in 1956 at the Sprinter Café,

Charleroi with ex-world champion and Tour de France stage winner Meulenberg (also, incidentally, Belgian team manager in the 1955 Tour of Britain). Above all, *chapeau* to the Scot, John Kennedy, who trained day in day out on the pavé with former world professional champion, Brik Schotte. John married a Belgian girl and became resident in Kortrij. Only true love could have prompted him to abandon the lovely lochs and heathery hills of his native Scotland for that industrialised Hell of the North.

For Belgians, all vagaries of road and climate were meat and drink. They were born with pneumatically sprung bodies and special hardship genes: one for cobbles, another for cinder paths and a third for rain, wind and snow. They were reared to love those very things that made life miserable for normal human beings. Through his coal miner's mask of grit and grime, the sashed kermesse winner would grin devilishly, lofting his victor's bouquet as he planted a kiss on some local belle's cheek. For her part, I guess, she would cherish this filthy imprint and soggy embrace, and go unwashed for weeks in a heroic conspiracy of hardship with her champion. Male and female alike, those Belgians were in it together when it came to hardship.

When British hardship tangled with Belgian hardship, it was no contest. What chance did I have, a council estate lad reared in savage, poverty-stricken South Yorkshire on a diet of soot-coated Shreddies? Little, it seemed. Their soot was superior. And it sniffed of amphetamine. Little wonder, then, I was shot off the back in two races, crashed in a third and my best result was twelfth, the only time I got amongst the prizes – though learn a lot I certainly did.

Despite some recent renovation, there was no disguising Café den Engel was a shaky old building, which quaked at the passage of tramcars and other heavy vehicles on the paved road outside. Five-star accommodation, it was not. A cobbled backyard enclosed a water pump, smelly earth-closet, caged rabbits and a fuss of hens, scratching the dirt. A barn, with a temporary makeshift boxing ring for the local youth to batter the hardship gene into each other, also sometimes doubled as a billet of the star minus category. None of this mattered a jot to us: we had come to Belgium in search of bike racing and adventure. On our low wages, we couldn't afford luxury. Anyway, it was a perverse pleasure to be crammed head to toe in a tiny basic bedroom and woken at dawn by cooing pigeons nesting in the air vents. The whitewashed walls were eye-catching studies for abstract action paintings, dotted and smudged in shades of red and brown where previous occupants had swatted the multitudinous pestering insects. It was interesting washing under the pump or out of a chipped enamel bowl and squatting outdoors in the stinking Belgian privy. Interesting too was ample Mama Beurick's dietary regime of boiled spinach, thick-cut chips and steak – horse steak, the bloodier the better. It was her duty to ensure we enjoyed our holiday and departed fitter than we had arrived. To this end she stood over us in the kitchen-diner as we ate, twirling her flabby arms in a parody of speeding bicycles, and crying '*Goed! Goed voor coureur!*' Occasionally, to emphasise the point, she would seize a chip, dip it in congealing blood and feed it to Spanky, her favourite.

Many Belgians had no single employment, but worked their socks off at several different jobs. Besides the café, the Beuricks ran what would now be called a recycling business, seemingly middlemen between the horse-knacker, a scrap-metal merchant and a glue factory. Piles of horse off-cuts, mainly hooves, lay around the backyard for Albert to skin and prise off the shoes. Did I just imagine that lingering odour of stable and decay? As an animal-loving Brit, I found this rather off-putting at mealtimes. Guilt-ridden visions of pitiful work-worn Black Beauties trooped sadly before my eyes as I chomped through those bloody horseflesh steaks, which, according to Mama, would build me muscle to rival world champion Van Steenbergen.

One morning we descended to a right royal rumpus, a scene from a cartoon comic. Albert was chasing a hen round the backyard, whilst Albert's mother, armed with a frying pan, was chasing Albert. For a joke he had crowned the hen with a portion of horse's skull, but its beak had jammed in the eye-socket and now the wretched panic-stricken creature was tearing hither and thither and in stooping circles, like a mobile memento mori, deprived of sight and squawk. With guttural screeches that would have done credit to a marauding Vandal, Mama caught Albert just as he caught the hen, and lashed him with the pan on his well-padded bottom to prevent him releasing its beak by unscrewing its neck. The hen belonged to Mama and she lacked a sense of humour where her property was concerned. Fearful for his own safety, Albert let the hen go, whereupon it promptly crashed into a post, no doubt seeing stars like Daffy Duck, and liberated itself from the skull.

In some respects this tiny enclave of domestic bliss could be deeply rural, though only a tram-ride from bustling, neon-lit Ghent. Whilst Mama stuffed us with equine protein, Albert acted as spare-time courier. Apart from finding us races, he introduced us to the nightlife of bars and dance halls, where occasionally our entrance would provoke the local lads to scarce-concealed hostility as 'their' girls giggled and conferred, fascinated at this unannounced foreign presence. Albert, well known everywhere, poured oil by shifting his imposing bulk from group to group and explaining we were OK British racing cyclists. To be British *and* a racing cyclist was doubly OK. Cycle racing was Belgium's top sport, and the British still basked in the heroic afterglow of liberating Europe from Nazi tyranny. Sadly, since then, it is our binge-drinking yobs and hooligans who have liberated *us* from this fount of European goodwill.

The dance halls jumped to music from the latest polychromatic American jukeboxes. It was that up-and-coming wild anarchic sound they called 'Rock 'n Roll'. At home, our own dance halls were fighting a rear-guard action to preserve the waltz and foxtrot, and signs proclaimed, 'Jivers will be ejected'. Here this Canute-like folly was exposed as so much pissing into the wind. We all jived and gyrated like crazy to sequinned and pompadoured Little Richard's 'Long Tall Sally' and 'Tutti Frutti'. The slower numbers were by arrangement with a singer named Elvis. Oh baby! This was the future, all our futures. Already the seismic Swinging Sixties were heaving up from under the dance floors of Ghent.

Here, at a race, Albert introduced us to Renilde, a cycle-racing fan from Bornem, who invited us to visit her parents' home and watch the West Flanders Championship. Albert conducted us part way. My abiding memory is of him squashing the life from his sports cycle, as he ducked and weaved, pushing bottom-gear up the slight incline to a canal bridge, Ghent's answer to Mont Ventoux: 'Zees fucking bike no good!' he gasped, sweat pouring down his rubicund cheeks.

Albert, friend to Tom Simpson, was a good-hearted guy, and hundreds of British racing cyclists, who found home from home at Café den Engel, will remember him and his mother with great affection, as I do.

That Christmas I received a card postmarked Bornem. It was from Renilde. 'Come and stay with us whenever you like,' it said. 'We at Bornem love coureurs.'

Bornem – the High Street. Stooping left, Mr Vergauwen.
Beside Van Overmaet stand Josephine and Renilde Vergauwens.

The Falcon RC visits Bornem, 1956. (L to R) Gary Bamford,
Ted Wren, Tony Hewson, 'Spanky' McFarlane, Tom Mayfield
Renilde Vergauwen (seated).

7

'They're English and they've brought along their tea-making equipment!' Hoots of laughter pursued us up the hill.

'Do you reckon she really meant it?' Jock was at my elbow in the Paris *bureau de poste* as I completed the telegram. 'People say things like that at Christmas: "Oh do come and visit!" And when you oblige, they've got a face like a second-hand fiddle and can't stop looking at their watch.'

'It's our only hope, unless you've got a better idea?' I passed him the telegram. 'Does this sound all right?' I had written: 'Coming with friend to stay. Arriving this afternoon. Hope it's OK with your parents. Tony.'

'It's a bit curt!'

'It's a telegram, not a love-letter. Now who's putting the damper on?'

It was my turn to be positive.

Bornem was a thirty-mile cycle ride north from Brussels railway station. The case-balancing act was a real ordeal over the pavé and we reached the small town in late afternoon with our forearms aching and fingers skinned. With somewhat embarrassed trepidation I tapped lightly on the door of the trim house opposite the café in Nieuwe Kouterstraat, wondering what sort of reception awaited us.

We had no need to worry. A beaming Renilde flung open the door and ushered us in to a welcome worthy of a long-lost milord at his ancestral pile. The whole family had gathered in the spotlessly clean Flemish kitchen to shake our hands. Their delight was so evident that bowing and curtsying would not have seemed amiss.

Apart from Renilde, no one spoke more than the odd word of English and, as we spoke no Flemish, it took time for us all to become acquainted. There was grandma, who hugged the stove, knitting socks, and younger sister Josephine, at school, who helped out evenings in the family café. Plump Mama Vergauwen, aided by Renilde, was a bustling, jolly domestic, consumed by housework.

49

Mr Vergauwen was a total mystery. He either owned or managed the café, open all hours or by arrangement with the last tipsy reveller. But his fleeting visits to the homestead – sometimes with a bulky satchel, sometimes an official-looking peaked cap – indicated an admirable variety of subsidiary employment, all marked by a sense of clock-watching urgency.

We were allocated a large bedroom under the eaves with a comfortable double bed – and immediately felt guilty. We were displacing Josephine, forced now to share with Renilde. Worse, their father refused any offer of rent and only reluctantly accepted small sums to cover the cost of food. In the face of the family's daylong industry, our part-time though energy-consuming occupation hardly seemed a proper job. We would need to prove to them that we were committed professional cyclists, not merely 'cowboys', playing at it.

Yet, descending 'early' at 8.00 a.m., we were the last to breakfast. The kitchen was deserted apart from grandma scowling by the stove. She would mime for us to tuck in to plates of bread, sausage meats and Gouda cheese. But when we grew tired of this stodgy, repetitive fare and requested porridge, she was dismayed. Porridge wasn't the proper Belgian breakfast. It took her an hour to prepare 'properly', during which time it often steamed dry on the stove. Our polite request for milk to revive it was then deemed 'wasteful'.

Each morning we hit the road, or rather the road hit us: the pavé began at the garden gate. Within a mile we were shaken to bits. The dirt paths came as relief, but oh, the boredom, as we wound our way between flat, never-ending fields of vegetables, the only 'hills' being bridges over canals or dykes, and always a teeth-chattering bitter wind blowing on one side across Europe from the snow-bound Urals, or on the other from the freezing North Sea. After the Côte d'Azur we were ill prepared for this assault on our morale. Far away across this bleak-green landscape waved the smoke banners of Antwerp's factory chimneys. Peasants tilling the land would pause to unbend their backs, processing our fleeting images through their memories for a pro-star match. We rode along in grim silence, increasingly saddlesore, wishing the miles away, the only respite from tedium being some surreal vision of a ship steaming across the fields, its watery medium concealed beneath our sight line.

Flanders, for me, was hell. The people were generous, and plentiful races with good prizes made for a decent living; but its appalling roads, flat landscape, grey skies or grudging, watery sunshine and the bizarre sensation of everywhere in the countryside being lapped by industrial pollution depressed me. How I longed for the wild peaks of Derbyshire or the Midi. I soon realised this was a country where I could never feel at home or bear to live for long. Jock confided to me exactly the same feeling.

Nevertheless, we were disciplined in pursuit of our careers, clocking up some rides of 120 miles. In Provence I'd averaged 500 miles per week; now, in this unfavourable environment it was only slightly less at 450.

Twelve days into our stay came our first race, the 98-mile Eerste Omloop Vrije Volkblad at Berlare, a vicious battle over cobbles and dirt paths under hours of freezing rain. I wore two long-sleeve jerseys interlayered with brown paper to keep out the cold. Somehow avoiding falls and punctures, we approached the finish in a small leading group, chasing a lone breakaway. I was no master of Belgian racing, but I'd learned a trick or two from my previous visit. With three hundred metres left, a railway bridge crossed the road at right angles. I noticed there were two separate tunnels, one for path, one for road. From the back I gambled on taking the opposition by surprise, jumped onto the cobbles and darted off out of sight under the bridge, re-emerging to a lead of several lengths and easily winning the sprint for second place. Jock was fourth.

My trophy flummoxed Papa Vergauwen. Our joking relationship with him revolved around his few words of English. Our tea-drinking ritual – the first thing we did after a training session was to brew up – amused him as an extravagant affectation. 'Your English tea too dear!' he would joke. 'In Belgium our linden tea is voor nix!' They made infusions of *tilleul* by gathering the pale-green leaves off lime trees. Now he examined my Vrije Volkblad trophy with sober respect. It was proof we were serious contenders in Belgium's national sport – and with less affectation than he'd imagined.

That was the high tide of our Belgian venture. Next came farce. It was that early-season classic of the professional racing calendar, the 250-kilometre Flèche Walonne, which then ran back to back with Liege–Bastogne–Liège in the Weekend Ardennais. The preceding day, to save on rail fares, we cycled the 56 miles to Charleroi and stayed at a café recommended by the Vergauwens. Breakfast next morning was late and, underestimating the distance to the race HQ outside of town, we barely had time to sign on for our numbers.

The baggage truck was by now two miles away at the hilltop start. The whole field, including Robinson and Elliot, was stripped for action and streaming up this hill, as we tore past them, hot and flustered, carrying our bags. This was the cue for mass leg pulling: 'Look how strong they are, racing with luggage! – It's all their food for the *ravitaillement!* – They're English and they've brought along their tea-making equipment!' Hoots of laughter pursued us up the hill.

We tried to take the jokes in good part, but it ended with the baggage-truck driver spurning us with the excuse that the doors were sealed. As no team or press car would help us out, we stood there feeling like idiots, bitterly humiliated as the race got under way.

But we had the last laugh. En route back to Bornem, snowflakes began to coat our faces. Snow lay so deep on the road we were obliged to finish the journey by train. Sitting in the station waiting room, munching jam sandwiches spread with spanners from our tool kit, we pitied those poor souls ploughing through an Ardennes blizzard so severe that most would abandon. The victor was Impanis, obviously a Belgian in possession of the bad-weather gene.

This fiasco marked the low point in our first attempt to break into continental racing. Going it alone was proving to be impossible. We had little money left and sensed we'd already outstayed our welcome at the Vergauwens. Despite Renilde's denials, it was plain we were becoming a burden on her hardworking family, taking up space and getting under their feet. Josephine had turned against us; naturally, she wanted her room back. Moreover, her jealous boyfriend was convinced one of us had designs on her affections, and together they conspired over the counter of the café bar, scowling as we played table football. It was time to move on, and lacking finance, there was only one place to go: England and home.

We rode in one last race, the 5 Bergen, (Kemelbergen, punctures, crashes and all!) and then announced our decision. Renilde was tearful, but we sensed a wave of relief sweeping over the rest of the family.

8

'How was I supposed to train, when it took me an hour to get out of the city and I had to carry the bike up and down six flights of stairs?'

We had failed. It would have been easy for us at that moment to give up on our ambition. It had been a brave effort, but surely time now to face facts and admit failure. Received wisdom asserted you needed a lucky break to penetrate the magic circle of continental professional road racing. Brian Robinson's break had come from the springboard of his expenses-paid year abroad with Hercules. Shay Elliott had had the luck of the Irish to catch Micky Wiegant's eye in the Route de France and be nurtured through his apprenticeship, otherwise 'he'd be back in the Emerald Isle, digging praties.' Talent and endeavour weren't enough, the argument went: success had to be written in the stars.

Yet, Jock and I were convinced we would discover our own brand of luck. It was a matter of perseverance and continued self-belief. Back we came to rejoin the British semi-professional circus, travelling the length and breadth of the country by public transport just to get a race – one week Sheffield, the next the Lake District, then Kent, then the Midlands. It seemed like a step backwards, but, in fact, it was more like *reculer pour mieux sauter*. We kept in close contact and used each other's homes as training bases. Far from giving up on our dream, we analysed our predicament to decide what lessons were there to be learned.

Top of the list came accommodation: having to rent an apartment was too expensive long-term. We needed some cheaper alternative that would assure our independence and didn't involve scrounging off kind-hearted folk like the Vergauwens.

Second came transport. It was ludicrous to be wasting precious energy cycling to races (56 miles in the case of Flèche Walonne) when the opposition arrived by train or car and started fresh. We were handicapped enough by our inexperience without gifting them a head start into the bargain.

Cash – the lack of it – was the essential problem, especially the question of how to gain rapid access to our winnings. Though I'd won decent prize money in France and Belgium, I couldn't claim it immediately. The system demanded its transfer into NCU coffers first, a process that took months. Living off dwindling savings for a whole season awaiting prize money to trickle through wasn't a viable option.

Jock had read in J. B. Wadley's *Sporting Cyclist* about the British professionals Bedwell, Greenfield and Scales residing briefly nearby in a caravan in Belgium, and argued we should follow their example. After the initial outlay, it offered the cheapest way to live abroad. The other plus was mobility: we could move around until we discovered our ideal location, and then the car, unhitched from the caravan, would serve as our transport to races, killing two birds with one stone. But then we did our sums. It was June already and we had no paid employment. Unlike Jock, I couldn't live off my relatively impoverished parents, and my savings were exhausted. There seemed little chance of us raising the necessary funds by December, unless we both immediately commenced full-time work – and Jock didn't seem keen to curtail his season.

Meanwhile, it was a return to racing in Britain – an uninspiring experience. Gone the continental buzz, the ferocious competition on crowd-filled circuits, the spur of media interest. We were back to participating in a Cinderella sport amidst a near publicity vacuum. It was depressing to feel passionate about a sport the public largely ignored, and feel powerless to change their perceptions. In fact, as long as the sport remained disunited, nothing could change.

Then something happened finally to crack my morale. It was in the Tour of Kent, hosting the cream of Britain's professionals and independents. The first stage, Dartford–Dover, proved indecisive, leaving the top spot on GC still to fight for. The second stage, a time trial over a bumpy 53-mile circuit, would surely determine the final outcome. Time trials weren't my speciality, but on this occasion I got the bit between my teeth, went head down and flew. At the foot of the steep climb out of Folkestone towards Dover, the traffic lights were at red. Checking the crossroads carefully, I raced through them and stormed on to win the stage and top the general classification board. An hour later I was disqualified. A race official skulking in a shop doorway had reported me for jumping the lights. I argued my case, but got nowhere. I suppose officialdom was right to deny my appeal, but it left a sour taste. On the continent the bike race had precedence over other traffic, and this incident simply served to underline that British cycle sport was a low prestige Mickey Mouse game, and I had lost patience with it.

To feel properly valued as an athlete, I must return to the continent. To do that, I needed money. I needed a full-time job.

The 'Jobs Vacant' columns of the Sheffield Star were full of Get-Rich-Quick opportunities of the door-to-door selling variety. One such caught my eye and I signed up with National Utilities to sell vacuum cleaners on commission. The training course made it appear like taking candy from babies, but the reality was very different and explained the high job turnover. It was hard work at unsociable hours, requiring cheek and the gift of blarney just to get a foot across the doorstep and plug in the machine for demonstration. Then pressure had to be applied to overcome sales resistance and obtain that all-important signature on the hire purchase agreement. It was not for the faint-hearted. Tricks of the trade included never asking permission to enter someone's house as this invited refusal. Leaning lopsided at the doorstep under the weight of your boxed cleaner, you doffed your trilby (then a badge of respectability), introduced yourself by name and took a step forward. You presumed your right of entry. The person facing you (usually a housewife) would take an involuntary step backwards and, hey presto, you were inside setting up your demonstration and nattering away chirpily to cover your tracks.

Those crime-free post-war years favoured doorstep selling. Working class people were trusting to the point of gullibility, and few had vacuum cleaners, so there was a ready market for this competitively priced product. It wasn't difficult selling to the diligent housewife, sick of slavery with brush, pan and carpet-beater. But her more sceptical husband held the purse strings, and returning again in the evening to sell the machine to *him* was another story. It often exposed underlying marital tension and you had to avoid igniting some unholy row that would scupper the sale. It required diplomacy and patience.

Somewhat to my surprise, I became a successful salesman, earning myself over £20 per week. But the long, unsociable hours soon had me looking for work elsewhere.

My second job 'on the knocker' was bizarre. I answered an advertisement for Catholics to sell 'a product with moral appeal'. It turned out to be a lavishly illustrated and expensively bound *New*

Testament. The sales team benefited from having direct leads in the form of a list of parishioners, prised from the local priest by our golden-tongued Irish supervisor, a man who could talk whisky from a snowflake. With no licence or driving experience, he conned the company into giving him a car. Collecting this brand-new Morris Traveller from a garage in Manchester, he drove it thirty miles across the Pennines in first gear until the over-heated engine locked solid. Yet, far from sacking him, the company paid for driving lessons and supplied another car. Even then he scoffed at the idea of taking a test. He saw nothing wrong with bribing priests or threatening sales-resistant parishioners with hell-fire and damnation or, indeed, for himself, an inveterate con-artist, to be selling *bibles.*

Of more immediate concern to me was his reckless booze-fuelled driving. After he skidded the sales van off the road close to a tree, I decided it might be wise to quit the job before life quit me. Later I learned Paddy was in hospital after one night leaving the pub legless and overturning his vehicle. Petrol leaked everywhere, and awaiting the breakdown services, he lit a fag inside the fume-filled wreckage and experienced at first hand the poetic justice of hell-fire.

In my final selling job I opted for the safety of shank's pony, lugging a case of Kleeneze brushes and polishes from door to door.

Five months had passed since my last race and the velo was gathering dust in the shed. I hadn't so much as cocked my leg across the saddle much less gone for a ride. It wasn't divorce, I told myself, but a trial separation. I needed a complete break to recharge the batteries, and selling had helped to fill the void, each sale celebrated with the élan of a cycling triumph. Both occupations were forms of competition. To sell a product, I had first to sell myself and in the process become another person, someone more talkative and self-assured than the rather shy, laconic bike rider of my alter ego. It was my first intimation that personality could be multi-layered like an onion and I had discovered hitherto unsuspected abilities. A sales supervisor remarked that I wasn't in the normal run of salesmen: 'You don't bully and bluster,' he said. 'You charm the clientele into handing over their cash. You're more like a gentleman highwayman.' He was offering me promotion in a vain attempt to stave off my resignation, so perhaps laying it on thick.

I was tempted to make a career of selling, but in November Jock wrote reminding me of our other plans. Unlike me, he had continued racing throughout summer both here and abroad, including another spell in Belgium staying with the Vergauwens, and in Paris where Rensch had found him a totally inappropriate top floor room in the grubby city centre. 'How was I supposed to train, when it took me an hour to get out of the city and I had to carry the bike up and down six flights of stairs?' It had been a miserable, lonely experience and he couldn't wait for us to link up again. But he hadn't saved much money and there was a P.S. 'I've met this Vic Sutton bloke from Doncaster who wants to join us. He's a carpenter. He says he could convert a van for us to live in – cheaper than a car and caravan. What do you think?'

9

*'Coureurs — cyclistes — anglais?' He savoured each word as if it
were a pastille to be sucked. 'Et vous courrez en France?'*

It was February 13th 1958 and a mountain of luggage was piled on
the kitchen floor of my parents' council house: a racing cycle with
mudguards, spare sprint wheels and tubular tyres, a suitcase of
clothing, blankets and a cotton youth hostel sleeping bag, some soot-
black pots and pans, a storm lantern and paraffin heater and several
cardboard boxes of food-stuffs, including tins of steak, packets of
tea and my precious Shreddies, sufficient for the first weeks of our
expedition. It was 11.00 a.m. and the ambulance, to be driven from
Thorne by Vic's father on the first stage of the trip to London, was
already an hour late. I was becoming rather anxious. An accident
now would wreck our plans.

Eventually, to my relief, I heard an engine throbbing outside the
front gate. The delay was because it had become bogged down in
the field where it was parked. Not for the last time, we benefited
from Jock's advice to affiliate to the AA, Vic's SOS call bringing out
a tow truck to drag the ambulance from where its rear wheels had
dug themselves into the mud. But on terra firma another problem
surfaced in the shape of a greenish puddle collecting underneath the
radiator, and even two tins of Radweld only reduced this dribble to
a drip. It was a serious development calling for expert opinion.

In Tolworth, Jock pulled a face. 'Nope, there's no way I'm driving
around the continent with a leaky radiator. And it's not as if it's a
regular vehicle. Finding a spare over here will be difficult enough.'
He was right. Next morning he spent an hour ringing around to
locate a reconditioned exchange unit, and another collecting it
from a distant garage in his father's car and several more fitting
and testing, by which time the day had gone and our departure for
Dover Docks postponed until the morrow. Vic, Derek and I spent
our first night in the ambulance. The bunk beds were comfortable
beyond belief and only the roar of commuter traffic on the nearby
A3 aroused us next morning. I lay awake dully comforted by the

knowledge that they were bound for the diurnal grind of work; we for the great adventure of France.

We had spent the previous evening interchanging sums of money in a financial settlement resembling Monopoly. My pile grew gratifyingly large. I had paid £75 up front for the ambulance, £27 for tax, insurance and AA membership and £44 for the return ferry crossing, whilst Jock and Vic had contributed the cost of their materials. As my outlay was being recouped, holidaymaker Derek, sharing only in day-to-day running expenses, sat on his hands.

Already the enterprise had blossomed beyond budget. Even before we embarked, we were looking at a shared bill of £165. Jock had managed to scrape together £100, Vic and I, from working full-time to the last minute, somewhat more. The cash left after our settlement would have to fund all our living expenses. We calculated it might last three months. What then? We crossed our fingers. Certainly we could afford no more costly repairs.

They were still crossed as we set out next day for Dover, listening intently for any warning of mechanical failure. Apart from the stench of the radiator burning new paint, there was nothing to fault and soon we relaxed and began out-bellowing one another as we swayed in unison across the bench seat in a rendition of Lonnie Donegan's 'Rock Island Line'. When the Channel breakers hove into view, we squealed like excited kids on holiday.

But as we queued at Dover East Dock amidst a scatter of Bentleys, Daimlers and their tweedy *Harper's Bazaar* accoutred occupants, a sniffy duffel-coated port official brought us back to earth. It seemed our outlandish vehicle was in the wrong place and lowering the tone. We should depart forthwith to the West Dock and join the other vans, lorries and common-or-garden freight where we belonged. Useless to flourish our booking document; the AA, he insisted, were in gross error, impugning my honesty with a parting shot of 'not their fault, of course'.

Thus delayed, it was gloomy mid-afternoon before we cleared Dunkirk. Immediately the cobbled, pot-holed roads signalled their hostile intent with a cacophony of sliding bottles, cans and cases from the rear, putting us into prime Froggy-bashing mode. This was the route of the BEF's 1940's retreat, harrassed by German dive-bombers, and when a '*Route bombée*' road sign appeared, I scoffed, 'Tin hats on, lads! The Stukas are back!' In fact, *bombée* simply meant 'arched'.

The road possessed a steep camber and driving against the ditch's magnetic pull set my arms aching fit to bust.

Then came an even weirder triangular warning sign. *'Betteraves!'* Beetroots, I chortled! For heaven's sake, what had beetroots got against the human race? But maybe these extremely clever French knew something the rest of us didn't concerning this malevolent root vegetable? Maybe these lowly unprepossessing globes were about to rise from the fields and stuff themselves down our throats in a desperate bid to boost their popularity? Maybe — Wheeyih! Worzel Gummage! My daydream was interrupted as our back wheels suddenly slid down the camber.

'For Christ's sake, watch it!' Jock yelled as I fought for control. I'd completely overlooked a dangerous skidpan of squashed beetroots tumbled off a farm trailer, presumably coming out of winter storage. Now the sign made perfect sense – *Vive La France*.

Our AA approved route bypassed Paris via Cambrai, Soissons and Auxerre to link with the main N6 south. Money being tight, we opted to camp at the roadside, for which my cautious, civil service mind advised seeking official permission. What folly! At a village gendarmerie, two surly *flics* scrutinised our passports before escorting us at breakneck speed through the pitch-black night miles back the way we had come. They deposited us in a remote lay-by. By torchlight we drained the radiator into a bucket (thus saving a few pence on anti-freeze), lit our storm lantern and ate our first meal in a cosy fug of paraffin fumes. We were tucked up snug and snoring by ten o'clock, ready for an early rise.

But after breakfast as we repacked, a squeal of brakes heralded the return of *les flics* – a different and even less friendly lot. Straightening their hats and patting their holsters, they demanded to know what we meant by camping here? Couldn't we read? One forced apart the overgrown bushes to reveal a cunningly concealed blue enamel sign: *'Defense de camper!'*

'But it was your comrades,' I explained, in my most diplomatic French, 'who directed us to this very spot.'

Outrage.

'Ici? Nos camarades? Jamais! C'est impossible, Ils n'ont pas le droit! Ici, c'est a nous!'

As if their comrades would pull such a trick, escorting us onto their neighbouring associates' patch, where they knew camping was forbidden! Absurd! Totally absurd!

'Vous n'êtes pas gitanes?' queried the most thrustful *flic*, nosing suspiciously around the ambulance and making it sound as if the crime of wrongful camping merited the guillotine, but being a gypsy something far worse.

'*Non! Nous sommes coureurs cyclistes anglais!'*

'*Coureurs – cyclistes – anglais?'* He savoured each word as if it were a pastille to be sucked. *'Et vous courrez en France?'*

Here we go again, I thought. The two men exchanged an amused glance. To them, this absurd conceit rivalled the first one about camping here with police permission.

They riffled through our passports, thankfully without discovering that I was an FLN terrorist with an ambulance of dynamite primed to blow up the Palais de Justice.

'*Allez vous en!'* The chef flicked his head southwards. Through the rear-view mirror I watched them sniggering together, until a bend in the road hid them from sight.

I had learned my lesson. No more pandering to the cops! Next night we camped, without permission, in a hilltop field overlooking the shimmering lights of a village. It was a magical scene. A ring of steaming horses stood silhouetted like Neolithic stones against the star-filled sky as the sweet scent of wood-smoke crept up the hill. Frost glittered on the grass. Soon it grew intensely cold and with the ambulance becoming a freeze box, we opted to leave the paraffin heater burning through the night, a decision that almost cost us our lives. Around 2.a.m. I woke up coughing in a cloud of acrid fumes. I rolled dizzily from my bunk and crawled across the floor through pools of condensation dripping off the ceiling. I forced open the door and fell outside. The heater's blue flame had turned a lethal smoking white. I tugged the others out, coughing and spluttering, onto the whitened grass, where Jock promptly vomited. We were all deathly pale and very shaken. It had been a near thing and a salutary lesson never to leave the heater burning untended.

We were young and could turn most setbacks into a joke, but next day's equivalent of a binge hangover severely limited our chortling, that is until crossing Lyon at rush hour where a saluting traffic cop waved us through a busy junction on the assumption that our illuminated ambulance sign was for real.

Here was our first experience of the lunatic law of *'priorité à droite'*. Vehicles, even cyclists, hurtled in from the right, whether from main roads or alleyways, never checking, becoming apoplectic if you failed to give them precedence. *'Priorité à droite'* was their Napoleonic Right and, death or glory, they assumed it. The worst case was a kamikaze old peasant tractor driver further down the N6. Towing his tottering trailer, he pulled out of a field (a field, for God's sake!) right into our path. We skidded to avoid him and ended up on the mud from whence he had just emerged, whilst he pootled off to his farmyard with never a backward glance. *Mon Dieu!* You had to admire their crazy French pluck.

Five such days of driving in our almost brake-free, overloaded, dodgy ambulance brought us to a campsite on the coast near Menton, overlooking the gross villas of swanky Cap Martin and the blue Mediterranean. It consisted of sandy terraces in the sprinkled shade of pine trees. We expected the proprietor of such a picturesque site to turn up her nose at our pitifully shabby appearance, but she was most welcoming, probably because it was out of season and she had few other clients. She was even still smiling later when she apologised for a temporary loss of lighting in the washroom – an electrician was on his way to discover the cause. We kept mum. The cause was that long length of cable spanning the entrance and now tangled around the bikes on our roof rack. Barefoot Derek had been absolutely right about that unique shudder of joy he experienced as we passed beneath.

After settling in, we began to assemble our new tawny-orange Fred Dean frames. Jock had negotiated with cycle trader Fred, whose shop was on York Road, Wandsworth, to supply us all with bespoke frames and racing jerseys – that was all, no cash, no contract. It was a gentlemen's agreement with a small cycle dealer, but the nearest thing we had to sponsorship. On the back of Jock's later success, Fred milked it for all it was worth. He advertised in the cycling press in block capitals 'WE ARE THE ONLY FIRM IN BRITAIN TO HAVE A PROFESSIONAL ROADMAN' – not strictly true since by then Jock had been a Mercier professional for four months. But who could blame him? The 'Jock Andrews' model frame set was priced at sixteen guineas and worth every penny. (I still possess mine and I rate it a classic.)

Training began in earnest and by the end of our third week we'd already covered 1,250 miles, much of it in the mountains. A stone overweight after my seven months lay-off, I was really struggling. Gone was the old *coup de pedale* of 1957. Far from picking up where

I'd left off, I realised I would now have to become the Comeback Kid.

Fatigue snowballs as the body strives to adapt to a sudden rigorous regime change. Two hours after training, my heart would still be racing at 80+. Some sleep-disturbed nights, it hammered away to dawn. In hindsight I came to realise this shock treatment did more harm than good and at this low level of fitness I'd have done better to ease myself back into training by accompanying bohemian Derek on his gentler solo rides.

10

'Breeteesh OK. Jeepsy no good. You comprehend? Gitanes no good.'
When he pronounced gitanes it sounded like shit-on, a word spat
from the mouth like a bad oyster.

Our first race was the 90-mile Grand Prix Ville de Cannes and I surprised myself by finishing close to Jock and Vic in the bunch. But a week later the altogether tougher Ronde de Monaco saw me 'blown off the back' after barely thirty miles. In the Tour du Var, where the previous year I had been a major contender, a second stage puncture mercifully relegated me to the sag wagon to gripe over my loss of form. Even with 2,000 miles in my legs, I remained a few pounds over racing weight.

Ron Coe and Stan Brittain were holiday training on the Côte d'Azur prior to returning to England for the 1958 season. Ron was third and Jock sixth in a bunch sprint at the finish of the first half-stage, but they ran up a deficit of over twelve minutes in the afternoon, and this was the height of their challenge. On final general classification, headed by Rene Privat, Vic ended up 13th, Ron 18th, Jock 19th and Stan 23rd. The 'unknown' neophyte Vic had amazed Jock and me, and whatever qualms we had once had about his ability were now dispelled.

One afternoon a large bluff Englishman stuck his head round the ambulance door. Jock knew him as Bill Lovelace, one time reporter for *Bicycle* magazine, a great cycling fan and celebrity photographer who had reputedly done work for *Picture Post*. He was on assignment to photograph Winston Churchill's villa on Cap Martin and had been alerted to our presence by the caretaker, who lived locally. Curiosity pushed him up the hill to bridge the social divide between Churchill's affluent life-style and ours of near penury. It would make a wonderful feature, he said, snapping us all alongside the ambulance, but doubted whether his conservative editor would agree. Sadly, he must have been right. We heard nothing more of it.

The Côte d'Azur, still associated in the 1950s with great wealth and celebrity, sprang to prominence a century earlier when English nobility dubbed it 'The Riviera'. The royal connection had waned, but it retained its stamp of exclusivity, plain to us, exclusively the only bicycling English, as we pedalled the opulent boulevards of Monte Carlo, Cannes or the Promenade des Anglais past swish hotels fronted by uniformed doormen, with chauffeured Rolls and Mercedes parked in close attendance and slick-party yachts bobbing at anchor in the marinas. We joked about these 'Lords and Ladies', debutantes and playboy plutocrats, their expensive toys, their lives of purposeless indolence, mimicking their plummy English accents.

The shoreline from Nice to Cannes was quite another salt-spray workaday world with its hauled-up fishing-boats curtained by nets, white paint-peeled snackbar shacks and rickety blackboard easels advertising *bouillabaisse*. Spinning past on hard-pumped tyres, our wheels communicated that loose arhythmic chatter of the vagabond existence – free, unpredictable and strangely exciting. We were not inspired to envy the plutocrats.

Then the brief racing season was over and it was decision time. I was desperate to stay in France, but to be assured of earning our living, where in that vast country should we go? Where were the cycling hotspots? Brittany had been suggested, but Jock and Vic were running low on cash and we couldn't afford to gamble, so we opted for the only dead cert, cycling-mad Belgium, the devil we knew. En route back north, we paused in Frejus for the Circuit du Theatre Romain, a hundred-laps of a one-kilometre parkland circuit with two acute hairpins every lap, 200 corners of sprinting. It was like a *kermesse* minus cobbles, and good practice for Flanders. Soon the snake of riders was snapping at its own tail and I resigned myself to a place mid-bunch alongside Vic. Sprinter Jock, more ambitious, contested the up-front primes over-enthusiastically, touched a wheel and crashed heavily, tearing open his arm and shoulder.

Sadly, another day that would neither put bread in our mouths nor help slake the ambulance's ravenous thirst for petrol. Experience was our only prize.

Despite Jock's injuries, we couldn't hang around, so we snacked hurriedly and drove on the N7 to beyond Aix-en-Provence, where off-road I discovered a quiet spot to camp inside the walls of an isolated quarry. We badly needed a restful night, especially Jock, now in some pain and regretting shrugging off the first-aid officer's advice of hospital treatment. Quiet? Restful? Local youths soon materialised from nowhere and started circling the ambulance on their popping *velomoteurs*, whooping and yelling in argot. It was like being ambushed by redskins on the Oregon Trail. As darkness fell and they showed no signs of departing, Jock stepped outside and stripped back his shirt to reveal the deep gash bleeding through his bandage.

They crowded round. *'Oh là, là! Le pauvre gars!'*

'Nous sommes coureurs cyclistes,' I explained. *'Il est tombé.'* Heap big brave! They were suitably impressed and left us in peace.

With Jock still in pain, it was up to me next day to do all the driving. Down the Rhone valley the Mistral blasted straight at us, tearing at the roof rack. Top speed became 35mph. Rain sheeted down the windscreen, almost obliterating the road ahead, making radar a desirable optional extra. Worse, our one and only windscreen wiper suddenly packed up in a puff of foul smoke. Fortunately, those sophisticated Austin designers, on the cutting edge of 1930's technology, had thought of this: not quite radar, but manual operation of the wiper from inside the cab. As I drove, Derek leaned across and did the business, so raising spirits no end amongst oncoming motorists, who mistook his side-to-side hand movements for cheery waves. *Salut! Salut!* They waved back. The depression associated with the Mistral, reckoned to be as much mental as meteorological, doubles the regional suicide rate. Thus I leave it to your imagination to calculate how many lives were spared on that drear day by our accidental spread of bonhomie.

We had covered about 500 kilometres, the equivalent in our tortoise conveyance of travelling to the asteroid belt and back, and at dusk pulled into a field off the N6 south of Auxerre. I felt absolutely whacked, the imprint of rain-drenched road and Derek's hairy penduluming paw still confronting my vision. We conjured up some sort of spaghetti meal, left the dirty plates to soak in a bucket and collapsed into our bunks.

Outside, just as dawn broke, came a loud whistling. It sounded neither like birds nor Derek's snoring. Gruff voices shouted our alarm call. Vic parted a curtain and then remarked casually, 'We're surrounded!' Sure enough, dragging on shirts and trousers, we stumbled out to face a ring of plug-ugly peasants armed with hunting rifles and shotguns. *'Restez là!'* one cried, waving his gun like some crazy desperado out of Viva Zapata.

Mean-eyed, dishevelled, uniformly hatchet-faced, they resembled in-bred B movie Montana hillbillies after a night on the moonshine, majored in the schools of lynching and kidnap. What had happened to *Liberté, Egalité et Fraternité* regarding brother strangers, I wondered?

'*Que faites-vous là?'*

Their guns were pointed menacingly in our direction. Plainly they believed our unauthorised presence on their land gave them licence to lump us as targets alongside rats and other vermin.

I explained we were racing cyclists on our way north. English – racing – cyclists. I was getting really good at this by now. I stressed each word carefully and pointed to our bikes, then to our AA approved GB badge. But this only drew the usual dumbfounded response: '*Coureurs – cyclistes – anglais, eh?'* Yes, indeed, I know. It took some believing. But at least they lowered their guns.

They held a brief confab. Then their Numero Un, sporting cartridge belt over jacket stained with blood and goose grease, his flies held together by a safety pin the size of a hand grenade, stepped forward and addressed us in pidgin English.

'Breeteesh OK. Jeepsy no good. You comprehend? Gitanes no good.'

When he pronounced *gitanes* it sounded like *shit-on*, a word spat from the mouth like a bad oyster. It wasn't wise to stand too close in case you were flecked with venomous saliva and suffered the death of a thousand shit-ons. They nodded and disappeared off into the mist. There was to be no fraternal handshaking. Some time later, from way up on the hilltop, came the popping of guns and mocking cries of '*Vinston Shershill! La Reine Elisabeth!'* as they targeted the bunny rabbits.

There and then we learned that not every French peasant was a cycling aficionado, much less anglophile.

In Paris, unnerved at being repeatedly mistaken for gypsies or potential terrorists, we opted for an official campsite, a rather barren and exposed field on the high eastern fringes of the city, which we shared with a scatter of caravans and tents. The place had a sad air of desertion as though stricken by sudden plague. Apart from *monsieur le gardien* and us, the only sign of human life came from a tiny bivouac tent where someone unseen hacked and coughed continuously night and day. For a person so plainly ill to shut himself away in a canvas coffin in this wintry god-forsaken hole was perverse. Weren't there easier ways to do penance or commit suicide? The calendar said April, but there was nothing spring-like about the hoar frost and freezing fog that gripped the city.

Well wrapped up, we cycled to Vincennes to register for Sunday's minor classic, Paris–Orléans, and then continued for another 80 miles of training to Rambouillet and back, reconnoitring the hills of the Vallée de Chevreuse where many a Bordeaux-Paris had been won and lost behind phut-phutting Derny pacers. Jock's shoulder had begun to heal, but heaving on the bars still brought a grimace to his face and bloodied his bandage.

The day of Paris–Orléans dawned cold but clear. We were up at 5.00 a.m., forcing down a pre-race breakfast of steak and pasta. For me, in such poor physical condition, it felt like a condemned man's futile gesture. Hoar frost thick as snow still coated the fields. Despite sunshine, the arctic air snatched at our breath as we cycled into Paris for the 7.30 a.m. start. Our lips were freeze-sealed, but if anyone had said, 'This is madness!' we might have turned round and gone back to bed. That's how I felt anyway, but I didn't intend to be first to show the white flag. We'd come this far through thick and thin, setback and injury, and our dream was still intact, if only just. So, I thought, let the brass-monkeys Seine freeze over and be damned. We Brits are made in the right-on-to-the-end mould, every one of us a Scott of the Antarctic. It was the cold talking.

Then I reconsidered. Hang on. Hadn't Scott tried to outdo the Norwegians at their national sport of walking through snow, for Christ's sake, and perished in the attempt? And here we were in Paris, France, Britons trying to beat the French at *their* national sport. *Merde alors!*

Paris–Orléans was a race in which Shay Elliott had once shone for the ACBB. The flat 100 miles course suited the sprinter-roadman and ordinarily Jock should have excelled. As it was, none of us warmed up fast enough to make the break and we had to be content with places in the bunch. I could settle for that. On present form, just to complete a rapid race of this quality was an achievement. Indeed, pedalling 52x14 in the nose-to-handlebar lineouts, there were moments when I sensed my renaissance.

11

'We would be greatly honoured for you to join us, unless, of course, you have other plans?'

Belgium! Here I was once again in the land of cobbles and dirt paths, the land that Time forgot. But what was the alternative? The races were plentiful, and perhaps, just perhaps, we might earn some much-needed cash.

At the border customs post, uniformed officials had us open up our suitcases from under the bunks. Searching for smuggled goods, seemingly a profitable cross-border racket, they tapped the hardboard panelling for anything hidden behind. Armed gangs at night would run butter in ice-packed vans from the Netherlands across the network of lanes into France and Belgium. Finding nothing that smelled of pasture apart from Jock's haircream, they scrutinised our passports and I watched warily as one sucked his lips over my Iron Curtain visas before the entry stamp thumped down and we were admitted.

Jock and I knew Belgium well enough not to set up camp in the Hell of the North. We drove on past Cambrai and Valenciennes before forking east through Mons to Charleroi, where we stopped on a patch of waste ground beside the Sambre. This gave us the option to train on the smooth roads and hills of the Ardennes whilst putting the racing hotspots of Flanders within reasonable travelling distance. Our roof rack of bikes attracted immediate attention from passing barges. Their crewmen hooted and waved, and on deck their lines of washing semaphored fellowship with our own, strung between trees.

Here the ambulance was exposed to both river and road, yet we gave little thought to security. Only a flimsy Yale lock protected us from the opportunist thief whilst we were absent training. But we were never broken into and, truth to tell, there was little *worth* thieving. Cash, passports and bikes, our only possessions of real value, accompanied us everywhere.

One day, however, we returned to find a police car parked beside the ambulance. It looked like bad news and I geared myself up to jump again through the familiar *coureur-cycliste-anglais* hoop. But these officers weren't hunting illegal immigrants, gypsies or smugglers. Instead they indicated a large white building on the hillside. It was an old folks home. Some busybody with a spyglass had read our ambulance sign and panicked the residents with a malicious rumour that we were stationed in waiting to speed the deceased to the morgue. They believed some lethal epidemic was about to sweep through their home and the authorities weren't letting on. The policeman was most apologetic. Crazy, yes, but would we mind departing?

The ambulance on the banks of the Sambre (Belgium), 1958.

Mistaken so often for undesirables, now we were being elevated to the role of mythical ferryboatmen across the Styx. At a low point in morale, we joked about snaffling this chance to do some part-time undertaking.

Fortunately, this coincided with our first race, at Astene. We enquired of the organisers for a campsite and were told of an anglophile family living in Boorsbeke, a village near Alst. These good folk shared the belief, common then throughout liberated Europe, that they owed their freedom to the British, and so were happy to share the extensive grounds of their lovely old 17th century house out of Vermeer (De Oud Huis Van De Vuyst) with a bunch of nomadic racing cyclists. On their rear lawn pecked over by hens and conveniently close to the kitchen pump, we stayed long enough to race twice in Brussels and once in Bossuit, where we performed well, but not well enough to raise morale from this low ebb.

A couple of succinct sentences in a letter home to Falcon Road Club secretary, Ted Wren, framed our despairing mood: 'Just a few hurried lines from Belgium. Weather lousy, morale low and no form – that's the story.'

Jokey, bitchy, devil-may-care on the surface, we hid our real feelings. But with cash running low and our performances mediocre, failure was on the horizon. I asked Ted to forward me a list of races in England.

Perhaps we might have wandered round Belgium for a while longer, then, penniless and defeated, retreated home. But so much in life is down to luck, and now came our lucky break. This semi-permanent address in Boorsbeke allowed letters to be forwarded from England, including one from Ian Brown who, with fellow independents Bernard Pusey and Dave Ricketts, had been sporadically active on the continent. It was an invitation to compose a British team for the five-day Tour de Champagne, centred on Rheims in late May, preceded by the Tour de L'Oise, starting from Creil. Naturally, we jumped at these chances, without then knowing that the Tour de Champagne would provide our breakthrough.

Already engaged to race twice in the Belgian Ardennes (Ronde Meuse et Ardennes and Circuit Dinantais), it made sense for us to remove closer to the French border. Apologising for deep tyre ruts in our hosts' lawn, we quit Borsbeke for the forests towards Phillipeville where an old problem arose. Days of rain had left the ground soggy and springs overflowed the road. We couldn't risk pulling off only for the ambulance to dig itself into the mud. At last we chanced on a seeming dry spot under the dripping pine canopy and after stamping the wet bracken chose it for our campsite. It had the advantage of proximity to a crossroads with its tiny shop-cum-post office, where we could buy food, collect our forwarded mail and negotiate to draw water from the pump.

Despite the dreary drumming of rain on our roof, it was heaven to be back in the hills and on good roads. We performed well in the Ardennes races and trained hard, covering 1,150 miles between 19th May and 1st June, an amazing 82 miles per day average that rose to 96 miles if the two 'rest' days spent motoring between races are factored out. In the light of modern sports science this was probably far too much. But cycling then was a tough sport, in which resting equalled weakness and pandering to fatigue. Like Greek Sisiphus, true champions were supposed to shove the boulder of fatigue up the mountainside over and over again until they dropped.

Without access to newspapers or radio and blissfully ignorant of world events, we crossed into France on May 24th 1958 amidst a manifest sense of political crisis. The Fourth Republic had just collapsed under threat of civil war over Algeria and De Gaulle had been hustled back into power. The border was crawling with tanks and heavily armed troops. Officials almost pulled the ambulance apart before admitting us.

Nevertheless, the 300-mile two-stage Tour de L'Oise went ahead next day in Creil as planned. Putting in a last-ditch solo attack on the second stage, I was caught just at the stadium entrance. It was disappointing, but my excess weight had fallen off and at last I felt myself getting back to form.

We arrived in Rheims long after dark and parked on the town square – unwisely. Thoroughly exhausted from racing and travelling, we needed sleep, but were woken early by a tremendous hubbub from outside. We were surrounded yet again, not by huntsmen but stallholders shrieking their wares. It was market day. A jobs-worth in a gold braid cap rolled up to demand rent for our stall. 'Stall?' I pointed to the chaotic kitchenette. 'What do you imagine we have to sell: old pots and pans, a greasy rusting stove?' First we were gipsies, then undertakers, now market traders! Whatever next? I wound up the gramophone: '*Nous sommes – coureurs – cyclistes – anglais.*'

'*Ah, mais oui!*' he beamed. '*Ça va! Vous êtes ici pour le Tour de Champagne. Bonne chance!*'

He shook my hand and was gone. Teetering from shock, I almost chased after him. Had he misunderstood? Not only was our presence here totally unauthorised, but we were British racing cyclists about to pit our miserable talent and inexperience against the excellence of his compatriots. Had he no respect for bureaucracy and where was that superior Gallic snigger he was supposed to bestow? Somehow I felt cheated.

We signed on at race headquarters, the offices of *L'Union*, a regional newspaper born out of wartime resistance to Nazi occupation. The Tour was in its fifth edition and had grown in size and quality each year. The field of ninety riders included teams from Denmark, Germany, Switzerland, Belgium and Italy as well as French regional teams, the strongest from Brittany and the South West. A special eight-page edition of the newspaper carried details of course and riders and promised a 'passionate' contest with 'a spectacular finale in the Montagne de Reims'. Some Jonahs had been predicting the demise of cycle racing. The editorial challenged them to explain why each year there were more riders and bigger crowds. The twin hedges of spectators bordering the final 80 kilometres in 1957 certified the race's increasing popularity.

And popular it certainly was. Next morning, through a press of autograph hunters and shower of paper hats scattered from the topmost office windows of *L'Union* onto Place Drouot, we shoved our way to the *Départ*, grinning like Cheshire cats. I waved in the direction of Pusey, Brown and Ricketts beside the *Ravitaillement* tent. 'What d'you reckon?' called Jock. 'Isn't this bloody marvellous?'

The first day was a split stage, a 44-kilometre team time trial in the morning and a 150-kilometre road race after lunch. The initiated recognise the team time trial as the real race of truth. Differences in ability and fitness cannot be hidden and an off-day exposes you to the shame of not being able to pull your weight and becoming a passenger, or, worse, getting dropped. Our team of six crossed the line in 6th place at Épernay as a foursome minus Ricketts and Brown. The steep climb of Ville en Selve and a persistent crosswind had done the damage.

With tired legs evident, predictably the afternoon stage to Troyes produced a bunch sprint, won in his hometown by Ramella, Breton Le Bigault becoming race leader.

*Tour de Champagne, 1958. Jock Andrews leads Pusey, Hewson and Sutton up
the Côte de Ville en Selve during the team time trial.*

Preceding the 210-kilometre stage to Chalons, we witnessed the departure of the publicity caravan in a hullabaloo of klaxons and accordion music. Wherever crowds gathered, this raucous troupe would dispense free samples and product miniatures amidst clouds of diesel and crackly ballad. The La Slavia Brewery van carried a giant cutout of a swim-suited girl clasping a foaming phallic-shaped beer bottle to her bosom. Via a hidden speaker, she intoned orgasmically *'Oh La Slavia, c'est la biere des sportifs!'* – repeatedly, prompting the deep-felt urge to throttle. Yes, size mattered. On the roof of the Bottes Badou van sat a giant goose-stepping boot, which I immediately christened Herman. Likewise an immense cartwheel watch ticked a-top the saloon of Altitude Precision Watches, *'assurant le chronométrage officiel du Tour de Champagne.'* Some vehicles were positively sci-fi in appearance. The *Pernod Fils* bus resembled a multi-portholed ocean liner fronted by the observation room of a mountaintop ski-café. The Conord trailer attracted the envious gaze of housewives everywhere with its plastiglass see-through display of the latest domestic appliances. In contrast to all these juggernauts, the white-wall tyred, chrome-sleek saloons of Kleber-Colombes purred and glided in a show of masculine appeal. I tried to imagine this unbridled display of commercial exuberance rolling up to a dawn time-trial back home, shocked officials agog at such sacrilegious intrusion on their private ceremonies. Here it served to reinforce the impression that cycling and the everlasting bourgeois fête of *La Vie Française* were joyously at one.

It was this unity of patriotic, sporting and commercial sentiment that explained why continental cycling enjoyed such widespread support, not just with the populace, but also at every level of society: government, local authorities, police, big business and the press. In Britain for too long the motto had been. 'Cycling for cyclists' in the paranoid belief that amateur sport would be 'polluted' by association with commerce and devalued by cooperation with outside bodies. The BLRC, to its eternal credit, opposed this absurd prejudice and did much to drag the sport fifty years forward into the twentieth century.

It was time to remove dowdy stick-in-the-mud Britain from mind, as an official with hand-held speaker strained to read the start sheet: 'Andrev – Bru-en – Hevson – Poozey – Sooton – Rick-ett –'. Then we were off. It was to be a good day, with Dave Ricketts finishing 8th, Vic 11th and the team placed second.

Next day the hills of the Ardennes turned the general classification on its head as rain and hail poured from puce-coloured skies. Jock seemed to have picked the good break, until a closed railway-crossing gate at Monthois intervened. The riders raced the approaching train, jousting with death as they dragged their bikes under the barriers, but their rhythm was broken and the bunch hunted them down. Jock persevered with another attack to finish 10th, two minutes behind winner Jo Bianco. The rest of us followed ten minutes later in the storm-drenched peloton.

The following day, en route to St Quentin, Jock was off again and this time I joined him. Soon we were a seven-strong group, driving hard. The burly Breton, Gainche, roared us on with '*Roulez! Roulez!*' as the yellow jersey dropped into his lap. Tamburlini, 1954 Tour of Britain winner, added his exhortations. With three strong teams blocking behind, it was an irresistible combination and we built a twelve minutes lead. Jock and I both felt strong enough to jump away in the final kilometres, but each time Gainche and Tamburlini brought us back.

In a hotly disputed sprint-finish, the verdict went to Gainche from Jock, though the subsequent photo showed the two men thrusting for the line wheel to wheel. A dead-heat would have been fairer. I was delighted with my sixth place just ahead of Tamburlini. Jock leapt into second on GC behind Gainche and I was now 7th.

To put Jock's achievement into context: Gainche later outsprinted Darrigade to win a stage of the Tour de France.

During the night I developed a high temperature, perhaps from standing around too long in sweaty kit, awaiting Vic and the others. On the final stage through 'the mountains of Rheims' I clung on until a crowd-packed 1-in-5 cliff face 40 kilometres from the line, when I lost seven minutes and was relegated to 16th on GC. Vic had been in mediocre form throughout and ended up 31st. It was a bad day for Dave and Ian who both abandoned. But for Jock, mounting the podium in second place between Gainche and Tamburlini, what a triumph!

Tour de Champagne, 1958. Gainche versus Andrews at St Quentin.
A dead-heat, surely? No! The judges gave the verdict to Gainche.
Hewson (partly masked) is fifth.

After the race a dapper moustachioed Frenchman approached us and introduced himself as Pierre Joliveau, president of the Bicycle Club of Reims. He had a proposition and over delicious ice-cold Oranginas at a nearby café-bar came straight to the point. 'The BCR is one of the oldest clubs in France, if not the world.' His blue, white and red enamel lapel badge bore the image of a penny-farthing bicycle and the date 1880. 'We would be greatly honoured for you to join us, unless, of course, you have other plans?'

At a stroke our immediate future was decided. The club would pay our campsite fees to stay in Rheims and arrange winning bonuses through their sponsors, Rasoir Remington. After the rebuff Jock and I had suffered from the ACBB, it seemed too good to be true.

'The racing in this region – is there enough for us to earn a living?'

'Naturally! Why else would I invite you?'

So began our long friendship with Pierre and his beautiful wife, Eliane, which only ended with their deaths just before the Millennium.

We felt cock-a-hoop. We would slash our living expenses and in Pierre have someone with local knowledge to organise our racing calendar. Even better, training in enchanting Champagne with its forests, vineyards and chalky escarpments reminiscent of the Downs would be an absolute delight after the depressing drudgery of Flanders.

The deal on which we shook hands cut two ways. The BCR, despite its glorious history, had fallen on hard times, especially since its star attraction, Roger Hassenforder, had left to turn professional. It was in competition with other clubs for membership and believed its glamorous association with 'Les Britanniques du Bicycle' would be the publicity coup to attract new blood. What was proposed was a partnership. The club would promote us and we would promote the club's revival by building on the media cachet from our success in the Tour de Champagne. With luck it could become a win-win situation for us both.

12

Now he was really in awe of us, and went round telling all his friends, 'Ces Anglais, heh? Extraordinaires!'

At the pleasant leafy municipal campsite east of Rheims, life soon fell into a reassuring pattern of training, racing and domesticity, bringing a welcome sense of stability to our nomadic existence. As spring turned to summer, the weather grew hot and Vic erected his grocer-father's canvas awning outside the ambulance to give us more space for cooking and washing up. Exposed to fresh air, the interior gradually divested itself of winter's accumulated odours of sweaty bodies and burned meat. Our personal hygiene improved, too, under the cold showers of the ablution block, and washing our togs in a hand basin was much easier than over the breakback bucket. We soaped and scrubbed the chamois inside our shorts, or treated it with surgical spirit to prevent the build up of bacteria that caused saddle boils, airing all our clothes on a line strung from the roof rack to a nearby tree, a rule infringement the good-natured warden chose to ignore. With Derek returned to England, there was more space available inside the ambulance, and a spare bunk – not that sleeping was ever a problem in that cosy womb-like interior. Wrapped like mummies, we slept a healthy nine hours each night on Jock's well-sprung mattresses.

By and large we shared equally the domestic chores. A simple nutritious menu was agreed informally along the lines of 'Steak, spaghetti and carrots tonight. O.K?' Disagreements over chef's choice were rare, unless perhaps to suggest, 'How about stew for a change?' Carrot râpé in a dressing of olive oil and lemon juice was the favourite hors d'oeuvres. For dessert we chopped up bananas, apples and oranges into a salad topped with delicious, creamy Danone from glass pots on returnable deposit – an exciting discovery, since yoghurt was 'a disgusting foreign mess' virtually unobtainable in Britain. And then, of course, there was our breakfast staple of bread – *baguettes, flutes*, dainty *ficelles*, all crisp, chewy and warm off the baker's rack, good enough to eat ungarnished, but even better spread with jam or honey. Speaking good French, I was responsible for shopping and keeping account of expenditure, which on food amounted to about four thousand old francs each per week (£3). At regular intervals we reached a financial settlement. We lived well, yet inexpensively, on a diet rich in carbohydrate, protein, fruit and vegetables, but low on fat. It would still pass muster among top athletes nowadays – except for its high meat content. 'Give us this day our daily steak' was the racing cyclist's gospel.

With meat being expensive, a butcher club member suggested buying directly from the abattoir, quoting him for a discount. Making a detour from training, we trod gingerly between ranks of hooked carcases dripping blood, our shoe-plates clacking in the claustrophobic gloom of the concrete slaughterhouse, to beg service of a disgruntled assistant in a besmirched apron. His curt manner signalled that dispensing slivers of meat to impoverished foreign cyclists was not his top priority. He chose the toughest cast-offs and tossed our coins disrespectfully into his gratuity bowl. Subscribing to the creed that steak was more nutritious undercooked (*saignant*), we chewed dutifully at these fibrous bovine ironclads until our jaws ached, yet still swallowed indigestible gobbets the size of small boulders. It was tougher even than Belgian horse-steak and our enthusiasm for this discounted battle armour soon waned.

The more expensive alternative was from Monsieur le Boucher himself. But his shop was out of our way and, moreover, he shut early for his lunchtime siesta and had to be roused at the back door where a ferocious German guard dog was chained to its kennel. Inching flat to the wall just out of range of this raging hellhound's enormous comic-strip fangs was not exactly an experience to whet the appetite for raw meat. At the gate we debated whose privilege it was to lead the way.

'It's your turn.'

'No, yours. I went last time.'

'It's no good me going first. I can't speak French.' (Vic!)

Armed with cycle pumps, we entered in team line. But, ultimately, terror overcame resolution. Saving a few francs might cost literally an arm and a leg, and bowing to convenience, we bought from a butcher nearer to the campsite.

Not surprisingly, living cheek by jowl in Third World conditions, our inter-personal relationships were not all sweetness and light. Tensions arose around the division of domestic chores and how well and quickly they were performed. Jock could be quite acid with Vic, whom he suspected of being a North-country bumpkin, especially as Vic had once complained: 'Steak and spaghetti is all right, but when can we have some good old rice pud with custard?'

'Coostard?' Jock roared, trying but failing to copy the northern vowel sound. 'Coostard isn't good for you, Victor,' – he would only call him Victor when he was on his patronising high horse – 'and rice pooding is fatty stodge!' The fact that Vic weighed less than nine stones and could have passed through the eye of a needle didn't seem relevant to Jock. Approaching mealtimes when it was Vic's turn to cook, he would make a big show of studying his watch, before commenting sarcastically, 'Are we likely to be eating before midnight this evening, Victor, or do you want me to chef yet *again?*'

These tensions never developed into full-blown rows or feuds, though middle class, privately educated Jock adopted a quizzical attitude towards Vic that showed he'd relegated this plain-speaking northern lad to the bottom of his pecking order. National Service spent in barracks amongst other men taught us the importance of basic hygiene and fending for ourselves, and that compromise was better than squabble. Yet even though we tried hard to endorse the Three Musketeers' maxim of each for one, and one for each, Me-Me now and then reared its ugly head. It was easy to understand why some later British combines with big egos trying to copy our venture quickly fell apart.

Our second stage race came within the month. It was the four-day Circuit des Ardennes (winner in 1961, John Geddes), not of international importance like the Tour de Champagne, but a top-class regional event nonetheless. Big hills were to be expected, but not the incessant unseasonable rain, icy mountain downpours in mid-June. Ten riders abandoned on the first day. The sadistic organisers had handpicked some narrow lanes that became rivers. It was bad enough being blinded by mud and dung showering up slosh into your face without having your front pocket sandwiches flavoured with stinking cowpat relish. At one point we raced across a straw-strewn farmyard, pot-holed and cobbled, cows, geese and hens scattering in panic. Perhaps we were off course – who could tell in that thick hilltop mist? Experiencing punctures (eight in my case) and crashes, we took to carrying three spare tyres as service vehicles were often stuck beyond call behind the splintered field. In the twisting forested or hedged lanes it was difficult to read the race. A break could be minutes up before anyone realised it had gone.

The first you knew was from a chugging motorbike dropping back through the mist with its information board of rain-blurred chalk figures. Crumbs! What's that? Is the gap three minutes or eight? Is that pre-race favourite Tamburlini's number? Without on-bike computers or radio contact with a team car, we could only guess from time elapsed what distance remained to be covered.

It was a magical mystery tour, each stage a tough strength-sapping 125 miles. Out of 100 starters only 25 finished, though the prize list extended to 30th place (which, in grasping France, says much!). We plugged on to the end with climber Vic a commendable 6th on GC, putting it down to 'experience' and wryly re-christening this confrontation with raw nature: 'Le Tour de Merde'.

Fortunately for our finances, things were going well in smaller races. In the Prix Biscuits Rem, we delighted our French backers by winning the team prize. Next day at Laon, we enjoyed a clean sweep: Vic first, Jock second and me third. In the Circuit de Bairon Jock won, I was third and Vic fourth.

Such races were our bread and butter, but with ambition to be more than local heroes, we had to keep in touch with the leading professionals. An opportunity came with the Circuit des Remparts at Boulogne. This was a nocturne under streetlamps, a mind-numbing 60 laps (105 kilometres) round the ancient ramparts against the likes of Darrigade, Stablinski, Hassenforder, Elliott and other seasoned pros. Ill-lit nocturnes were potentially lethal. The corners, in a cyclorama of deceptively swirling shadows, prompted nervy over-braking and called for 100% concentration. We finished equal 10th just behind winner Darrigade, and Jock and I snatched two prime prizes. It was a meritorious performance and, we felt, another step towards catching some influential *directeur-sportif's* eye. In our hearts we believed recognition would happen one fine day. With all our effort and dedication – it simply had to. Afterwards, camped above the winking lights of Boulogne, too tired to make a proper meal, we settled for tea and sandwiches in the paraffin light's glow and talked up our prospects before turning in.

Next morning's return drive almost sank our little ship of optimism. A sudden horrendous bang from under the ambulance's bonnet, a puff of blue smoke, the clatter of a football rattle.

Jock grimaced: 'Sounds like a piston's blown.' We limped home and unclipped the bonnet to reveal the innards fuming like an old bonfire, with a gut-wrenching stench of burned oil. Watching our hard-earned winnings going up in smoke, we felt pretty sick.

This was a problem we could do without. The ambulance wasn't just our transport, but our living quarters, our home. We couldn't afford to pass it to a garage for repair and move into a hotel. So, time for a spot of good old British DIY. Employing our odds and ends box of ancient chewed-up spanners, Jock and Vic stripped down the engine and removed the fragments of shattered piston. I wrote to the AA for a spare, and when it arrived a fortnight later and the engine was reassembled, Vic and I stood by holding our breath, with everything crossed, as Jock pulled the starter. Once, twice, the engine turned irresolutely, then roared back to life, ticking over like a metronome. We were jubilant.

A motor as well as cycling fanatic, Pierre had been much impressed with our dominance of local racing, but all along sceptical of the competence of self-taught mechanics. DIY repairs were practically unheard of in conservative pre-*Monsieur Bricolage* France, where respect for professional expertise ruled supreme. Even adding water to his radiator was something Pierre left to a hydraulics expert. We had some chutzpah coming over here and muscling in on his national sport, but *Mon Dieu*, repairing this big beast of an engine in the middle of a field with the sole assistance of a manual and some clapped-out spanners from the scrap museum – this would surely be our Waterloo. Now, hearing rumour of our success, he rushed round in his new Citroën DS19 to witness our triumph of improvisation. Cocking his ear to the smooth-running engine, he puckered his brow in concentration. *Bravo!* he exclaimed. *'Rolls Royce!'*

Now he was really in awe of us, and went round telling all his friends, *'Ces Anglais, heh? Extraordinaires!'*

13

He attacked every hill in a rage of effort, as though at each pedal thrust to stamp on his own frustration and avenge an insult. Take that and that and that!

Our settled domestic routine was paying dividends in results, and being licensed to a French club had immense advantages. Our racing programme was organised for us, and our travelling expenses negotiated. Without the club's provision of transport, the ambulance's protracted breakdown would have cost us dear in lost opportunities to race. The big bonus though was being able access our prize money. By mid-May our cash was running low. Few ordinary people then possessed chequebook bank accounts and there was no such thing as the credit card. Cash was king. Jock, in particular, felt the financial strain and before the Tour de Champagne had his suitcase packed ready to return home. Without affiliation to the BCR, his £100 prize-money would have passed direct to the NCU and remained out of reach until the season's end. But now, inside the month, our winnings awaited claim from the Rheims branch of the *Federation Française du Cyclisme*. We simply presented our licences, signed on the dotted line and emerged clutching our wad of banknotes. The joy of that first big payday! It was more than money. It was tangible evidence of a success that no one could gainsay. That day we walked on air.

Annie and Francine, two very attractive *demoiselles,* worked behind the counter at the FFC where, to the envy of all their friends, they got to meet lots of bronzed, muscular, sexy Frenchmen, racing cyclists all. But we were special, or so we thought. We were English, the only English, and they seemed to enjoy having us chat them up. It was bold-as-brass Jock who suggested inviting them for an evening meal in the ambulance. 'Have a drink, have a drink, have a drink on me,' he sang, an out-of-key Lonnie Donegan, as heads together behind a filing cabinet they pondered their decision. The idiot's going to scare them off, I thought, and was astonished when they emerged to say, *'Oui, ça va.'*

As the great day approached our anticipation gave way to anxiety. What would these chic French girls make of our rudimentary living quarters – especially the greasy stove and kitchenette littered with bottles and cans? And what had swayed their decision? Was it just curiosity – the chance to go slumming in a menagerie? We went into an absolute frenzy of tidying and cleaning, swabbing the floor, scrubbing the grime-encrusted pans, folding our blankets and stuffing them with all our other meagre possessions out of sight under the bunks. Remember, as ex-squaddies, we were trained in the arts of 'bull'. But nothing we did could disguise the fact that our ambulance was simply a boys' hostel on wheels.

We strove mightily to impress. A big questionmark surrounded the choice of meal. Our self-appointed master chef Jock volunteered himself to prepare his *pièce de résistance* of steak and spaghetti, preceded by a hors d'oeuvres of grated carrot in an oil and vinegar dressing, with dessert of fresh fruit salad. Finger-kissing superb! Such unexpected *quasi-français cuisine* would knock them cold with its calculated sophistication. Furthermore, to demonstrate how deeply we were embedded into French culture, we purchased a bottle of cheap *vin de table*. We showered, shaved, dressed in our best clothes, Brylcreemed our hair and with increasing nervousness sat on our bunks to await their coming.

Haute cusine nomade style

84

They arrived by car, late, heralded by peals of laughter. Nerves, we assumed charitably, – unless, of course, clapping eyes on the ambulance for the first time, they were in real hysterics. Maybe they were more scared of us than we of them, since they were accompanied by an apologetic driver/chaperone, somebody's brother or cousin, who hung back, smiling fulsomely, whilst looking repeatedly over his shoulder as though ready to do a runner if we took offence at his uninvited presence. We all shook hands rather awkwardly. Then the giggling recommenced as we gave them a guided tour of the ambulance, bumping bottoms in the confined space. We demonstrated the folding table and bunks doubling as benches, on which they were expected to sit and eat.

'It's very basic!' I apologised. 'Absolutely!' said Annie. 'But full marks for effort. You are, after all, men living alone.' It sounded like a well-rehearsed comment and, exchanging glances, they suddenly doubled up again into paroxysms of uncontrollable laughter.

'Oh, you must excuse us, please!' they spluttered. But the more they excused themselves, the more they laughed over whatever secret it was they shared and had no intention of disclosing. And the more they laughed and tossed their heads and their luscious hair glinted in the soft glow from the storm lantern, the more beautiful they appeared. How could we possibly take offence? In fact, the comedy was so infectious that extrovert Jock unashamedly began to play himself for laughs.

The girls observed his preparation of the meal with critical amusement, as he pretended to count each stick of spaghetti like a miser, demanding, *'Combien en voulez-vous exactement?'* and then, with a pantomime gesture, tossed the steak in the pan as if it were pancake.

'Attendez!' exclaimed Francine. *'J'ai quelque chose.'*

She dashed off to the car and returned with a covered dish, which she revealed as the most exquisite quiche decorated with tomatoes and olives. The appearance of competition distracted our chef long enough for his steak to curl up and burn, something we were only alerted to when smoke began drifting into the ambulance. Vic tried to waft it out and tripped over the table-leg. Cutlery and plates slid onto the floor. Nothing was broken, but for a while hysteria reigned and then redoubled as, to demonstrate our high standards of hygiene, I washed the floored items in a bucket of cold, soapy water and wiped them on our one stained tea towel. The steak wasn't the only culinary disaster. In the confusion, Jock forgot the pasta, which overcooked until it resembled a tangled pudding fit only for the pig bin.

Perhaps unsurprisingly after all that, their perfumes drowned in cooking odours, the girls picked politely at their plates and ate almost nothing. They drank none of the wine, though Annie swirled hers like a connoisseur, sniffed the glass and held it critically up to the light. (Plonk!). From their handbags they had produced napkins to cover their knees. First the chaperone, now the napkins – was some self-defence mechanism at play, I wondered, predicated by someone's *Maman*? What exactly was it they feared: food poisoning, kidnap? For our part, napkin-less exiles from John Bull's island, we showed them the ravenous bikies' way, gobbling everything: burnt steak, sloshy tangled spaghetti and especially Francine's delicious mouth-melting quiche.

'*C'est bon!*' we assured the girls and their embarrassed chaperone.

'*Mais bien sûr!*' they chorused, pushing their full plates aside.

Really they were very sweet and couldn't have thought too badly of us, for afterwards we were invited to see where *they* lived and we all squeezed into the chaperone's cramped car, the girls sitting delightfully across our knees, for a bumpy sensuous tour of the suburbs. In the eyes of Vic and me, council estate lads, Annie's parents' comfortable bourgeois dwelling, with its nice Louis Quinze reproduction furniture, oil paintings and polished parquet floors, looked enviably sumptuous.

Nothing much came of this encounter. We remained good friends with the girls, but our ambitions left small space for romantic involvement. For their part, young and chic, they had wide choice, so why should they be bothered with apparently penniless comedians, whose prospects, to say the least, were questionable?

When Pierre and Eliane came to hear of our little soirée, they too roared with laughter. Clearly, in our naivety, we had missed the true depths of this comedy, which had something to do with Englishmen cooking badly in the land of *haute cuisine*.

Nevertheless, we rated this as the best and happiest evening we ever spent in the old ambulance.

Not everyone in the BCR was as welcoming as Pierre and Eliane. André had been the club's one and only real star until we blew into town. He was an excellent rider, a later winner of the 'Tour de Merde' and the coveted *lanterne rouge* of the Tour de France as member of a Paris-Nord-Est team; also he was somewhat acquainted with our island, having raced there in the 1954 Tour of Britain as *domestique* to the victorious Tamburlini. However, he wasn't exactly joyous in our presence and his aloofness spoke volumes: the publicity and acclaim surrounding our successes had been to his detriment and, sick of sharing top dog spot with a bunch of foreign interlopers, he determined to put us in our place.

One day he invited us for a training ride. 'He will show you the countryside around Rheims,' Pierre said reassuringly. Taking this to mean a gentle, sightseeing tour, we made no special preparations, arriving at the pre-arranged rendezvous in sweaters and full-length trousers strapped up below the knee. We carried bulky musettes. Our bikes had mudguards. There to greet us was an André stripped for action: shorts, vest, racing cap, spare tubular criss-crossed over shoulders, chain dripping oil. He shook hands without dismounting and then took off like a greyhound from the slips.

A modest 16/17 mph of side-by-side cycling with interludes for chatting was our normal training mode. Frequent racing took care of any need for speed-work, and turning recovery rides into races seemed to us a formula for burnout.

But now we *were* in a race and no mistake, with André storming off at the front. His chosen route was through the Montagne de Reims, slope after sun-drenched slope ablaze with verdant ranks of venerable gnarled and twisted champagne vines. Whenever the road ahead rose, so did André, straining every sinew out of the saddle to drop us. Honour demanded we stay with him, whatever the cost in pain. He attacked every hill in a rage of effort, as though at each pedal thrust to stamp on his own frustration and avenge an insult. Take that and that and that! This, he seemed to be saying, is my cycling fiefdom and my master class.

Two and a half hours later, every pore exuding, we squealed to a halt before the towering Rheims cathedral, where we were christened honorary *champenois* in our own holy sweat. In all that time, not a single word had passed between us. We must have covered over 90 kilometres. The landscape had flashed by in a golden blur of lanes and dusty by-ways, and clinging to André's back wheel, we had paid no attention to signposts. So much for 'showing us the countryside'. Our limbs throbbed from heat and fatigue.

André's strained salt-lined face told of his impressive efforts to show us the way. *'Alors, ça va?'* he growled, extending his hand. I felt a bit like a public school fag after taking a beating from prefect Smythe-Major – was I supposed to shake it and say thank you, Monsieur André? In fact, that's exactly what happened. *'Oui, merci, André!'* I replied. *'Ça va!'* And we all solemnly shook hands and he pedalled off.

We never trained with André again. But thereafter his attitude towards us visibly softened. His indignation must have been requited; he was much less aloof and on occasions even greeted us with a smile.

The quasi-British team at the start of the Tour de l'Ouest, 1958.
L to R: Lach, Pusey, Andrews, Hewson, Ricketts, Brown,
the masseur, Bartrop, Sutton, Mater.

14

'What was she like?' we demanded.
'Like the blooming Karma-Sutra,' he replied. And that was all we
ever got out of him on the subject.

After La Grande Boucle and Paris–Nice, the seven days Tour de L'Ouest ranked alongside Le Dauphiné Libéré as the third most important stage race in France. A tradition dating back to 1931, excellent sponsorship and publicity from large regional newspaper, *Ouest France,* big prize money and a star-studded field were all to its credit. Its list of previous participants read like a Who's-Who of cycling history. Each August, Europe's sporting journalists would clink their glasses of apple-brandy Calvados in recognition of Normandy, over whose fertile rolling hectares the race ran towards Le Mont St Michel and the rugged Brittany coastline so favoured by French holidaymakers and the better-off English.

Having made headlines in the Tour de Champagne, we were now invited to front a seven-man British team alongside Ian Brown, Dave Ricketts, Dick Bartrop, my Falcon club-mate over from England, and Stephane Lach, an up-and-coming Frenchman from Troyes, who for this week became a nominal subject of her Gracious Majesty, Elizabeth the Second.

In opposition were top trade teams – Mercier, Geminiani-St Raphael, Helyett-Leroux, Peugeot and the Belgian Groene-Leeuw – and stars such as Cazala, Everaert, Hassenforder, Mastrotto, Roger Rivière, Gérard Saint, Defilippis, Scodeller, De Cabooter (solo winner of the 1955 Grand Prix of Essex), Darrigade and Forestier.

Peugeot-owning Stefane gave us a lift from Rheims to the departure town of Lisieux, a religious site of divine intervention to rival Lourdes – given the star-studded opposition, we debated whether to fall on our knees at the hotel or defer our prayers to the start-line. With its domed Carmelite Basilica and cathedral, Lisieux was the centre of pilgrimage to miracle-worker Saint Theresa, 'The Little Flower of Jesus', second only to Joan of Arc in the French hagiocracy; and every second person in the bustling town centre, which had been almost totally reconstructed following a post-D-Day bombardment, was a rosary-beaded nun or cleric.

Welcoming us at our hotel was our French manager, bespectacled André Mater. What struck me immediately was his warmth of personality, what the French call *'sympa'*. He appeared to be cycling-savvy, softly spoken, a good communicator and listener and gratifyingly attentive to our requirements.

As a French speaker, I shared rooms with Stefane. I was rather untidy, used to improvising out of a jumbled suitcase, whereas Stephane was twelve hours ahead in preparation and fastidious in personal grooming. Before retiring to bed, he stacked his racing gear for the morrow on a chair in precise order of dress – each garment pressed and folded, polished shoes beneath, racing cap and opened-out sunglasses on top. After each stage he scrubbed himself from tip to toe with eau de cologne 'to remove impurities from the skin', and before breakfast always sipped a glass of beaten raw eggs in sherry: *'très fortifiant'*, he claimed in defiance of received wisdom that eggs were bad for the liver. His professional dedication was eventually rewarded by 2nd places in the Tour of Morocco and the Tour du Sud Est, a stage win in the Tour du Var, 3rd behind Darrigade and Anglade in the 1960 Isle of Man International and three good results in the Tour de France itself. But that was for the future. Here, like us, he was still a scholar.

The race opened to sudden torrential downpours. 'Oh no,' we said, 'not another Tour de Merde.' But there were few lanes and we were spared the cow-shit showers. Nino Defilippis won the first stage and we all ended close up in the bunch, except for Jock, who punctured. As he was with a small group of pursuers in similar plight, Mater saw no point in ordering anyone to drop back and help, though if he'd foreseen Jock was to become his main man, he might have decided otherwise.

Jean Bobet, brother of revered triple Tour de France winner Louison, animated the 2nd stage, 184 kilometres from Granville to Rennes. Besides the filial connection, Jean's other claim to fame was as a certified *professeur d'anglais*, a rare intellectual amongst the rough and ready cycling elite of that era (though, unlike dumbed-down tabloid-blitzed Britain, France cherishes its intellectuals, once bestowing pop-star status on the philosopher Sartre). Even more of a curiosity was 1930s Paris intellectual, Edmond Heuse, professor at the haughty *École des Beaux Arts* and member of the *Institut de*

France. His alter ego enrolled at the *Academy du Strip-Tease* and *Crazy Horse saloon, Avenue George V*, and he counted amongst his former employments circus clown, cabaret dancer and – yes – professional racing cyclist.

Jean had studied at Aberdeen University and spoke excellent English. Never mind that, the peloton stigmatised no one and *'sympa'* intellectual Jean, meshed effortlessly into its backslapping, joking camaraderie.

Jean began the race-winning breakaway at 70 kilometres when a previous break, including Vic, had just been caught. To launch an attack at such a moment is a standard manoeuvre of the bike race. After a successful high-speed chase, the peloton yearns to catch its breath and reward itself with food and drink. Then bang! Another animator, here Jean, sprints off and catches everyone with their psychological shorts round their ankles. Flesh being weak, the peloton may well pause to compute the danger before organising another chase.

By kilometre 100 an eight-man group including Scodeller, Novak, Everaert, Jean Bobet, Gérard Saint and our Jock held a two-minute lead. By kilometre 130 it had doubled. Then, following Italian and Belgian counter attacks, the lead was cut to around a minute. The break seemed doomed. It was carrying passengers, amongst whom a tired Jean, who in the frenzy had delayed eating. Now psychometabolic disaster as his supply of instant energy, a packet of sugar lumps, fell from his quivering fingers onto the road. When Pierre Everaert and Jock attacked up a sharp incline, he was dropped.

Ouest France took wry note in next day's headline:

LE PROFESSEUR D'ANGLAIS JEAN BOBET FUT 'ASSASSINÉ' PAR UN – BRITANNIQUE! (English teacher Jean Bobet slaughtered – by an Englishman!)

Reinvigorated, the break held steady and on the Rennes velodrome Saint led out team-mate Everaert to victory. Novak was 2nd and Jock 3rd. I finished 33rd at one and a half minutes, with Vic and Stefane 37th. Our other team members were less fortunate: Pusey, Brown, Ricketts and Bartrop all suffered mechanical trouble and fell foul of the time limit. Though Mater argued strenuously, officialdom demanded its sacrificial victims and they were eliminated. At a stroke, and after only two stages, our team was chopped in half.

*Tour de l'Ouest, Stage 2. Andrews leads the break containing
Saint, Novak, Scodeller and Everaert.*

The unknown Jock had hugely impressed the press. Until 1959,
when Simpson became race leader, the only other Brit to have shown
such verve and promise was Brian Robinson, 4th in 1957. *'Mister
ANDREWS, qui êtes-vous?'* the newspaper demanded, supplying its
own answer by means of an interview with Jock himself.

The first law of cycling dynamics (*peloton + pluie = chute*) was
illustrated on this stage under unusual circumstances. The so-called
Prince of Jokers, Hassenforder, acting as a sort of mobile arm-waving
news service to the peloton, alerted us to the imminence of the
famous landmark, Le Mont St Michel. Following a shower, farm
vehicles had greased the road with mud. As we crested a cliff-top
rise, Hassan shouted, *'Regardez!'* Far below, pinned to the shining
sea by a shaft of sunlight, lay the fortified abbey, its dark granite
ramparts and towers like some beautiful pop-up illustration from a
fairy tale. So enchanting was this vista that a rider beside me crossed
himself in religious awe. Next second came the mad Harpo tinkle of
his front wheel spigot lever engaging with another's spokes followed

by the muffled thud of flesh and bone hitting tarmac. Glancing back at the subsequent stack-up of bodies and bikes, Hassan spread his arms in a gesture of self-exoneration. *'Alors?'* How come his 'good deed' had resulted in such chaos? (Moral: cross yourself, but never wheels.)

Without his first day woes, Jock would have been riding high on general classification. Nevertheless, he was in cracking form. The tactically brilliant Mater read the race to perfection, ordering him to 'recuperate' for two days in the peloton, and then go on the attack over the final stages. The result? – 4th at Brest and 12th on the last stage ending at Saint-Brieuc, keeping himself firmly in the public eye.

The rest of us weren't displeased either. Stefane was 9th at La Roche sur Yon. My best placing was 16th. Vic, Stefane and I showed up well on final general classification (the great Tom Simpson could only manage 18th place in 1959). Once again we'd proved we were worthy to rub shoulders with the very of best bike riders and our DIY gamble was justified.

We had far exceeded Mater's expectations. He was delighted. Team managers were as much in competition as riders. He had started as a no-hoper underdog but ended basking in the reflected glory of Jock's publicity, which, we fondly imagined, would promote him up the league of *directeurs-sportifs*. In the hotel at Saint Brieuc, we toasted our success in champagne. Clinking glasses, he said, 'Whenever you pass through Paris, be sure to drop in to see me.' He handed us a business card, which read *'Jacques Mater, Bijoutier-Joaillier, Rue Sainte-Anne, Paris 2eme.'* On the back he scrawled, *'Hotel L'Escale, Rue Blondel'*. At first sight we overlooked the 'Jacques' (his son?) and mistook André for some well-to-do jeweller-hotelier, doubly blessed as a top cycling manager. Our respect for this Frenchman with twinkling eyes knew no bounds. Only later we realised our mistake: André was no jeweller. His was a totally different business as we were about to discover.

Perhaps sooner than expected we took up his invitation. At the last minute, Stefane chose not to return via Rheims, so we took the train. Crossing Paris between stations, we decided on the spur of the moment, as much out of curiosity as anything, to drop in on André. A street plan located Rue Blondel linking the 2nd and 3rd *arrondissements* near the Strasbourg St Denis metro.

It was a sultry August afternoon and abnormally quiet as most Parisiens had quit their stifling sewer-perfumed capital for annual vacation on the coast. As we neared Rue Blondel, so the neighbourhoods became meaner and stars tumbled from the hotel ratings. We passed one of those pill box urinals on a corner, its rounded fly-postered walls affixed with a blue *defense de cracher* sign, a couple of sad deserted bars, their sullen proprietors staring out over empty counters and worn moleskin banquettes, before turning into a dingy street of barred windows. Rue Blondel. Here came our first intimation that things Mater were not all they seemed. A line of girls, resembling a bus queue, stood chattering together like budgerigars on a perch. They wore a uniform of skimpy nipple-taut blouses in saucy hues of tangerine, scarlet, electric blue and pink. They slouched back, one foot propped on the building behind, their gymslips split open to the thigh (the pre-Mary Quant miniskirt!). There was nothing else for it: the hotel lay beyond and we must run their gauntlet. As our presence registered on their antennae, they fell ominously silent. Then one spoke for all, '*Alors, cheri, qu'est-ce-que tu veux?*' Embarrassed, I could only mutter an inanely apologetic reply of '*Non, merci, mademoiselle. Merci, non.*'

Imagine. We considered ourselves to be men of the world, but it was the prudish illiberal world of 1958 where sex was never discussed in polite society and even our most vulgar newspapers hid behind coded references to 'intimacy'. (No sex please, we're British!) Here, not just one, but a whole posse of whores was brazenly soliciting us in broad daylight on a public thoroughfare in a European capital, albeit gay Paris. Unnerved, we scuttled past to where a scruffy neon sign indicated '*L'Hotel Escale*' and darted inside – to be barred in the lobby by an old crow of a concierge, who flapped up from her cane chair with arms outstretched as if to contain a panicky flock of geese. I presented Mater's card, and she conducted us upstairs to a second-floor landing. Moments later she emerged from a grand double door, leading a chic and elegantly coiffured woman who coldly enquired our business. My explanation that we were '*les coureurs anglais de Monsieur Mater*' hardly produced the anticipated welcome. Had we strayed into the wrong building by mistake? She condescended to invite us into her sumptuous apartment, whilst she made a phone call from the desk, her input consisting entirely of '*Oui, d'accord!*' and '*Bien sûr!*' her interlocutor clearly someone of authority, possibly Mater himself. When she hung up, her demeanour changed. *'Faites comme chez vous!'* she smiled, putting the hotel at our disposal.

Over French-style lukewarm milky 'tea' with petits-fours, we passed time in chitchat about England and our Royal Family, in which she was expert. She spoke a mixture of French and fractured English and my skills as interpreter were on constant call. Her refined gestures prompted a rattling of bangles; she was bedecked with brooches and rings, all expensive jewellery to my untutored eyes. Every now and then she excused herself to answer a tap at the door. No word passed, but on each occasion she exchanged a frilled white towel from a tall housekeeper's cupboard for a handful of banknotes, which she deposited in a safe-box in her desk drawer, the keys swinging sensually from a thick golden chain at her waist.

I was puzzled. What did this ritual signify? Then the penny dropped. How naïve we'd been! Of course, the girls outside – this was no ordinary hotel, but a knocking shop with swift turnover, a bordello, *un hotel de passe*, where the tarts – *cocottes, poules, putains, gonzesses* (French has a hundred expressions for them, including *les grandes horizontales* for those playthings of the old aristocracy) – paid a levy to bring their clients: no incriminating paperwork, but cash for receipt of a towel.

I was desperately trying to square things in my mind. What did this make of the charming and *sympa* Mater? Had we been team-managed by a brothel-keeper? Surely not? But then what exactly was his connection with this unsavoury trade, and how did it tally with his passion for the healthy, athletic, open-air pursuit of cycle-racing? The two activities seemed poles apart, a schizophrenia that outdid even that of the *Beaux Arts/Striptease* academic, Edmond Heuse.

Afterwards, in the bedroom given over to us, as knocking and door slamming, snatched conversations and nervous laughter continued long into the night, Jock and I discussed this enigma without ever arriving at a conclusion. Vic had struck up a relationship with the bejewelled Madame and we saw no more of him until breakfast. Broad hints were dropped that the girls were at our disposal gratis, an offer we politely declined, confiding to each other that we were not that desperate for sex. Our libidos were suppressed by seven days of hard racing. Where on earth had Vic found the energy to go at it, we wondered? Maybe he was living out one of his boasts: 'I feel as strong as a bull.' There was concern also of contracting something nasty: pre-antibiotic remedies, the 'sweep's broom' treatment of venereal disease could be humiliating and painful. In our eyes, the enterprise wasn't worth the candle, so to speak.

If we had studied the history of prostitution in Paris, we might have been less surprised. Licensed brothels (euphemistically called *maisons de tolérance*) flourished in the 1930s, associated with art and literature and glorified by celebrated writers like Anaïs Nin and the 'scandalous' Henry Miller. Requisitioned to serve the exclusive needs of Nazi officers during the war, they fell foul of the Resistance and in 1946 Marthe Richard of the Municipal Council of Paris, a fervent opponent, closed them down. Did that end prostitution? Of course not! Brothels simply metamorphosed into 'tourist hotels', like *L'Hotel Escale*, with the 'no vacancies' sign a permanent fixture to ward off genuine tourists. Now the girls touted on the streets instead of receiving their clients in the anonymity of the salon. A trade once conducted discreetly behind closed doors, licensed and regulated, with proper health checks, was embarrassingly exposed to public view and totally unregulated, the very opposite of the good Marthe's intentions and an example of law scoring an own goal. Corruption thrived: police action was at best fitful and half-hearted. But this was France, where law often opposed reality, a Feydeau farcical mystery to the outsider.

I call this visible flouting of the law mysterious, but it is only mysterious to Anglo-Saxons. My French godson boasted a glove compartment stuffed with unredeemed parking tickets. I was horrified. They represented a small fortune in unpaid fines. 'Aren't you concerned the authorities will have you arrested?' I asked. '*Mais non,*' he replied, 'our bureaucracy is monstrously inefficient. And anyway, the law in France is merely an ideal, to be looked up to, not obeyed.'

I heard similar stories from French friends, sometimes expressed with sadness, sometimes glee. One even accounted France's post-war economic success to its relaxed attitude to the law, especially EU law. Perhaps there is truth in the widespread tabloid belief that we play cricket whilst they play catch-as-catch-can.

L'Escale signifies relaxation. Blondel was a French minstrel of the 12th century who sang of courtly love. Here we were in the *quartier* of Saint-Denis, long noted for prostitution and pre-war haunt of liberated writers and artists, not least Monsieur 'Prick on Wheels', Toulouse-Lautrec. Nowadays some of these former brothels are lovingly preserved as monuments on the tourist trail – which I take to be another fine example of that wry, delicious, tongue-in-cheek Gallic sense of humour concerning matters sexual.

Next morning there was much leg pulling over breakfast, when we were reunited with a sheepish, bleary-eyed Victor.

'What was she like?' we demanded.

'Like the blooming Karma-Sutra,' he replied. And that was all we ever got out of him on the subject.

As for Mater, he never materialised. When asked, Madame merely shrugged: '*Il est très occupé avec ses affaires.*'

What affairs, we wondered?

Tour de l'Ouest, 1958. Jean Bobet in conversation with our Directeur Sportif, André Mater. L to R: Lach, Mater, Andrews, Bobet, Hewson, Sutton.

15

'These devilish English never feel happy unless they have a nice little hill under their tyres –'.

Meanwhile, the chalky slopes of the *Montagne* reflected heat and the grapes swelled and sweetened, promising the champagne barons a bumper harvest. It was time to celebrate and many towns and villages celebrated with a bike race organised by a *comité des fêtes* aided by a local cycling club. Sponsorship came via shopkeepers, farmers and small businessmen, and races were titled accordingly: Grand Prix des Commercants à Tergnier, Grand Prix Biscuits Rem, Grand Prix Slavia-Sedan: a union of small shopkeepers, a biscuit factory, a brewery. Whether or not the prizes were grand, 'Grand Prix' usually figured somewhere. The bicycle race wasn't just a spectacle to attract visitors to the *fête;* it was a means for local business to present itself as public benefactor number one, and for communities to unite around a project of mutual self-interest.

A typical côte in the Montagnes de Reims.

Not every race was open to us as semi-professionals. Nevertheless, we raced on average twice a week, usually on Saturday and Sunday back to back, and we were earning enough in prize money and expenses to put our early–season financial woes behind us. There was much for us to celebrate.

And the French excelled in celebration. Our curiosity value as cycling subjects of Her Royal Majesty (the French media was absolutely obsessed with Royal tittle-tattle as the British media is now) brought invitations to attend the odd municipal and commercial gathering. These often took place at our teatime and were occasions for speechifying bonhomie accompanied by canapés and sweet biscuits washed down by bottle upon bottle of 'Veuve Clicquot's little accident' as champagne was sometimes called. Champagne fulfilled the role of our afternoon tea and was drunk with great style, exuberance and pride in its hometown. As our French-speaking representative, called upon to say a few words, I found a glass or two beforehand lubricated the larynx, fructified the brain and gladdened the heart. We soon acquired a taste for these free samplings, served with due ceremony in the right setting, the right glass and at the right temperature. Despite our arrogant conviction that Britain led the world in most things, we had to admit a sneaking regard for French style on such ceremonial occasions, its elegance and easy formality. Though as foreigners we never integrated fully into French culture, little by little, over the next three years, each in his own way, we began to 'go native'.

A champagne reception in Reims with the manager of the newspaper L'Union and the President of B.C. Remois.

Champagne was delightful, but when it came to catering for *our* British passion, tea-drinking, French restaurants and cafés were a disaster area. Ordering tea risked being presented with a brimming cup of tepid, anaemic-looking liquid, the colour of wrung-out long johns, swimming with leaves and accompanied by a jug of boiled processed milk, skin and all. It tasted absolutely foul, as if the tea had been stored with garlic and brewed from lukewarm mineral water. A polite request to the waiter to rectify these failings would be enough to provoke a diplomatic incident akin to spitting on the floor of the Louvre or wiping one's feet on the tricolore. Gallic pride forbade French cuisine ever to be challenged. Even with something as basic as making tea, chef rated himself above reproach.

Jock was going from strength to strength. His sprinting prowess meant he had only to be with the race leaders approaching a finish to be almost certain of victory. The newspaper *L'Union* extolled his enviable record in banner headlines:

Andrews triomphe à nouveau a Signy-le-Petit ou seul V. Modric a résiste jusqu'au bout aux trois Anglais du B.C. Remois.

And, after yet another Andrews win, his third that week,

ANDREWS, avec un brio extraordinaire, enlève à Tergnier sa 3eme victoire en sept jours!

The report beneath made comfortable reading for us all:

In this peloton there were some men of class such as Andrews, Loof, Hewson, Sutton, Sauret and the combative Valentin Modric, who dreamed of taking his revenge at Tergnier on the three Englishmen who had made him suffer at Signy.

The report described our efforts to shake off the opposition on the climb of Septvaux: 'These devilish English never feel happy unless they have a nice little hill under their tyres…' Rubbing more salt into French wounds was Jock's self-confident approach to the sprint finish, 'Andrews sat up for a moment and spruced himself up in preparation for the kiss of victory!' Another bouquet and embrace from a pretty girl were his due rewards. He had discovered the knack of winning.

For knack it was, that explosive surge, the spring of the tiger, leaving Vic and me to pick up the crumbs. At Signy I was 3rd and Vic 4th. At Tergnier I was 4th and Vic 9th. A bike-length in a race of 100 miles separated winning from being an also-ran.

And so Jock became the first to realise our dream. His second place in the Tour de Champagne and aggressive performances against the established stars of the Tour de L'Ouest had propelled him to the notice of one of France's premier *directeur-sportifs*, Mercier's well-respected Antonin Magne. Magne, like Pélissier, had been a *costaud* of the 1930s. This dour, steely-nosed professionalism now informed his managerial career. Contracts were normally arranged during the close season, but when Jock won the prestigious Grand Prix des Quatre Vents, a selection race for the French amateur world championship team, beating the flower of French amateurs and independents in the process, Magne jumped to the phone before some rival beat him to it. This undiscovered rider out of backward England, at present a raw self-nurtured talent, might, with proper support and guidance, become another Elliott or Robinson, or better. Magne decided it was worth the gamble and telephoned his offer via Pierre Joliveau.

It happened so quickly, all within a few weeks, as if some fairy godfather had waved his wand and said, 'Jock, you shall go to the ball!' Jock had cracked the oyster and Vic and I couldn't help feeling a tinge of envy as we saw him off by train to Paris to confer with the great man.

It was late afternoon two days later, when this nifty-looking Simca with chrome bumpers and whitewall tyres rolled up beside the ambulance. Vic and I did a double take to recognise the man behind the wheel as our comrade. Gone the stained crumpled trousers, checked shirt with threadbare collar and scuffed sandals. He was dressed *à la mode* in a brand new casual outfit, with styled haircut and sunglasses to match. At our prompting he did a sheepish twirl. He had returned from the ball with a demonstration of his new spending power – part contract advance, part prize money, blown on transforming himself from rags to riches. As for the Simca, Magne had warned him to be prepared to race anywhere in the country at short notice, so he needed his own transport

With a sudden shock we realised this was a parting of the ways. Henceforth Jock would be working to his own agenda, no longer sharing our enterprise, hardly our comrade. It was such a profound change that neither Vic nor I quite knew how to feel. We were happy he had confounded those Jonahs back home who said reaching the heights under one's own steam was impossible. Yet we were also envious that he had 'made it' and we hadn't, when so little separated us in ability and performance. He possessed that mysterious and temporary gift of form that bred confidence, aggression and good judgment. His finishing kick had done the rest.

Magne's rush to sign Jock up for Mercier had been partly to meet the deadline for the World Professional Road Race Championship to be held on the Gueux Circuit near Rheims. This was a venue for Grand Prix motor racing, with a stand for spectators at the finish and triumphal arch over the carriageway. The circuit was half on smooth flat roads and half on the hilly lanes of the *montagne*. The combination of hills and heat was destined to splinter the field.

Vic and I had also hoped to participate, but at the last minute the UCI withdrew permission for independents and we ended up as spectator-helpers, passing up drinks. At the start Jock was unusually twitchy. He had had a spat with British team manager Benny Foster. As Jock drove out to Gueux that morning, the NCU team car overtook him with a jersey trailing from a window. Apparently, it had been worn in the previous day's amateur championship and was now being 'aired' for Jock's benefit, the only spare being allocated to Robinson. According to Jock, Foster tossed the jersey in his direction, saying, 'Here, that's for you!' Outraged, Jock threw it straight back. 'It's damp and stinks of sweat. I'm not wearing that.' Why hadn't it been laundered and dried at the hotel the previous evening? Why were there no spares? It was disgraceful that a professional was expected to represent his country wearing secondhand kit.

Jock's action (or Foster's inaction) could have cost him dear. The ban on commercial advertising in world championships ruled out wearing his Mercier jersey. Instead he took a chance on the more anonymous Fred Dean, an infringement that somehow escaped the adjudicators' eyes, and seven and a half hours and 172 miles later, finished 13th, four minutes behind solo winner Ercole Baldini (*Il Sputnik della Route!* as Italian banners proclaimed, likening him to the Soviet space capsule in orbit around Earth). Many stars, Anquetil included, abandoned in the heat. Amongst others that Jock beat to the line were De Filippis, Geminiani, Coppi, Scodeller, Planckaert, Adriaenssens, Elliott, Robinson and Graczyk. It remains one of the best achievements ever by a British rider in a World Professional

Road Race Championship. But from reading the team manager's self-congratulatory autobiography, *The Benny Foster Story*, you would never guess. Two pages devoted to the race praise Robinson and Elliott, but never mention the Englishman who beat them both. Foster's petty revenge was to edit Jock completely out.

The *Miroir Sprint* journalist/photographer who turned up to interview us at the campsite was intrigued. It was unprecedented for three young British cyclists to reside in France and compete at the highest level, let alone live together from hand-to-mouth in a converted ambulance. He had us pose for photographs in the galley kitchen amidst our rudimentary culinary paraphernalia. He faked us under the open bonnet 'repairing' the engine, and again sitting around on the grass whilst I 'played' my guitar. From all this emerged the idea of a gypsy life-style and the accompanying headline *Les Nomades du Velo Anglais*.

I took the opportunity to enquire about Mater. Without mentioning Rue Blondel, I asked about his standing as a *directeur sportif*. Was he highly regarded? 'Very much so,' the journalist replied. 'He knows the business and has a good record. He'd love to be put in charge of the French national team in the Route de France, but there's no chance of that happening. It would cause a scandal.'

I pushed him to explain, but he was reluctant. 'It's a question of perceived morality,' was all he would add. It was ironic, I thought, that this 'perceived morality' proved no bar to his appointment as manager of a *British* team. I was tempted to add that our gracious Queen would not have been amused.

Despite Mater's dodgy *métier*, it was impossible to dislike him as a person. That autumn he visited our campsite and we spent a pleasant afternoon reminiscing around the Tour de L'Ouest and acquainting him with our future plans. As ever he radiated warmth and charm. *L'Hotel Escale* was never mentioned. I wondered whether giving that business card was an indiscretion he now regretted, or simply his way of being open and honest: this is how I am – take me or leave me.

That was the last time I met André. Whether he had much of a future in French cycling I very much doubt.

16

I hated the thought of her ending up in the embrace of a scrapyard crusher. 'She' had acquired an identity with more emotional resonance than a mere lump of recyclable metal.

A rectangle of trodden yellowing turf marked where the ambulance had remained ever since our ill-fated trip to Boulogne. Meanwhile, transport to races was by courtesy of the BCR, an arrangement that suited us well and usually worked like clockwork. Once, I forgot my cycling shoes, but our chauffeur made a return trip to retrieve them just in time – ever afterwards Pierre obliged me to tick off a kit list before leaving.

Sometimes transport to distant races was provided by club sponsors La Slavia Brewery. It was no comfortable cushioned ride. We had to squat on upturned crates in the back of this monster delivery van as it bumped at snail's pace through the French countryside. The windowless metal interior was sweltering hot and, unable to see outside, we were entirely reliant on the driver's navigational skills. One Sunday, returning from the Ardennes, the vehicle suddenly halted. Good, we thought, maybe it's a café and we can buy a snack. But stepping out, we found ourselves in the middle of nowhere. All was quiet up front, suggesting the driver was answering a call of nature in the bushes, so we slaked our post-race thirst from a soft drinks crate slung beneath the chassis. But when five minutes of silence became ten, I was sent forward to investigate.

I found the man slumped in his seat, staring at the fly-bespattered windscreen. Always monosyllabic in conversation, it was now as if a catatonic fit had struck him dumb. Worse still, the van rested across the middle of the road, and as I stood at the open cab door, passing vehicles skimmed my elbow, their occupants hooting and gesturing disagreeably. Some were big trucks being driven on sidelights post the late afternoon aperitif. Dusk was falling. This was no place to park.

Vic and Jock joined me, equally puzzled. We discounted a heart attack or stroke: his problem was apparently mental or emotional.

We tried to cajole him into action by punching his arm, but only a thick vein pulsing at his brow indicated he was still in the land of the living. At last, in desperation, we shoved him across the bench seat and I took his place behind the wheel. He made no resistance. With a seeming corpse at my side, I proceeded cautiously through the moth–filled dusk, having in mind I was uninsured to drive.

At the campsite we unloaded and left him sitting. Over a cup of 'rosy' we debated what to do with our 'guest'. We could hardly leave a sick man alone in his cab all night, and yet we hesitated to call for help. Fortunately, the decision was made for us. The van roared back to life and Rip Van Winkle disappeared without lights in the direction of the camp exit.

It still presented a moral dilemma. If we put the incident from our minds, it might well be repeated with more serious consequences. If we 'grassed', the poor man could lose his livelihood. In the end we left our problem with Pierre.

Some days later Monsieur Linglet, the La Slavia proprietor, paid us a visit to apologise. The man, it seemed, was manic-depressive and prone to attacks of nervous paralysis. He should never have been allocated to driving duties. 'You won't sack him, will you?' I enquired. '*Oh mais non!* He has a wife and family. We'll put him on light duties in the brewery.'

This humane solution – remember, before EU employment protection laws, bosses had a free hand – won Linglet our deepest respect. He was not only a well-to-do cycling enthusiast, but also a man of genuine compassion.

As the season drew to a close, something else was decided. We had considered saving money by making do with the ambulance for another year. But returning from a three-days' racing trip to the Luxembourg border, the old girl pitched into one deep pothole too many and let out a crack of doom. It was a broken spring. She was left tilting at an alarming angle with a huge strain on the steering. We limped back to Rheims with me cursing that my winnings from a second place at Longwy, intended for homegoing presents, would now need to be spent patching up a vehicle that was past its time. We found and fitted an approximating Citroën spare from a crashed van at a local scrapyard. She still listed as if from a torpedo strike, but at least was driveable.

That decided it. The old ambulance, once our panacea, was now an unsustainable burden that had to go. First though we must get her back to England.

Petrol was expensive in France. At Dunkirk the dipstick suggested we had just enough fuel left in the tank to see us on and off the ferry. That proved to be over-optimistic. The engine spluttered and died and, embarrassingly, we had to be towed off last of all on disembarkation. Though we felt like idiots, it may after all have been a blessing in disguise. I was illegally importing a cage-bird as a gift for my mother and Vic had stashed his personal wine cellar behind the plywood interior to evade paying duty, the free allowance being a niggardly two bottles. A customs official sipping his mug of tea waved us through, doubtless concluding that no self-respecting smuggler would risk being out of fuel.

Vic volunteered to dispose of the ambulance. He had a contact in Thorne who 'will take her off our hands for £14' – and I was glad. I hated the thought of her ending up in the embrace of a scrapyard crusher. 'She' had acquired an identity with more emotional resonance than a mere lump of recyclable metal. She had been our home through ups and downs and rain and shine, where we had entertained Annie and Francine and been dubbed *Les Nomades du Velo Anglais*. She deserved better, and she got it, going straight back into service with a farmer in need of a mobile chicken house.

Farmers can be slow to rid their land of junk. Perhaps, just perhaps, our ambulance still reposes in some corner of a boggy field, rusting away quietly to eternity on rotted scarecrow tyres – at any rate, the romantic in me would like to think so.

17

'Rheims is OK,' he said, 'but there are better places for you to make a living.'

We had good reason to be pleased with our first full season of racing abroad. Jock became only the second Briton in history to win a contract with a top continental team and Vic emerged from nowhere to reveal his talent as a climber. My results had been consistently good, once I burned off the fat from my lay-off. We had won more in prize money than we could possibly have earned from our jobs back home and we felt we had hardly begun to scratch the surface. Vic and I reckoned we had much more to learn and give. Consequently, it wasn't a question of whether to return to France, but when and how.

No sooner were we back than we began making plans for 1959. We had some tough decisions to make. Should we replace Jock with someone else or stay as a twosome? Should we buy another van for conversion, or go for the car and caravan option, using the cash surplus from our winnings? Though we still needed to budget carefully, the penny-pinching of 1958 was behind us.

With our income on tap, we could, like Jock, have rented an apartment in Rheims, but we decided instead to retain the roving option. There were other parts of France to explore and, indeed, a cycling enthusiast from the Southwest had already made us a tempting offer.

Lucien Desnos had been travelling in Champagne when a newspaper headline caught his attention. It concerned three young Englishmen who were the favourites in a local cycle race. Curious to discover why Englishmen were cycle-racing in France, he came along to watch us at Signy le Petit and when we did well, as the press predicted, finishing 1st, 3rd and 4th, he was mightily impressed. He sought me out after the race and made an offer. 'Rheims is OK,' he said, 'but there are better places for you to make a living. My region, Charente, for example, bordering the Correze, Limousin and Bordeaux – lots of races and after the Tour a criterium almost every day, with contracts, travelling expenses and good prize money. As Britons, you'd be in demand and people would come to see you race. You'd be very welcome to stay and camp free of charge in the village of Saint Claud sur le Son, where I work in the pharmacy. Think it over.' He left me with his card.

To be in demand both in Rheims and the South West was very flattering. But for the moment we were content to stay put – that is until Jock's contract with Mercier threw everything up into the air. Even then Vic and I decided to keep matters on hold until after our visit to the Côte d'Azur in the spring of '59

That winter I found temporary work with Henry Holmes Cycles. Henry had three busy shops in and around Sheffield and ran a mail-order business. The arrangement suited us both. Though the pay was poor, he allowed me time off for training, and under his expert tuition I learned some much needed mechanical skills, including the art of wheel building. For his part, he was banking on my name and reputation attracting customers.

For much of 1958 I had struggled to recapture fitness lost during the previous year's lay-off. That six months 'rest and recuperation' had been a mistake I wasn't about to repeat. I kept the pedals turning. The mileages were necessarily modest, because now my body was genuinely crying out for rest and recuperation after sixty-one races in seven months, plus many thousands of training miles. This relentless grind typified the life of the professional racing cyclist of that era, whose income was gleaned mainly from prize and appearance money. Some, like fabled hardman Rik Van Steenbergen, took no winter break at all but raced on the six-days circuit or flew around the world to garner contracts. Many bike racers were country boys who swapped slavery on the land for slavery on the bicycle in a romantic bid for fame and fortune. Some succeeded, but for most, at best *domestiques,* it was a case of scrabbling for crumbs at the feet of a star. To make a living, they had to race anywhere and everywhere, whereas today's well salaried professionals can pick and choose, formulate a balanced programme and nurture their condition to a peak. Cycling has always been a tough sport, but there is tough and tough.

Meanwhile our preparations went ahead. Falcon Road Club's Alan Huntingdon, a successful independent rider keen to improve, replaced Jock as our third member. Vic and I knew he could be relied on not to get cold feet and pull out at the last minute. Also, being Tykes together, we spoke the same language.

Sharing costs, we three could now easily afford a car and caravan, and I eventually purchased a medium sized second-hand tourer. Vic had also been busy. He had found a suitable car, a pre-war Wolseley 12, which the seller described as powerful and reliable. He had had a tow bar fitted and passed his driving test. Now three drivers would share the burden of driving.

We planned to return to the Côte d'Azur in mid February. In the meantime I tried to clock up some training on English roads, but bad weather intervened and I covered barely 300 kilometres in January, before contracting flu.

The Asiatic flu epidemic of 1958/9 was the worst since the 1918 pandemic that had killed millions. There was no combative vaccine. I spent a week in bed, shaking, sweating, coughing and vomiting, a trip-hammer trapped inside my head. The doctor was sanguine: all the hospitals were full, and anyway youngsters like me had reserves of strength to pull through.

He was right, of course. After eight days I was back on my feet. But cycling was out of the question and I had barely enough energy to pack and complete preparations before Vic arrived with Alan and the Wolseley and we hitched up to the caravan. Soon the roof rack was weighted down with bikes and spares, the caravan loaded with suitcases and boxes of food, pans and crockery. But something was plainly wrong. Car and caravan should have been in horizontal plane. Instead they presented a shallow V shape, the caravan tipped forwards and the low-slung Wolseley tipped back, its towbar almost scraping the road and bonnet assuming the angle of a heavy bomber taking off. Re-arranging our luggage to form a counterweight made little impression.

'Chocks away!' Vic joked. Then I noticed something else, a little inky pool of oil forming beneath the engine.

Alan looked sceptical as I said to Vic, 'Are you sure this engine's OK?'

'Course it is. The guy told me all about the engine. It does use a little bit of oil, but I've got plenty in reserve.'

He certainly had: a five-gallon drum of 'reconstituted', the cheapest slurry obtainable. A bit of oil! We would spend months pouring oil in at one end only for it to exit at others, leaving behind slug-like trails and clouds of oleaginous black smoke.

We stayed that night outside Jock's house in Tolworth, parked beside his Simca. Our erstwhile motoring expert cast a critical eye over our latest acquisition. 'Did you buy this heap of scrap, Vic?' Diplomacy wasn't Jock's strong point. He laughed theatrically. 'How far do you imagine you're going to get with this old wreck?' He jumped on the vestigial running board with his pretend machine gun and mowed us all down. 'It belongs in a gangster movie!'

True, but there was little we could do now: we were stuck with oil-guzzling 'Rosy Lee', as she was later christened by Pierre, like it or lump it.

Before the MOT test intervened, many such lamentable pre-war wrecks still chugged around on Britain's roads. In France, a sharp contrast existed between countryside and town. Out in the sticks wartime petrol shortages had produced some weird and wonderful Heath Robinson contraptions, wood-burners that smoked like Mississippi paddle steamers, others with roof-slung billowing reservoirs of gas. There were also many elegant, low-slung Citroëns of Inspector Maigret fame, nowadays lovingly restored to become sought-after vintage trophies. Bernard Pusey possessed one such and after our abandonment in the Grand Prix Fourmies, demonstrated his driving skill, with me as heart-in-mouth passenger, by shoving into the tyre-squealing pack of team cars and jockeying for position with the maddest of wheels-on-the-verge, dust-kicking *directeurs sportifs*.

By 1959, the *nouvelle vague* of Citroëns was loose on city streets. Pierre had two, a bouncy *deux chevaux*, with dashboard gear change, for his electrical business and also a stylish DS19 (aping his hero, De Gaulle!) with its innovative lifting pneumatic suspension that made him feel, he said, like a Roman emperor charioteer. And that was how he drove, one-handed, bowling over the Rheims pavé and wolf-whistling the girls – '*Oh, regardez, la jolie fille!*' Once, hurtling at 160 kph down the N51 towards Charleville, he advised, '*Attention les flics!*' superfluously since lumbering Rosy was never likely to trouble traffic cops. In the back seat, his long-suffering wife Eliane murmured resignedly, '*Incorrigible!* 'e eez just leetle boy!'

Rosy's tow bar scraped the cobbles as we dipped and lurched over Northern France's *routes bombées*, the caravan tugging behind like a reluctant whale. Each morning Rosy accepted her oily breakfast with a grateful glug-glug only for most to be farted back out through the exhaust.

It was bitterly cold, the roads practically deserted and shrouded in mist. Trees were hung with long icicles, like giant chandeliers, which our oncoming airwave brought clattering down on the caravan roof. Many lorry drivers sat huddled over roadside braziers, waiting for the *barrière de dégele* to be lifted. This was a law to prevent heavy vehicles from damaging thawing road surfaces (it was repealed only when some financial genius concluded that paralysing commerce cost more than road repairs).

We camped west of Nice, close to the presentday airport and juncture with the N202, at a rent of only 2000 francs per week (under £2). We had the campsite to ourselves for the whole five weeks of our stay, one reason being perhaps a large pen of gobbling turkeys, a clamorous wake-up call at dawn, or the equally sleep-disruptive braying from the marshland of frogs a-courting.

No more franc-pinching trips to Uniprix in Nice and humping back loaded haversacks. Nearby were some excellent village shops, one specialising in fresh pasta, catering for the Franco-Italian taste of the border regions. The ravioli was to die for! The only ravioli obtainable in England outside London was the tinned 'heartburn' variety in a tomato sauce like battery acid.

Most Britons (including most athletes) gave little thought then to diet. Pappy white sliced bread, tinned foods, eggs and bacon fried in lard, boiled beef and cabbage: these were the norm. In his misnamed *Scientific Training for Cycling* of 1954 Dr Christopher Woodard warned athletes off bread, rice, bananas, spaghetti and dried fruit because, he said, they were fattening (an early exponent of the Atkin's Diet!). Not until the 70s did 'pasta' creep into English dictionaries. Two years of exposure to French cuisine and a thorough reading of Louison Bobet's book, *En Selle*, had me discounting Dr Christopher's misinformation and ensuring we stuck to a fat-free, carbohydrate-loaded diet with fresh fruit and vegetables. I still possess some of those shopping lists informing the basics of healthy eating – bread, oats, rice, pasta, greens, fruit, yoghurt, margarine rather than expensive butter, cheese and ham (but not eggs, 'bad for the liver') – all are there. Lacking a fridge, we used fresh ingredients.

We diverged from the modern athlete's ideal diet in the amount of red meat consumed, usually steak, lightly fried to retain the protein and mineral content. But there was a snag: undercooked meat might harbour live tapeworm eggs. Once ingested, these hatched and grew huge, feasting off the contents of the gut and accounting for many a cyclist's loss of form. Recently meat has had a bad press. Even before the BSE catastrophe, it was being associated with bowel cancer, and dieticians began recommending alternative sources of protein, especially fish, said to explain the low incidence of heart disease amongst the Japanese. The myth that meat was essential should have been exploded by the feats of our 1940s top athlete Sydney Wooderson, a vegetarian. It certainly was when Francesco Moser won the 1984 Giro d'Italia on a mainly cereal vegetarian diet.

Well recovered from my bout of flu, I slipped easily back into training and with barely 1,000 kilometres in the legs felt confident enough to start and finish in the Grand Prix Ville de Nice on 23rd February. Vic too was riding well, but for Alan the speed and aggression of continental racing was an eye-opener.

With a good financial buffer we could afford to be more relaxed in our approach to training – less of the cols of Braus and Castillon and more of the easier coast-hugging routes. I was determined to build up gradually and so was paying more attention to recovery. I experimented with yoga as practised by German ace, Rudi Altig, though fighting shy of limb-twisting poses in favour of the relaxation techniques. After lunch, I would stretch out on a sunny patch of grass, rid my mind of distracting thoughts, and visualise myself floating weightless to the point of merging with space. This mental visualisation was quite the opposite of falling asleep and maybe more beneficial as I 'awoke' after half an hour feeling thoroughly de-stressed. Vic and Alan, reposing in more traditional ways, contemplated this stratagem with wonder and amusement.

18

Anquetil — As we crouched and crossed in the line-out, the flowing trick of rain and light made it hard to distinguish where the man ended and machine began. It was as if they were forged together at birth from the same shining material.

In 1957, Derek had introduced us to an Italian cycle dealer named Barale, whose shop in Bordighera on a cliff-edge was within sound of the waves. It was crammed to the ceiling with Campagnolo and other gorgeous star-spangled Italian gear, arguably the best, and here at discount prices. I had commissions from Pierre and friends at home, and two trips were necessary to bring all these goodies back past wary French Customs officials.

I enjoyed this undulating 60-mile return ride through Nice and Menton, with a soft briny breeze blowing off the sea. We took advantage of a bureau-de-change near the customs post offering an excellent rate of exchange. The unstable Italian currency was on a post-war low and we traded pristine pounds sterling for saddlebags of the most disgusting used banknotes you could imagine: crumpled, torn, scribbled-over and so grubby they might have been mashed up in a bowl of sick at a Mussolini pasta party and left on a waste tip to dry.

Barale eyed our filthy wads with cupidity.

We communicated via an odd mélange of Italian, English and French, together with lots of pointing, gesticulating and scribbling on his Martini notepads. Wizened Barale was always good for a haggle, though once bargained down, prices needed the cement of writing or they slithered back up. After testing the tread on my teeth, I bought a dozen Pirelli Corsa Leggera eight-ounce tubulars at a discount of 30 per-cent on the British price. Barale claimed they had been seasoned for six months at the factory and then hung for a similar period hardening off in his showroom. Whatever the truth, the rubber was as tough as rhino skin, making them extremely puncture-resistant.

'Bar Ale', as Gil Taylor comically christened him, turned out to be something of an anglophile expert on our sceptred isle. It rained non-stop (tick); London was shrouded in fog (tick); you risked having your pocket picked or throat slashed in the East End (double tick); all roads were cobbled (what?); every inhabitant wore a stovepipe hat (hang on!); England was pancake flat except for that hilly bit where the phantom dog roamed. He communicated all this by mime and words plucked randomly from our three languages. The phantom dog was a savage howl and 'Basker-Ville' pronounced like Deauville.

'*Ingelterra* not flat,' insisted Gil. 'Lake District is in *Ingelterra*!' He demonstrated hills with his hand surfing up and down dolphin-like. I threw in my own two penn'orth of dolphins: 'Pennines! Cotswolds!' Derek plugged on about Beachy Head. For him, anywhere north of Hove was Border Country.

'You joka me!' Barale scoffed. *His* hand zoomed up high in a gesture resembling a Blackshirt salute. '*Alpi!*' He stood on tiptoe. '*Appen! Alpi Dolomitiche!*'

We were bowed and humbled. He was talking real hills, Stelvios, not pimples like Holme Moss and Birdlip.

Whence had he gleaned all this nonsense about Britain? Apparently from watching period-costume films like 'The Hound of the Baskervilles', 'Great Expectations' and 'Wuthering Heights'. In this pre-TV-documentary era, it wasn't uncommon for foreigners to imagine our country was trapped in some nineteenth century Wuthering Heights time warp and peopled by phlegmatic eccentrics who made great warriors but lousy lovers (double tick?).

On our departure, he wished us bon voyage. Unlike his verbose and raucous Italian customers, we represented his paradigm of the soft-spoken English gentleman – and what a pleasure to take our cash. He scooped up the piles of filthy currency from his counter like something the dog had left, and stuffed them into his bulging till, where the germs were probably already conjugating like rabbits.

Before the EU, there was something cloak and dagger about crossing the Franco-Italian border that gave rise to a pleasurable frisson of concern. Italian officials barely bothered, but the French made our passports the occasion for deep philosophic study. In 1957, despite our shoulders being swathed in brand new tubulars and our musettes stuffed with equipment *Campagnolo*, customs officials accepted all was for our own use and not intended for resale. We were waved through.

But in 1960 the mood had hardened. Jock's Simca was pulled out of line and minutely searched. Even the seats were removed. All our purchases from the genial Barale were laid out on a table, alongside the receipts, for forensic scrutiny. They were having a purge. Several people had been arrested for smuggling cycle equipment into France and selling it on for profit. The price difference could add up to a nice little earner for the smuggler and, indeed, one notable Monsieur Big had recently been hauled before the courts, and jailed.

The assiduous search uncovered nothing covert; nevertheless we were slapped with a bill for customs duty. I protested – we were professional racing cyclists and the equipment was for our own personal use. The officials looked askance and one said, 'Professionals, eh? So your sponsor supplies all your equipment. Therefore this must be surplus to your requirements and for resale at profit.' – impeccable logic, but, unfortunately for us, not true.

We were stumped. Then suddenly Jock dived into his jacket pocket and produced a postcard. *'Regardez!'* It was of the Mercier team with Louison and himself standing together in line.

'Ça, c'est moi! Et ça, Bobet!'

They took the postcard and passed it round, rocking their heads – *Alors* – swelling visibly with Gallic pride. *'Vous gardez,'* Jock said, and he autographed it for them. They pinned it up on their notice board, saluted and waved us on our way. The bill was junked.

So what had happened to impeccable French logic? It seems national hero Bobet had trumped it. Any friend of his was a friend of theirs.

Italy was a world apart from France, noisier, more vibrant. Motorists lived on their hooters and could never overtake without giving full blast to their intentions. On a busy road this non-stop hooting would provoke us into angry, hand-over ear gestures, astonishing the Italian drivers: after all, they were only doing what came naturally.

In France the ear-splitting velo-moteur reigned supreme and in Italy the Vespa scooter. For sheer dare-devilry Italians took the biscuit, placing their faith entirely in some little token metal effigy of the Virgin or Saint Christopher strapped to the petrol tank, road safety being an alien concept. You would see amorous couples riding together, the girl on pillion, their hands intertwined and the steering and braking taking care of themselves. We were once astonished to see a Vespa delivery boy freewheeling no-hands downhill, the engine cut to save fuel and his arms packed to the eyebrows with floral bouquets. How could he possibly see where he was going or control the machine? He cornered by leaning. Short of dropping his cargo, how did he propose to stop on reaching his destination? With such inspiring exemplars, no wonder so many Italians made suicidally great descenders.

In some isolated country districts time seemed to have stood still: no electricity or mains water, no telephone. The twentieth century had passed them by. Many peasant women washed garments in the river, thrashing the dirt out on boulders, and spreading them to dry on hedges and walls. In other places there were communal washhouses fed by running spring-water. As we cycled past, the women would be sloshing up to their elbows in some great stone tub, singing and chattering, a sense of happy community overlaying their apparent poverty. Sometimes they paused long enough to smile at us and gabble something unintelligible in the twanging Provençal lingo. Asked what they said, I always gave the same joking answer: 'They're admiring our personal qualities!' Wherever we went, especially in the countryside, the locals would gawp, surmising we were perhaps *les as*. Brian Robinson has commented sadly:

'We used to sit and chat with the fans in villages. Now the riders are surrounded by bodyguards, totally separate.'

The only time I can recall anyone back home taking such an intense interest was once as I climbed out of a Derbyshire village and overheard a small boy asking, 'Mummy, who's that man?'

'Just a silly cyclist, dear! Ignore him!'

That pretty well summed up what you could expect in England.

On March 22nd we raced in the Souvenir Eusebi and next day hitched up the caravan and headed west to explore what Charente had to offer.

But now, in warmer weather, oily perfidious Rosy gave notice to take nothing for granted. Rounding a narrow blind bend in some Provençal village on the N7, an enormous horn-blasting truck suddenly came at us with trailer in tow. Vic hit the brakes and we stopped, squeezed between the truck and a tall building, just a Rizla from being crushed into a Dinky toy. Towering above throbbed this juggernaut, its driver expressing dour-faced devotion to his Divine

Right of free passage on his *route nationale*. If someone had to back up, it certainly wasn't going to be him.

Unfortunately, darling Rosy chose now to stall and play dead. Pressing the starter button served only to turn a lifeless engine. By contrast the juggernaut's engine was thundering in our ears, demanding a swift end of delay. We crawled through a rear window and lifted Rosy's bonnet to be met by a wave of ferocious heat. Wisps of steam leaked from hosepipe unions. Dripping oil patterned the dust at our feet. From his lofty throne the truck driver gazed down contemptuously. It seemed the carburettor had boiled and evaporated its fuel and we must wait for it to cool.

A small crowd gathered to proffer advice. Why not remove the top off the carburettor and fill it with spare fuel? (We had none.) Why not use the starting handle to save the battery? (Because it had a habit of kicking back and breaking one's wrist.) The truck driver wound up his window, sealing himself from the rabble and no doubt thinking: this never happened when the Germans ran the country. Traffic was piling up in both directions and we expected at any moment to hear the sound of a police klaxon. Deeply humiliated, we were about to unhitch the caravan and manhandle it backwards, when Rosy suddenly relented and staggered back to life, emitting clouds of oily smoke. It had taken ten minutes. We reversed and the juggernaut inched past, dragging behind a long queue of traffic. For miles afterwards, drivers overtaking made that gesture that says 'Foreign Idiots!' Alan, two-fingered in response, angrily demanded of Vic whether Rosy's previous owner had mentioned stalling, alongside oil consumption, as being 'a bit of a problem'? But if Vic knew, he remained tight-lipped, refusing to be drawn.

We were overwhelmed with indifference by our first sight of tiny Saint Claud sur le Son. Parking on a cinder strip beside the communal pump, we set out to explore what little there was to see. An avenue of chestnuts led to a cemetery where gravestones bore tinted photographic images of the deceased beaming at us in the fulsome prime of life. Ancient houses bordered a square containing a war memorial and two serried ranks of trees. Over the roofs poked the tall spire of a church, its walls sprouting tufts of grass and weed, beneath which patron Saint Claud was ensconced in his medieval crypt. A few small shops, a small hotel and filling station, a blacksmith's, roads to north, east and west – and that was it, not exactly the city of Rheims. 'What are we doing here?' Vic murmured.

But first impressions can be deceptive. Within days, in the square, workmen began erecting an impressive spectator stand. It seemed this 'backward' village was the dynamo for the region's biggest professional cycling criterium, scheduled that year for March 30th – and we had just about enough time to warm up for it.

A short, softly spoken man with a pronounced limp, whom we remembered as Lucien Desnos, arrived to greet us, accompanied by the stout mayor, who joked that we were the first English visitors to the region since *Richard Coeur de Lion* lost his life from a stray arrow in 1199 whilst besieging the castle of Chalus, his mother being Eleanor of Aquitaine. 'So you see, we are all closely related. Our two nations once shared a queen.'

All the travelling had left us feeling stiff and lazy. Needing to snap out of our lethargy, we covered 100 then 220 kilometres on successive days, exploring the lush countryside under scudding white clouds. It was quite different from Champagne: far fewer vineyards, yet more bucolic, with a sense of remoteness from centres of industry and population, and a network of deserted lanes through forests and rolling hills that made training almost a pleasure.

Lucien had anticipated our arrival by entering us for two criteriums, at Saint Claud and on the day before at Bourcfranc in Charente Maritime, site of the richest oyster beds in Europe. Here at the fishing port the weather was foul. The 60 laps, one-kilometre course ran beside a rain-lashed harbour exposed to the full force of the elements. At the start a surprise was in store: sheltering under an umbrella, in the green and white jersey of Helyett Leroux, was the sleek figure of Jacques Anquetil. There was something feminine about Anquetil's slim physique that belied his wonderful masculine strength and courage, as the American journalist and Tour watcher Robert Daley has remarked: 'I would stare at him as if he were a girl – trying to understand where all that power came from.' We three each had a small *prime de départ*. But we too stared fascinated, wondering what jingling purse of gold had been offered to entice Maître Jacques to launch himself into this Atlantic storm.

I ended up 7th to Anquetil's 2nd and won several primes. I can still hear the slosh of tyres through that lake of a circuit and see the clusters of drenched spectators bowed beneath their brollies. But my clearest memory is of Anquetil himself. Football fanatics boast of their 'beautiful game', but here was the Apollo of the beautiful machine. Other stars – Bobet, Geminiani, Graczyc – bobbing and swaying, seemed perpetually at war with the bicycle. But this man, with his pedalling action so rapid, precise and apparently effortless, was all minimalist elegance. If he had spent half the night with his *copains*, smoking, drinking and playing cards, as legend decrees, there was no sign of it. As we crouched and crossed in the line-out, buffeted by wind, the flowing trick of rain and light made it hard to distinguish where the man ended and machine began. It was as if they had been forged together at birth from the same shining material.

But there was more than style to Anquetil. He was naturally reserved, which some journalists interpreted as arrogance, dubbing him 'Napoleon'. They preferred extrovert, voluble, warm-hearted characters like Geminiani, who always provided good copy. Yet ever afterwards out of this 'arrogant' detachment, with a little nod of recognition, he would register my presence on the start line, a minnow among sharks, as if to say, 'You too are part of this show!' something I have never forgotten.

Anquetil, born in January 1934, was almost exactly my age. There, of course, the comparison ends. Five times winner of *La Grande Boucle*, nine times of the Grand Prix des Nations, twice of the Tour of Italy, he was by light years the superior athlete. But in the race of life I have out-stayed him: he died of cancer at the tragically young age of 53. Perhaps his reputation for aloofness stemmed from his impatience at the probing of some journalists with only armchair understanding of the cyclist's brutally tough profession. After the drug-related death of Simpson on Ventoux in 1967, he remarked, 'You would have to be an imbecile or an idiot to believe no one takes drugs!'

Anquetil was always his own man, ferociously honest when it came to speaking out on the use of stimulants. To his credit he treated Death with the same honesty and wry sense of humour. To his once great rival, the 'eternal second', Raymond Poulidor, visiting him at the end, he reputedly drew on his last reserves of strength to say, 'I'm on the edge of the hole. Sorry, Raymond, but once again you will finish second.'

During his career, the French public and media disparaged Anquetil as a boring *rouleur*, uninspirational, too cautious and calculating, a mere accountant on wheels. Though made a Chevalier of the *Légion d'Honneur* by De Gaulle personally, he was not popular. But a generation later, with homegrown talent in short supply, his worth was recognised. On his death, the nation was plunged into mourning and Apollo's image was carried on all the front pages, even of *Paris-Match*.

St Claud sur le Son, 1959. A warm-up amateur race on the day preceeding the big professional criterium.

19

*'Voilà!' She cried triumphantly, loosening her restraining hand
from around my groin, and I felt the thickness of fluid being slowly
pumped into a reluctant vein. It occurred to me afterwards that
it must be like this for a virgin being ravished by an incompetent
lover.*

Amongst our prizes from Bourcfranc was a box of fresh oysters, big
fellows the size of saucers. As we had no appetite for *fruits de mer*, I
offered them to some true *gitanes* camped above us in the lee of the
cemetery wall. Swarthy, black-haired Pyreneans, they were sitting
around a stick fire close to their hoop-top wagon. They accepted
my gift with the guarded thanks of those more used to abuse than
goodwill. As dusk fell, their fire flared and a guitar struck up and
they began singing some plangent song in what sounded like Basque
or Catalan. With a bottle or two of rough wine, my hard-won oysters
were being serenaded, and I was pleased to think they had at least
brought some happiness to poor travellers with whom it wasn't that
hard for us to identify.

Next morning the site was empty. The gypsies had decamped
at dawn, leaving behind a ring of blackened ash on the trampled
grass. Of the oyster shells there was no trace. Perhaps even then, as
the wagon rumbled on, their children were busy fashioning them
into simple necklaces and bangles for sale? Unlike modern urban
man, these thrifty people made sure nothing that came into their
hands went to waste.

Now there followed seven weeks that I rate the best of my cycling
career. The cold, drenching rain of Bourcfranc continued next day
for the criterium at Saint Claud, where I won a 2,000-franc prime,
before Roger Rivière broke clear and lapped the entire field, causing
many, including Vic, Brian Robinson and me, to retire. Six days later
I won my first race in France, at Fontenay Le Compte. It happened in
extraordinary circumstances. At a crossroads, our semi-professional
peloton clashed with another from an amateur race coming from
the opposite direction. Some inter-regional failure of communication

must have occurred. The two pelotons, led by police outriders, briefly merged and confusion reigned. As we turned left, I made my escape with Vic and seven others. Two of these turned out to be infiltrators from the 3rd-category race, who were rapidly burned off. But we were never caught and, with Vic's aid, I was able to win the five-up sprint in Fontenay.

The upshot of this tale occurred in 1995 when one Henri Lumineau contacted me from France. He lived in the Vendée not far from Fontenay and was trying to trace former riders from the Tour de L'Ouest for a book he was researching (since published in Belgium as *Le Lexique du Tour de L'Ouest*). It transpired that Henri, now a firm friend, was one of those amateurs in that clash of bunches all those years before.

After Fontenoy I was twice second, at Le Coux and Langon. The course at Le Coux was unique in my experience, many circuits up and down the same road with dead turns around weighted wine barrels. Then, in late April, came the five-stage, 582-kilometre Tour de L'Aude, later an international women's race, but then for young professionals and independents.

As we were being paid *frais de déplacement* (travelling expenses), we travelled by rail to the departure town of Limoux. Lodged in a stuffy box-room at the hotel, I had trouble sleeping and was concerned next morning that a lapse of concentration might cause me to crash. Instead, despite sore eyes, I felt quite alert and the rolling terrain suited me well. From finishing in the bunch on the first stage, I leapfrogged through the general classification to end up 4th overall at Carcassonne, my best result since the 1957 Tour du Var.

A hidden border exists between workaday athletic fitness and 'form'. I now crossed this border without understanding why; and for the first (and only) time in my career, I felt myself to be 'flying' or 'floating' or possessed with *coup de pédale*. It was like experiencing a lifetime of buying lottery tickets without success, and then suddenly pulling the jackpot. All my previous efforts seemed a parody of plodding endeavour. I was blessed with boundless energy, pedalling with a rapid easy cadence, always in the right gear and almost inured from pain. My confidence fed off this condition and I strove to be at the head of affairs, close to the arrowhead of the peloton, looking always to attack. And in the break, I was the one driving it forward, nagging and cajoling the others to greater and greater effort.

I was in the form of my life and Vic and Alan were also performing well. But our immediate programme was complicated and required careful planning. Vic and I were still affiliated to the BCR and Pierre Joliveau was keen for us to race in Rheims, so we struck a compromise: most of May and June in Champagne, the rest of the season in Charente. Pierre had lined up the important Grand Prix des Cooperateurs for us on May 3rd and we planned to travel by train to Rheims, breaking our journey in Poitiers on May 1st for the 21st edition of Poitiers-Saumur-Poitiers. Then on May 7th and 8th we were due back south in the Pyrenees for the Tour de L'Ariège; then again back north for the Tour de L'Oise on 17th and 18th May followed by the Circuit des Ardennes and in mid June the Tour de Champagne – all in all, ten days of racing in May alone with much travelling between and little rest. A modern-day professional, commuting by airplane or team-car, might blanch at the thought of such a demanding schedule.

The Poitiers race (206 kilometres) had drawn a good field of amateurs and independents. It was serving the FFC as a pre-Olympic trial and consequently had attracted riders from the Paris school of excellence. Two of these, Colin and Sciardis, animated the first half of the race and at Saumur held a lead of over a minute. But they were reined in over the second leg and left for dead on the final hills. A bunch of 19 (from 53 starters) contested the sprint, led out by the Parisian Le Greves; but two Charentais veterans, Pras and Pallu, had his wheel and relegated him to 3rd place. I was 5th, taking primes en route, and Vic equal 11th. In 1948 Pras had been a stage-winner of the Tour de France at La Rochelle. Here he was, eleven years later, still performing; or as *La Nouvelle Republique* remarked caustically: 'It was significant that a race designed for our Olympic youth was won by veterans.'

Two days later, Rheims and another bunch finish, but under very different circumstances. The field split in the *montagne de Reims*, only to regroup on the flat run to the finish. Despite my recent efforts at Poitiers, I felt immensely energetic and soon established a breakaway. My mistake was to whip these riders into such frenzy that one by one they pealed off, only to reform into a vengeful chasing pack. I dropped the last man with ten miles to go, a bad miscalculation, for just when I needed help, boring into a head wind on a dead-straight road, I was alone and exposed, a sitting-duck target. I was caught within sight of the *Arrivée*.

It was depressing, but I tucked it into the big bag marked 'lessons learned' and moved on – to a complete change of scenery, the Pyrenees and the Tour de L'Ariège. Here was the stamping ground of Raymond Mastrotto, whom the press had nicknamed 'Bull of the Pyrenees' on account of his powerful physique, more like a rugby back than cyclist. The other giant of the sport, Anatole Novak, notable in an age of twiddlers for shoving enormous gears, was even bulkier, with the chest of an ox and thighs like tree-trunks; to Jock, Vic and me he was simply 'Mr Universe'. Growth-hormone drugs had yet to be exploited, so both these Gargantuas were naturals. And, amazingly, both could climb well, Mastrotto well enough to be considered a favourite for the 1959 Tour de France.

Doing battle with the Bull in his homeland, I put up a performance I rank better than winning the Tour of Britain. On the first stage (229 kilometres), Mastrotto broke clear to cross the line almost two minutes ahead. But on the second day I matched him on the 4,000-foot ascent of the Col du Port. After bulleting down into Tarascon, the race progressed through narrow, twisting lanes where the surface in parts had degenerated into sand, gravel and grass. It was ideal territory for the lone break and, still feeling perky, I scooted off, giving Mastrotto the slip. Ahead, I could glimpse the two leaders, Tour riders Gay and Polo, and eventually a desperate pursuit race ensued, climaxing on the route nationale. If only I could catch them, the Tour de L'Ariège was mine. But at the line they were still 45 seconds ahead, and though I had two minutes over Mastrotto's group, it wasn't enough.

Mastrotto had timed it nicely. He remained top of the leader board, with Polo at 21 seconds and myself at 1.03. Vic was 5th at two minutes. Alan still had to find his racing legs, but was satisfied just to complete such a hard fast stage, 234 kilometres in six hours and ten minutes, averaging 38 kph.

I had begun to feel like the Jock of 1958, thinking victory rather than survival. But, unfortunately, it wasn't to last.

I remember that evening meal of trout hooked from the river beside the hotel, and the celebratory bottle of *sauvignon blanc* that we shared. Unsurprisingly, I felt exhausted and turned in early. Lulled to sleep by the sound of the rushing mountain stream below my window, I awoke in the small hours, coughing. Suddenly I felt desperately ill. My brow was burning. Moonlight flooded through the open casement and in my befuddled state I mistook it for dawn, especially as the air was filled with bird-song. It turned out to be the trilling of nightingales, beautiful and eerie rising up over the tumbling waters. By turns burning and shivering, I began hallucinating that I was aboard a raft in the tropics, spinning uncontrollably down foaming rapids towards a waterfall.

Come the true dawn, my lungs were raw with coughing. We took the train to Angoulême and from there I phoned St Claud asking to be collected by car. Village barber, Raymond Helion left his salon to pick me up, and I spent the next week at his house, being nursed by his wife, Huguette.

Eventually, the fever passed, but leaving my lungs congested. A visiting doctor diagnosed bronchitis resulting from an influenza virus. I expected him to prescribe a British-style unguent cough cure, but instead he drew from his bag a dozen glass jars resembling yoghurt pots, which he proceeded to heat up over a spirit burner. He clapped these hot jars to various parts of my chest and back. It was an ancient and agonising remedy called *ventouses*. The object, apparently, was to loosen and suck out the congestion. After a few minutes, each vacuum was released with a sharp twist and popping explosion of air. It was painful and I was soon covered in round purple bruises as if I'd gone ten rounds with a boxer wearing plant-pots for gloves. ('Cupping' is now a treatment on offer at celebrity health clinics!) I began to dread the sound of the doctor's approaching footfall and several applications of this remedy out of Paracelsus's Bumper Book of Spells brought no improvement.

Meantime, slowly but surely, as one day of inactivity bled into the next, I felt my precious hard-won form slipping away. It was psychological torture, yet there was nothing I could do about it. Non-athletes rarely appreciate that physical fitness cannot be banked. Acquired through years of hard graft, this perishable commodity can simply evaporate like morning dew. I was sliding back down the greasy pole that had taken me an age to climb.

The psychological pressure to get back on the bike was immense. Already I was two kilos heavier, and visits from my healthy-looking companions with accounts of their long training rides were no comfort. After seven days, against doctor's orders, I moved back into the caravan and recommenced training.

I reasoned I had little choice since we were contracted to go north for the two-days Tour de L'Oise and fulfil our agreement with the BCR. On May 16th we left the caravan in community care and took

Rosy on the long road to Creil, north of Paris, where next day, in a cold fall of rain, I made the gesture of signing the start sheet. After 70 kilometres, soaked to the skin, coughing and shaking, I climbed into the sag wagon. Attempting to race with bronchitis in such harsh conditions had been a foolish and costly mistake, as I was to discover.

The BCR had rented us a 'house' in Trigny, a village 15 kilometres west of Rheims. It was a tumbledown, unheated, two-room dwelling with bare cement floors, water pump and earth closet, overrun by mice. But it came rent-free; and though the straw mattresses barely alleviated the discomfort of sleeping on unsprung iron beds, it was welcome as a place to rest our heads.

For the next few days, whilst my comrades trained, I did little apart from cycling into Rheims to seek Pierre's advice. He put me in touch with a city doctor, who confirmed that I had bronchitis, but laughed off *ventouses* as a country bumpkin's remedy. 'Medieval witchcraft!' he scoffed. 'Let's see what modern medicine can do.' He prescribed penicillin.

In 1959 anti-biotic treatment was still at the scattergun stage, one strain used to treat every ailment. Eventually, of course, abuse of this 'wonder cure-all' would uncover a downside in terms of damaged immune systems and antibiotic-resistant germs like MRSA.

But when I cycled out to see the district nurse for my first injection, I had high hopes of a speedy cure. The woman lived in a cottage outside Trigny and her living room doubled as her 'surgery'. The domestic environment made few concessions to modern hygiene. A cat purred dreamily beside an open hearth; and the breakfast things were still on the table as she produced a battered tin box buried under scarves, gloves and other bric-a-brac in a dresser drawer. It contained a two-bit hypodermic syringe, which she now reassembled. A middle-aged no-nonsense authority figure of little sympathy and few words, straight out of 'Carry On Doctor', she indicated I was to drop my trousers and bend over a chair, whereupon she thumped my buttock with a wad of cotton wool soaked in surgical spirit. If she'd been younger and less of a sergeant major, 'mooning' and being slapped for it might have provoked me to lofty embarrassment. But seeing her sterilising that old blunt needle by plunging it into a spirit flame, and knowing my posterior was to be its target, rather took the edge off sexual appetite.

The well-used needle was about as sharp as your average biro, and it took several lunges for her to penetrate my derrière. 'Relax!' she commanded each time I yelped with pain. 'Your muscles are too tense!' Through a mirror on the wall, I watched the proceedings with growing trepidation. As she pushed off from the dresser in a final do-or-die thrust, her face wore the grim, piggy-eyed expression of a charging rhino.

'*Voilà!*' She cried triumphantly, loosening her restraining hand from around my groin, and I felt the thickness of fluid being slowly pumped into a reluctant vein. It occurred to me afterwards that it must be like this for a virgin being ravished by an incompetent lover.

Eventually I returned from her tender grasp to the relative humanity of Vic and Alan, who gathered round to cluck admiringly at the swelling bruise on my bum.

Further injections were prescribed, but I 'chickened out', telling Pierre I already felt much better, whereas the truth was I spent half the night coughing up my lungs and feeling dreadful. Remedies ancient and modern had proved equally ineffective. The bronchitis waxed and waned with the stress I inflicted on myself. A few days' rest brought improvement, a return to hard training and racing and I was back to square one. In a normal job, you can live with this condition whilst it gets better in the natural course of time. But athletics is not a normal anything, especially cycle racing, which subjects the body to massive energy burn and long exposure to the elements – over-heating, soaking, freezing. Under such a harsh regime, a depressed immune system cannot easily recuperate.

I wasn't the only member of our crew to be baffled by French medical practice. The previous year Vic had gone complaining of constipation to Pierre and Eliane, our surrogate parents. Eliane dispatched him with a note to the pharmacist where, flustered and embarrassed by the female assistant's incomprehensible gabble, he simply nodded at everything she said. 'She gave me these, like huge bloomin' horse pills,' he commented later. Back at the ambulance he swallowed a couple for good measure — and within half an hour rushed outside to vomit them back up.

'You idiot!' Jock laughed, reading the label. 'These aren't pills. They're suppositories. You've put them in at the wrong end!'

His mistake was understandable. Suppositories, monsieur's et madame's medical ingestion of choice, were virtually unknown in anal-retentive Britain.

I managed to complete half the Circuit of the Ardennes before exhaustion forced me to abandon; then in early June four stages of the Tour de Champagne, each stage being a strength-sapping 160 miles. But I was simply a passenger, clinging to the peloton. My nights were spent in bouts of coughing and I felt permanently tired. It took all my will power just to sign on and line up. The attacking form of only six weeks ago seemed as unreal now as a storybook romance, and I was left with heavy legs and an aching heart.

I was desperate to get myself better. What now added to this desperation was news of my selection with Vic and Jock as members of an International Team to contest the Tour de France, starting in Mulhouse on June 25th. The dream of a lifetime was about to be realised, and in normal circumstances I should have been on cloud nine. But with the clock ticking on my health, the good news simply served to ratchet up my anxiety and present an awful dilemma: should I give up my place in the Tour to someone who was fully fit, or accept and gamble on the bronchitis abating in time for the start? I decided to gamble, but when I abandoned on the final stage of the Tour de Champagne, too ill to continue, it was June 13th and I had just twelve days left to pray for a miracle cure.

At least money wasn't of immediate concern; my early season form had seen to that. From Bourcfranc to the Tour de L'Ariège I had netted 340,000 francs in prizes, primes and expenses, close to £300 in five weeks. In sporting or any other terms this was good pay. To put it in context: the professional footballer at this time was paid £12 per week, whilst the average weekly wage for a workingman was £7–£8. At £60 per week, I'd earned five times the professional footballer's wages and eight times those of a blue-collar worker (in today's money I suppose maybe £1,500 per week or £75,000 per year). Brian Robinson has stated that he earned around £1,000 per year. Many good riders earned similar sums, and the stars, vastly more. It was little wonder continental youth flocked to cycle racing as a means of escaping the poverty trap. Ten good racing years could set you up for life, with enough money to buy a business, luxury home and top-of-the-range lifestyle – and all the adulation to go with it.

But in this cruel game of financial snakes and ladders, earnings followed form. The eight weeks after the Tour de L'Ariège saw mine plummet to 51,000 francs (or around £5 per week). With living expenses over the same period of 95,000 francs, I was, in business parlance, operating at a loss – unsustainable in the long term.

My hopes were raised by a change in the weather. At the end of a cold, wet May, the temperature suddenly rose and the greenish fungal damp stains on the walls at Trigny dried out. I prayed my mucus-filled lungs would follow suit, as had occurred in the 1955 Circuit of Britain when I raced myself back to health in a heat wave. Might I not do likewise in the Tour? I was clutching at straws to rationalise the seriousness of my predicament. But it was only when I finished amongst prizewinners in the Grand Prix de Soissons on June 22nd that I became convinced my gamble had paid off.

Yes, a 95-mile race three days before starting the Tour de France! Add to this my other training and you have a grand total of 600 kilometres (375 miles) for that pre-Tour week. From this platform of fatigue and illness, I proposed to launch myself into three weeks and two and a half thousand miles of racing against the crème-de-la-crème of world cycling. Modern training manuals would call this lunacy, and I can only agree. I should have been tapering, resting not racing, building up reserves of glycogen in the muscles, allowing the body time to recuperate before its next explosive outlay of energy, boosting my immune system.

David Millar commented in his 2001 Tour Diary (BBC Online Sports): 'My preparation has not been really ideal – I've been racing non-stop since mid April. If you are taking part in the Tour, you shouldn't really race in June at all.'

Absolutely! You can put your feet up if someone is paying you a salary. But I had no salary and churning at the back of my mind was the conviction that I had to make up for lost training and lost earnings. And one could never do too much to satisfy cycling's credo of machismo, the factor most to blame for Tom Simpson's death on Ventoux in 1967.

Rest? Cycling supermen must never surrender to such 'weakness'.

20

Prior to the invention of the bicycle the nineteenth century French writer George Sand described apprentices touring the country to further their employment prospects as being involved in a Tour de France.

Crowds throng the bunting-decked streets of Mulhouse to applaud one hundred and twenty 'supermen'. Alongside the current favourites for the 1959 Tour – Anquetil, Charly Gaul, Baldini, Rivière – stand the veterans Robic and Bobet, former winners long past their best. My Tour de L'Ariège rival, Raymond Mastrotto, wears his first tricolour jersey with pride – some even say he will finish in yellow. I check for other familiar faces amongst the mêlée of officials, reporters, photographers and associated hangers-on outside race HQ. There's Dotto, and there Busto, winner of the 1957 Tour du Var. Eddy Pauwels, so much fêted in Bornem by the Vergaughen family – now in the black, yellow and red hoops of Belgium. And my roommate from the Tour de L'Ouest, Stephane Lach — that diet of sherry and eggs has paid off.

Now there's a real buzz amidst autograph hunters as an emaciated figure stoops over the signing-on table? His colours are of the bullring: sand-yellow and blood red. I bring him to memory from magazine photos of tortuous mountain roads and snowy peaks. Of course, Federico Bahamontes, 'The Eagle of Toledo', looking uncomfortably out of place in this grey northern clime with its steady fall of rain.

Will the rain never stop? The presence of some men I can match, even beat on a good day, is reassuring, less so the prospect of another dousing. I fear for my weakened lungs. *Mon Dieu!* Where is 'flaming' June? Wherever I look umbrellas are unfurled and racing capes glisten. A gendarme dodges around the overspill from a broken gutter; riders check their tyres, spinning the tread through gloved hands. Just as well – these first days over wet roads will produce a record number of punctures. I have put my faith in Barale and his rhino-skin *légèros*.

Both national and French regional teams are contesting this Tour, the system favoured by organiser Goddet. In the long run it will be doomed by the internal rivalries of individual riders and their separate commercial affiliations: the twelve-man French team, for example, divided amongst Helyett-Leroux, Mercier, Bobet and Geminiani Cycles. *'La France surtout!'* is a noble ideal, but impracticable when push comes to shove in the scramble to snatch cycling's most exalted prize, with all the rich pickings flowing from it. Can intense personal and commercial rivalries really be buried in the national interest?

This formula, while it lasts, suits Britain well. Before the changeover to trade teams in 1969, up to ten Britons contest each Tour – ten Britons in a Tour de France, something only to dream of nowadays.

But for 1959 we Brits are still on trial in a cobbled-together International team under the direction of a Frenchman, Sauveur Ducazeaux. The team is composed of two Austrians (Christian and Durlacher), two Danes (Jonsson and Retvig), two Portugese (Batista and Cardoso), a Pole (Wierucki), an Irishman (Shay Elliott) and four Englishmen (Brian Robinson, Jock, Vic and myself). Given the problems of cooperation within the French national team, can such a diverse grouping succeed? The communication barrier alone (six languages) must be formidable. Strangely, it works far better than expected: there are no in-built rivalries and no big egos. As for communication, to varying degrees of fluency, everyone speaks French or English. Our major difficulties will be mechanical, due to the mismatch of equipment.

Tour de France, 1959 – the International team at Mulhouse before Stage 1. Anglophones in centre of picture: from l to R, Andrews, Hewson, Robinson, Elliott, Sutton.

131

And so, team-by-team, we are introduced to the crowd, as the oddly named *L'Harmonie des Mines de Potasse* (Harmony of the Potash Mines) strikes up a medley of national anthems. And at 10.30 a.m. sharp, before the Exposition Hall, the deputy-mayor of Mulhouse snips the tricolour ribbon, launching us into the city's wide boulevards. '*Allez! A Metz!*' cry the spectators, a prayer echoed by the more exuberant riders. At once, the downpour relents and racing capes are cast aside.

Ten hard years have brought me to this summit of ambition. From age thirteen when I first learned to balance a bicycle, through 'burn-ups' with school chums, joining the BLRC, becoming National Junior Champion, competing in Amateur Circuits of Britain and winning a professional Tour of Britain; through two years of continental apprenticeship and all those tens of thousands of miles of training and racing; the struggles with illness, the triumphs and disappointments – now here I am at last, wound up to the sticking point of endeavour and released like a whirring clockwork toy to run for as far as I can in this exalted company.

The police-outriders' klaxons assault the air as, like royalty, we are shepherded through the suburbs. I experience a frisson of pride at being part of a moment of history as this rocket of a race lifts from its launch pad. What unknown perils, what rewards lie ahead in space and time? Freed from the city's confines, Goddet, in the race director's lead car, with a great flourish withdraws the neutralising flag. '*Bonne chance!*' he mouths – and the gaudy-coloured rocket takes off towards Metz, accelerating, accelerating.

As much frisky bronco as rocket, the peloton has kicked itself out of Mulhouse and already at three kilometres unseated the 'Clown Prince'. The joke now is on Hassenforder and three of his French team who must strive eyeballs-out to rescue him from a puncture. As they speed back through the caravan to safety in the bunch, their grit-begrimed faces grin off their comrades' wisecracks. At Bussang (45 kilometres) I am mightily relieved to dispose of the first real test, a minor *col*, which I ascend with rapid fluency. I am not alone. At the summit, friends and team-mates reassure one another with shouts of '*Alors, ça va?*'

So far, so good! I plan no heroics. I am a debutant whose ambition is to ride back to health and fitness, keeping a place mid-peloton, as Ducazeaux has advised, and staying out of trouble.

But that is much easier said than done, for the peloton is a maelstrom of restless energy in constant flux without fixed centre. Television cameras nowadays present an illusion of stability when the real dynamic is of perpetual change. The balloon of ease becomes the arrowhead of pursuit, and then just as swiftly reverts to its original shape as the break is caught. The echelon forms against the crosswind only to become a snap-taut line as the finish approaches. Departures from the front and clawing back at the rear only add to the instability, whilst crashes come out of nowhere, like mortar shells, scattering the ranks and leaving the fallen dazed and bleeding, to disentangle themselves from the wreckage and give chase, if they can. To 'sit mid-peloton' is difficult amidst all these ebbs and flows of man and machine. To 'stay still' you need to go forward or you will fall back. There is nothing in between. Falling back is easy. But going forward calls for concentration, assertiveness, judgment and bike-handling skills of the very first order.

At the back you rub shoulders with a weary raggle-taggle of hangers-on, whose will to fight has almost lapsed. A convulsion up front prompts a chain reaction, snapping the link to the peloton and dropping you plop into some bullying wind, as the heedless caravan purrs past. All road racers have been there at least once in their careers: *'J'ai souffert une défaillance,'* they comment by way of excuse, as if afflicted by some nasty disease.

The exceptional Anquetil can often be found at the back – some say as a gesture of contempt for the opposition up front; others, that he is easily bored and likes to gamble against the odds.

I am no Anquetil. With effort I flow and ebb around mid-peloton, and my only clue that the winning break of 18 riders has departed from Nancy around kilometre 200 is the frenetic pursuit that flattens me onto dropped handlebars for an hour of top gear twirling. Sprinter Darrigade wins for France. The average speed for the 150 miles is a rapid 27 mph.

Despite some casualties – Vic, caught up in a crash, loses 18 minutes and the Dane, Jonsson, last home, 33 minutes – Ducazeaux pronounces himself satisfied with our debut. Things could have gone worse.

The next stage, 150 miles to the Belgian city of Namur, traverses the true industrial north, a smokestack landscape, scarred and pitted by mines and slagheaps, and made bleaker by rumbling storm clouds. The miners of Italian descent are out in force at the roadside, their placards inscribed '*Forza Baldini!*' Punctures proliferate under heavy showers as we cross into Luxembourg.

There is a truce as champion of France, Henri Anglade, is permitted to race ahead and vault off into the embrace of his grandmother. And another as we quit Luxembourg and Charly Gaul stops to kiss his wife. Perhaps the only French institution more sacred than the Tour is *la famille*.

Generally, the pace is moderate as the peloton traverses Bastogne, scene of Hitler's last fling in the 1945 Battle of the Bulge. Several half-hearted breakaways enjoy their fifteen minutes of fame through these forested hills, including the German rider, Altweck. His fate demonstrates how quickly fortunes can change. Race leader at kilometre 200, he tumbles on the slippery descent into Dinant and sustains an injury that forces him to abandon at Bordeaux. So it goes.

The stage climaxes in two kilometres of cobbled ascent to the citadel of Namur, high above the River Meuse. The first to these hairpins will profit from an unobstructed passage and a psychological shove from the crowd's urging. Attack after attack is launched beside the Meuse until eventually our own Shay gets clear and goes for it, death-or-glory head down.

The bunch, in hot pursuit, squeals almost to a halt and doubles back on itself up the first slope to the citadel, jostling for space. The same thing happens at each bend and the leaders pull further away. Shay had the right idea to go it alone. The spruced-up gendarmerie can barely restrain a huge crowd yelling its heart out. I sprint out of the saddle from corner to corner through a cavern of sound. My back wheel slides and spins each time I accelerate on the slippery cobbles, until my 150-miles-weary legs cramp up and I lose contact and one minute fifty seconds, finishing 106th just behind team-mate, Batista. The victory goes to Italian, Vito Favero, who has narrowly out-sprinted Gainche (Tour de Champagne winner). Brave-heart Elliott was caught a bare kilometre from the line.

Sterling performances from Brian Robinson (6th) and Shay (10th) help to mellow our other misfortunes. Jock and Retwig have lost over nine minutes – Jock, like me suffering from bronchitis, a shadow of the man who once came within a whisker of beating today's winner. An awful chasm has opened up between our team and the rest, with eight of us in the bottom twenty on general classification, still topped by Darrigade, who also holds the points leader's *maillot vert*. Ducazeaux's smile is becoming strained.

Next day, 206 kilometres to Roubaix, and we traverse the 'Hell of the North', an eternity of cobbles, cinder paths and *routes bombées*. Quitting Metz under yet more leaden skies, I feel apprehensive. All we need to crown this impending Flemish nightmare is a good lashing of rain or, worse, a nice light drizzle to mix with dust and diesel at every cobbled corner into a cocktail of treacherous slime. At the roadside a throng of rosy-cheeked novitiates on furlough from a nearby seminary leap like gymnasts and wave us on our way. I hope we've been included in their prayers.

Maybe so, for the roads are dry as we bump on over pavé past chemical factories stinking of sulphur dioxide and stagnant canals. I am bouncing around somewhere mid-peloton. The pace is steady, until suddenly, crossing Charleroi, the peloton kicks itself into a furious hell-for-leather chase. One moment I am cruising, the next fighting to hang on, pulse racing.

High-walled factories, like grim brick prisons, border the exit from Charleroi and a pall of dust and smoke hangs in the air as though a Wild West posse has just galloped through. The entire peloton forms a long squiggly line on the miniscule strip of tar that divides pavé from pavement. We are all racing flat-out in the right-hand gutter. Past us cruise the team cars, anxious managers leaning out to glimpse the action up front and divine the cause of panic. A break has gone, but who is represented?

I shouldn't have taken my eyes off the rider in front. It only takes a split second for him to switch and me not to react. There's a jarring bone-shaking thud, like a sledgehammer blow, and suddenly I'm flung chest down onto the bars. What saves me from a potentially fatal header is the almost instantaneous second thud that socks me upright as my rear wheel follows my front into the same drain-hole with its missing iron cover. There's just this big gaping hole in the gutter and I've dunked down it smack-bang twice for a sucker one-two punch.

Badly shaken, chest bruised, I stop and raise my arm in a distress signal for Ducazeaux. Both my wheels are wrecked. The field goes flashing past, crouching low, snorting and spitting like demons out of hell. I wave an arm at the parade of team cars, palm open, like a half convinced Nazi saluting the Fuehrer's cavalcade. No one stops. Ducazeaux takes an age to appear and, when he does, the mechanic fumbles around with my bike as if he's just been set some impossible intelligence test. Time and again he runs to and from the car. He can find no wheels to fit. Seconds become minutes. An icy despair creeps over me. The Tour, caravan and all, have long since raced off into the distance and here am I, chained to the spot. Other mechanics change wheels in seconds. Riders leap off and straight back on again into the caravan's shelter, their race hardly disrupted. I want to rage at this monstrous incompetence, but I realise it will do no good.

Eventually, the mechanic gives up on wheels and opts for a spare bike. More delay as he lifts it off the roof rack and adjusts the saddle height. Then Ducazeaux pushes me off with a promise of help. Already I'm in deep trouble, alone and minutes adrift of a raging peloton.

For all eternity, it seems, I time-trial on this unfamiliar, uncomfortable bike. Then at last ahead I spy some slow-moving figures, accelerating on my approach. Wierucki, Retwig and Jock. There's no time for greetings or explanations. Maybe they were blown off the back of the bunch and Ducazeaux has herded them together with orders to wait.

We set to work, relaying each other hard, but to no avail. We realise the peloton has gone for good, chasing the strong ten-man break that formed in Charleroi. My accident couldn't have happened at a worse moment. We are left to do an 85 miles team time trial to try to beat the time limit at Roubaix. Worse still, Jock, ill and exhausted, abandons. Then we are down to three.

In a stage race nothing is more depressing than committing precious energy to a hopeless pursuit. The effort is the same as if you were leading the field in a breakaway, but with none of the rewards. As the gap grows, spectators tap their watches and shout, '*Allez! Vous êtes à sept minutes.*' *Sept* becomes *dix*, then *quinze*, then *vingt*. The hanging dust that signalled the caravan's passage has long since cleared, the road empty but for a few squashed paper hats turning idly in the wind. Now and then some stray official vehicle poodles past and its occupants gesture pityingly in our direction, but we see nothing more of our team car and realise we have been abandoned to our fate.

Strangely, the *Mur de Grammont* comes as some relief. Here, as we bob and weave up the almost vertical 'Wall', the five-deep bank of spectators has lost none of its fervour. Guttural Flemish voices scream their appreciation of our courage. Some evade the gendarmes' outstretched arms to shove us from behind. It is heart-warming to realise we remain part of their Tour. Somewhere behind, the *voiture balai* limps and shudders in bottom gear, Jock its only passenger.

Roubaix. We circle the track to a ripple of sympathetic applause 29 minutes after winner, Robert Cazala, and just inside the time limit. Exhausted, demoralised, we make our way to the hotel, where in the bathroom mirror our haggard, bespittled and sweat-lined faces tell their own tale. Is Ducazeaux sad for us? Far from it: he is cock-a-hoop. Our man Batista has finished with the leaders, the Charleroi break that went all the way to a massive eleven minutes advantage over the favourites. Yesterday he was 105th, one place ahead of me. Today he is 6th and a hero. He has accomplished this reversal of fortune through being in the right place at the right moment (*chapeau!*), but certainly with much less effort than I needed to finish 117th.

That irony is a cruel twist. After dinner I lie on my bed, listening to my pounding heart and reflecting on the day's events. I am in a rage of frustration and want to salve my rage with blame. Blame Ducazeaux! Blame the mechanic! The unpalatable fact, though, is that I alone of that big field crashed down an open drain-hole. On reflection I have to admit I was part architect of my misfortune.

Three days gone and a new leader, Cazala. Our Batista lies 10th at three and a half minutes, with Robinson and Elliott at 12 minutes, but comfortably placed amongst the favourites. Christian, Durlacher, Jonsson and Cardoso finished in the bunch at Roubaix and remain in contention. Vic has lost 20 minutes. Jock has abandoned. The rest of us are rooted at the bottom of GC.

On the debit side, I feel desperately tired after the disaster of Roubaix, new fatigue heaped on old. On the positive side, my bronchitis has dried up and I am not without hope. A few 'easy' stages remain before the Pyrenees and if I can recuperate I feel confident of getting through the mountains and reaching Paris. Maybe, just maybe, I will ride myself back to early-season form. A top thirty position is now out of reach, yet I can still put my name in lights.

Anyway, no use brooding, there's another stage to ride. And another. Today is Roubaix-Rouen, 230 kilometres into a cold gusty headwind. A lowering sky threatens more rain as we sign up for our ration of sweat, tears and grub, stuffing our pockets, back and front, with rice cake, bananas, peaches, dates, sandwich packs and whatever else we fancy from the groaning food counter. A peloton pedals on its belly. Seventy miles down the road will come the *ravitaillement*, where at speed we scoop a musette of nourishment rather like old non-stop express trains scooped mailbags into the maw of their mobile sorting office.

The *ravitaillement* presents opportunity and danger! Approaching, you can feel tension rise in the bunch, jumpy riders standing high on their pedals, craning to survey the road ahead. For spectators this is the best show in town. Team cars are parked in battle array on the village square. Onlookers behind barriers jostle for a view, or stray across the highway to the anger of white-webbed whistle-blasting gendarmes. A phalanx of motorcycle outriders with ear-splitting klaxons precedes us. It is a maelstrom of movement and sound with everyone on peak alert. Ahead, blending semi-invisible with the crowd, the team helpers wait, a couple or three bulging musettes strung over each arm. One is for you, or maybe two, if you have orders to collect for the team leader. You strain to pick your man out. Sometimes you see him too late – he's standing on the left when he's promised to be on the right or vice versa. Riders start to freewheel and switch sides, even to turn back and ride in a circle. No wonder the *ravitaillement* is called *la valse des musettes*. The risk of tumbling from touching a wheel or rolling bottle, or entangling with a dropped musette is high.

Now someone uses this chaos as cover for an attack. Skipping the feed, they launch themselves into a bums-up sprint. No sooner have you scooped your musette, than you're racing on the rivet, unable to transfer anything to your pockets, with that damned bulky knapsack, weighted down with full bottles, bumping and ram-battering your spine until the attack is neutralised.

Today, Sunday, the crowds are even denser. Through each town and village, the church bells peal a welcome and we are doubly blessed. We have quit the industrial landscapes and appalling roads of *L'Enfer* for the smooth highways of pastoral Normandy. Better still, there's a headwind. A blessing? Assuredly. In the bosom of the slow-moving peloton, I can take shelter and recuperate. The attacks are few. When Dutchman, Piet Van Est, goes it alone at kilometre 28, no one reacts, leaving him hanging out to dry in the wind. By kilometre 90 he has eight minutes lead. Soon he will be yellow jersey on the road. But the French team have other ideas. Once Anquetil and Bobet return to the fold from punctures, the game is up. Now the peloton rolls and at kilometre 158 the sad figure of Van Est reappears in the middle distance. What glorious folly, a photographer's delight, distracting from the boredom of an otherwise uneventful stage; likewise the 'deplorable' crash of Moresi and Anastasi. Tomorrow's front pages picture the 'Flying Dutchman' alongside swooning Anastasi's blood-encrusted visage, the Aspro helicopter rushing him to hospital.

Bruni out-sprints Van Aerde at Rouen, with the whole bunch breathing down their necks at six seconds. Again the International team has stragglers in Retwig and Durlacher, but they lose only eight minutes at most. The rest of us are home, safe and dry, literally. I have hardly broken sweat all day and feel mightily reposed.

21

Leoni – wipes his oily hands on my bed sheet. He surveys my physique quizzically, as a Roman slave-master might once have studied a prospective purchase. How much work have I got left in me?

A dawdling bunch is ideal for observing the stars at close quarters. Unstereotypical stardom appears in different physical guises: tiny, elfin-eared Robic, bull-chest Mastrotto, tall, elegant Gérard Saint with his matinée idol looks. Yet common to all are those gleaming shaven legs, with their surprisingly delicate ankles and sculpted calves, the protuberant knotted indigo veins from a Da Vinci anatomical drawing, prematurely varicose through years of punishing pressure, gigantic quadriceps overflowing like cancerous growths, contributing to the trade-mark cyclist's walk of a fish flopping out of water. All contact points – ankles, knees, elbows, hips – bear scarred, purple witness to the violence of *le métier de la route.* Boxing is called a violent sport, but show me the boxer more scarred than the professional *coureur cycliste.*

As for temperament, the sport is a liquorice all-sorts, though a rider's speciality may be a useful guide, time-trialists tending towards the phlegmatic, sprinter-roadmen fiery and explosive. Being a member of the big, backslapping peloton doesn't require you to be extrovert or gregarious. True, some sergeant-majors give indiscriminate orders, riding no hands the better to assert dominance. But the majority is of quiet concentration, friendly but business-like. I know which I prefer.

Extrovert Geminiani, *le grand fusil,* exercises his self-adopted role of Elder Statesman, moving through the quiescent bunch and cementing allegiances with touches of diplomacy and conspiracy. Now he rests a brotherly arm on a comrade's shoulder and takes a tow as they exchange the time of day or a joke. Now their heads go together and voices drop. Maybe they're plotting a coup?

Clown Prince 'Hassan' is different, a cheeky-chappy big Alpha extrovert for whom the bunch is a stage to manipulate his publicity.

Good publicity equals lucrative contracts. He has created a good market for himself selling his zany unpredictable behaviour to the media. Even when poor form relegates him down the classification, he is rarely out of the news, a wisecracker, a one-man circus act, juggling peaches at the heart of the peloton, or pedalling one-legged, the other leg posited on the handlebars, '*en repos*'. Now he snatches a battered straw hat from a spectator and tries it on for approval before flinging it back. Now he halts to embrace some chesty mama, her ample bosom wobbling with laughter. '*Ma fiancée!*' he proclaims to the bunch. Probably not, but who cares? It's just another offering from King Anquetil's court jester.

Jester, but no fool! With Darriagade and 'Popof' (Graczyk, so nicknamed after being arrested in Fiji, of all places, on suspicion of being a Russian spy), he shares the title of top French sprinter-roadman with a string of victories, including stages of the Tour. Soon he will out-sprint Van Geneugden and Sabbadini at La Rochelle and blow kisses to his adoring crowd. Yet he is also an unselfish worker for the French squad, dropping back time and again to assist *co-équipiers* in trouble.

Frankly, the man is an enigma. To dismiss him simply as an engaging publicity freak would be wrong. One morning, during the 1960 Tour de Champagne, Hassenforder appeared at the start waving a hand-painted placard, which read '*Non au meurtre de Caryl Chessman!*' He harangued the peloton in a passionate voice demanding that we strike. And why? To protest against the execution of Caryl Chessman, an international human rights cause celèbre, who was due to go to the electric chair in California after conviction on 17 charges of robbery, kidnapping and rape. Chessman, a reformed criminal thug, had, over a period of twelve years, conducted a brilliant legal battle from prison and won eight stays of execution. He had learned four languages and written best-selling books against capital punishment, including *Cell 2455 Death Row*, provoking worldwide condemnation of American judicial methods. So far all appeals for clemency had fallen on deaf ears. Undeterred, 'Hassan', waving his placard, created such a sympathetic stir that the start was delayed until the organisers promised to dispatch a message of protest to the gaol, surely the most bizarre the governor there had ever received.

Did he really believe the pleading of a bunch of racing cyclists would succeed where the Great and Good had failed? Or was it simply another opportunistic publicity stunt? Whatever the truth, it counted for nothing. Chessman went to the chair on time.

At a daunting 286 kilometres (178 miles) Rouen–Rennes will be our longest day, the longest of my career, beating the 157 miles of Sheffield–Phwelli in the 1955 Tour of Britain. It will be a severe test of my stamina and my recuperation from the hammering of Namur–Roubaix. As tomorrow is the time trial, crucial for those with pretensions of overall victory, I hope for another easy ride. But as we sidle out of Rouen's brooding historic city square, in which – and let the English never forget this – '*Vous avez brûlé Jean D'Arc!*' a three-quarter headwind, purple skies, and violent showers do not bode well. My woollen jersey, soaked by rain, pockets front and back bursting with food, is a sagging dead weight each time I rise from the saddle. Spirits sag too in a subdued peloton and you'd have thought no one was in the mood to race. But there's always someone, and off goes the German, Reitz, 'doing a Van Est'. And – *Mon Dieu!* – who joins him in this lunacy but Rivière, tomorrow's time trial favourite, treating himself to a long warm-up.

Six kilometres later and they both are back. We slosh on through rivulets of rain and Jacques Goddet's brow furrows as the soaked and dispirited peloton falls behind schedule.

Normandy. I remember the Tour de L'Ouest – rolling country where you constantly crunch through the gears. The truce is broken at kilometre 60 when ten men snatch a minute's lead. The big bunch stirs and splits. A twenty strong group, including Bobet, Baldini, Gaul and Rivière, is briefly away. But by Argentan, tranquillity reigns, allowing Saint to acknowledge a rapturous reception from his hometown supporters.

Kilometre 160, the sky clears. A shockingly hot sun confirms our progress southwards. The peloton sections the highway in search of shade and a strange languor begins to overcome me, a worrisome heaviness of mind and body. The good break has gone, well represented by French and Italian sprinters, and so the pursuit is hardly frenzied. Nevertheless, I drift uncontrollably backwards until the caravan's drone fills my ears, drilling into my skull. There's no need to look over my shoulder to know I'm last in line, stuck in a listless daze, without strength to improve my position.

At kilometre 200 the break appears ahead ascending a distant hill. Now we are there too and climbing. The peloton accelerates. I fight the pedals, shoulders swaying. It feels like treading water. The cortège of vehicles behind changes gear, hustling me impatiently. Let go and be done with it, they demand. Then I do. One by one they pick me off until I hear a voice in my ear. *'Qu'est-ce-qu'y a?'* It's Ducazeaux.

'Je suis *épuisé!*' I gasp. *'Une défaillance!'* He accelerates away. Short of towing me to Rennes, he knows I'm a lost cause.

As long as I can hang in with the caravan, there's hope of recovery on the plateau. But the hill goes on and on until I fall through a hole in that bag of suffocating heat and fumes and a cooling wind licks my face. Save for the *voiture balai* I shall be alone now for 80 kilometres.

At the summit I sit up to feed my sawdust body. Freed from the fluctuating rhythms of the bunch to ride at my own constant speed, I feel better. But it's too late. All that remains of the race ahead is a lingering dusty haze and a few knots of surprised spectators who shout, *'Allez! C'est pas loin!'* It is a well-meaning lie. Rennes *is* far, very far. My sole thought as I settle to time-trial on the drops is to beat the time limit and stay in contention.

Tomorrow's newspapers picture me defying the brush-bearing sag-wagon. One caption reads, 'Hewson dares not look behind in case he follows the example of his team-mate, Andrews, who abandoned two days ago.' Another comments wryly, 'The Englishman does his time-trial a day early!'

At dinner that night I stuff myself with energy-loaded carbohydrate foods: bread, pasta and two caramel desserts. Only Vic commiserates with me. Brian and Shay stay quiet, thinking perhaps there's nothing worth saying. Call it what you will, 'hunger-knock', 'bonk', *'defaillance'*, everyone has been there. Least said, soonest forgotten.

But again, as I lie on my bed, events crowd in to trouble my thoughts. This isn't the first time I've suffered a *défaillance*. I remember the Tour de L'Ariège. It's destructive of confidence and might strike me down again and again. What am I doing wrong? How can I prevent it? The training manuals, such as they are, advise eating plenty and conserving energy, whilst hydration, replacing fluids and minerals lost in sweat, is barely mentioned except to say, drink sparingly and don't burden the body with excess water: folly, as we now know. I am also unaware that fatigue climaxes two days after its cause. So Rouen–Rennes is payback time for the disaster of Namur–Roubaix.

When Ducazeaux delivers the stage results, I feel even worse. The pace was a modest 35 kph. All but five riders finished in the pack, three due to a late puncture. I alone lost big. 35 minutes! Again I have escaped elimination by a hair's breadth, but I feel humiliated.

More humiliation as Ducazeaux tells the masseur to prepare our best hopes for the time-trial: Batista, Elliott and Robinson. The rest of us will be treated in descending order of GC. Time is limited. Vic and I miss out. It's understandable, but this tangible evidence of being bottom of the pile doesn't exactly raise our morale.

11.00 p.m. The sun has set, but my bedroom walls still radiate heat and are warm to the touch. Sleep is difficult. My limbs ache and my heart thuds on at racing speed, as though to compensate for its earlier shameful performance. Windows are flung wide to admit cooling air, and through them well the sounds of fête. Somewhere an open-air *bal-musette* whirls to the skirl of an accordion and *chanteurs* vie to recreate the Parisian music halls and *rive gauche* cafes of Edith Piaf, Gilbert Becaud and Juliette Greco – their heart-aching sad, cynical songs, so exquisitely bitter-sweet French, being applauded wildly like surrogate national anthems. Now a guitarist sings, 'Whatever they say, whatever they say, I will go my own way.' Maybe it's George Brassens himself. Bravo, George! Go your own way and let me go mine: to sleep.

Just as I'm drifting off, a vehicle on furlough from the caravan belts past, its loudspeaker intoning idiotically. 'Hello! Hello! Gondolo! Hello! Hello! Gondolo!' I wake with a start and lash out at something stinging my face. A hunting pack of mosquitoes hovers in a light-beam. Another worry! I remember being once blinded by a bite on the eye-lid. I don't really fancy riding the Tour one-eyed.

Midnight, and the intimate chuckling of a couple returning from the festivities. I catch a whiff of perfume and Gauloise. Soon their lovemaking will shake the city, whilst here I lie exhausted.

How does a mosquito make love? Like Dracula, in darkness, by prick and suck. I draw the sheet over my face.

I have a survival plan. I put it to Ducazeaux before boarding the transport to Blain for the start of the time-trial. I want to treat today as a 'rest day'. Of course I must still cover the 45 kilometres course – but not flat-out. What I propose is a fast 'training' ride to conserve energy. Today there is no time limit and as *lanterne rouge* I can sink no lower. My ambition is to be of service to the team and see it through to Paris. Ducazeaux approves.

Out in the country, families picnicking at the roadside toast your passage with *un coup de rouge* and polite applause. But the true cycling aficionados, in racing caps and sunglasses, are aflame with passion, passion for your speed, as if it is a debt you personally owe. They are bent double under great loads of this passion, brandishing clenched fists, and staring into your eyes, willing you on. *'Roulez! Plus vite!'* they cry. I am only the *lanterne rouge*. How will they react as aces Rivière, Baldini and Anquetil flash past? Like crazed dervish dancers?

I try not to be influenced and stick to my plan. Even as riders overtake, I resist the temptation to speed up. I maintain a rapid, easy cadence, using 52 x 16 and 48 x 14, never top gear, and if my legs ache, I ease off. Nevertheless, I achieve a respectable average speed of 25.37 mph, and avoid finishing last. That dubious honour goes to my Danish team-mate Retwig. Vic, (65 minutes, 51 seconds), never much of a time-trialist, beats me by over a minute, whilst winner Rivière (56 minutes 46 seconds) averages almost 30 mph.

Vic and I have earned our leisurely afternoon at the pavement café. We sip Oranginas and ogle the passing girls. This is the life, we say. Pity Jock isn't here to share it. Tour celebrity has briefly detached us from everyday reality. Now, relaxing and watching the world go by, we almost feel part of the anonymous human race – unobserved until some kids come hunting our autographs. Then it's time to return to the hotel and rejoin the circus. The cage door clangs shut.

Today Leoni has time for us. Leoni isn't his real name. In my memory he blends with all my other long-forgotten masseurs into this single composite: a short, wiry, sun-tanned man with muscular tattooed arms and huge hands, the better to pummel you with. He bends to his task with a fervour bordering on hatred and if you complain he's hurting, he ripostes with a shrug, *'Qu'est-ce-que-tu veux, mon brave?'* Do you imagine all that stiffness will quit your muscles of its own accord? No, it must be beaten out, as your famous English schoolmasters beat evil from their pupils. As he thumps and presses your agonised quadriceps upwards from the knee, as if to rearrange them closer to the heart and lungs that fuel them, you notice his lips moving in silent prayer, an invocation perhaps to the devils of weariness to take flight.

Coppi had a famous blind coach and masseur, Cavalla, who stroked and plucked his thighs like a violinist. He was elevated in the press to the status of magician. All masseurs have some magic in their hands. Jock speaks of Tarachon, the Mercier masseur, who works in a butcher's apron, brutal costume for one with such deft touch. Jock rates him the best in the business, but in 1959, when new UCI regulations are approved, he will be sacked. He possesses no formal qualifications for a skill acquired by a lifetime of touching and feeling. It is intuitive. Without a certificate to hang on the wall, no modern sports injury clinic would give our half-literate Leoni a second glance, his very appearance terrifying the clientele, and, anyway, what insurer would indemnify his uncertified magic against possible litigation? The great masseurs of the Fifties have passed into legend with storybook witches and wizards.

Leoni ceases his torture and wipes his oily hands on my bed sheet. He surveys my physique quizzically, as a Roman slave-master might once have studied a prospective purchase. How much work have I got left in me?

'*Alors, ça va?*' he demands dubiously.

'*Oui, ça va!*' I roll off the bed, feeling light and springy, as if he's cleaned my every sinew with a toothbrush.

Ducazeaux's fingers touch in a playful arch of prayer. I'm praying, he says, for a miracle. No punctures. No crashes. No dropping of *musettes* at the *ravitaillement*. No *défaillance*. Here he smiles at me and seesaws his head like a father to a recalcitrant son. I smile back and nod. I will do my best.

Perhaps Ducazeaux isn't a true believer, for his prayers go unanswered. Barely fifteen minutes into the race, with the flying bunch wind-assisted towards a new record time for Rennes–La Rochelle, I hear a team car nosing forwards. It pauses just behind me. There is urgency in Ducazeaux's voice. He shouts something and I hear Vic shouting back, '*Non compris!*' Then the team car creeps up to me. Ducazeaux leans out and says, '*Retvig a crevé. Tu dois attendre.*'

Punctured! Wait for Retwig? Is he mad? We've barely left Rennes. There are 180 kilometres to cover. The pace is frenetic. And he wants me to wait for the weakest member of the team and bring him back to the peloton. Alone! Does he imagine I'm Anquetil, Rivière and Baldini all rolled into one?

I drop back through the caravan to take stock. Behind stretches a flat emptiness of ruler-straight road. I twist my neck, straining to peer through the haze of heat and dust.

Nothing.

I drop further back. Fifty yards separate me from the last vehicle, now a hundred. It's still possible for me to sprint and rejoin the peloton, but any more and I'll be lost. Still no sign of Retvig.

Disobey! The thought flashes through my mind. Disobey! There's an overwhelming desire to hug close to the body of mother peloton. I cannot give Vic's excuse of *'non compris'*, but I could shrug at Ducazeaux and shake my head and mouth, *'Il n'est pas là!'* Yet something stops me. Maybe it's that last father-son look that passed between us. And my every instinct is to obey. My Catholic upbringing, school, civil and military services have stamped obedience into my very being. But something even stronger is at play on my conscience: the inescapable fact that I owe Retvig. He had the decency to wait for me on the Roubaix stage and now decency demands I return the favour.

The Tour slides away from me into the far distance. The caravan's roar gives way to birdsong. I am in No-Man's Land, like a World War One soldier going over the top, not out of fear of authority, but because of loyalty to his comrades.

It turns out to be a two-for-one pointless sacrifice. The *voiture balai* shimmers through the heat haze, trailing the blond-haired Retvig. Even at distance I can tell his pedalling is floppy. He's going through the motions, but, mentally, he's already abandoned. His relays are half-hearted and soon he gestures that he's giving up. I continue alone to kilometre 70, but it's hopeless. The gap to the motoring bunch is expanding. There's no prospect of me beating the *délai*. I join Retwig in the sag wagon. Now, unbound, the vehicle spurts off for mile upon mile of empty road, only to lurch to a crawl behind Champion (Paris-Nord-Est), who brings us home 28 minutes after winner Hassenforder. But not good enough! Monsieur Champion is eliminated despite his name.

Next morning I watch the Tour departing for Bordeaux. It's like that bad dream where that train you must catch leaves you on the platform, paralysed, its tail-lights disappearing. It's gone and there's nothing you can do. You've said your farewells to Vic, Brian and Shay and wished them luck. But you can tell your words have gone over their heads. They're pre-occupied with moving on, just as you would be in their place.

A British newspaper reporter accosts me. I explain in great detail how I came to abandon. His story, when it appears, gives flu as the reason.

What do I feel? Stultified, superfluous, like a lump of dough trimmed off a pie and tossed aside. Every instinct tells me I should now be pedalling. Instead I'm walking, with my cardboard suitcase number 126 drumming on my handlebars in slow retreat to the station. I have no heart even to buy a newspaper – for the moment I want to put it all behind. In the carriage, ordinary people conduct ordinary everyday conversations about the weather, or price of butter. After the high drama of the past few days, 'everyday' seems unreal, and yet The Big Bike Race is the very last thing I want to discuss. I conceal that tell-tale number 126 under my jacket on the luggage rack.

At Saint Claud, beneath its tree-covered canopy, the caravan I left six weeks ago seems shrunken into its own tiny world. The tyres have lost air. The door is flung back, Alan's bike propping it open.

22

It seemed a group of elite climbers had left the peloton and the
commentator was enunciating a crackly recitation – Anquetil, Gaul,
Bahamontes. He paused as if to check a number and fumble with an
unfamiliar foreign name – 'et le petit Britannique, S-oo-ton.'

Jock's grim forecast had come true: 'Get that engine rebored before
the valves drop into the sump!' he joked. From February to June,
we experienced a diminution of power until only jamming the
accelerator to the floor guaranteed progress. Then two weeks before
the Tour, Rosy subsided with a mournful groan, oily brown liquid
pouring from every orifice. There was nothing else for it but an
expensive engine overhaul.

The result was amazing. Driving back to Saint Claud, just as
the Tour got under way, Alan reported Rosy actually touching a
speed of 50 mph. Just as well, because without reliable transport in
rural Charente, we were scuppered. True, our hairdresser friend,
Raymond, sometimes closed his shop to act as our chauffeur. But
now with the season in full swing and three or more races each week,
we couldn't take such generosity for granted. He had his own living
to earn.

Four days after the Tour quit me, I raced again at Saint Séverin,
south of Angoulême. Passing through the city, I gave a lift to local
rider, Jean, a non-stop chatterer and mine of useless information.
As he rabbited on, I began to regret having him on board. Soon I
would regret it even more.

It was the usual mixed field of top class amateurs and
independents and a challenging course of 120 kilometres with a
steep climb each lap back into the village. Soon the lead group was
reduced to some half dozen riders, including Jean and myself. After
the long-distance stages of the Tour, 120 kilometres was a fleabite
and well before the finish I stormed off alone.

The village was *en fête*. At every passage the crowd cheered me
through. On the square a gold and blue-painted carousel emitted
the same ear-splitting song, Piaf's snarling rendition of *'La Foule'*,
that passionate ambivalent tribute to her adoring public whose

terrifying lust for her fame both encouraged and crushed her. The frantic waltz filled my head and imposed its own hypnotic rhythm. I raced harder and harder and won by a considerable margin.

'Congratulations,' Jean said afterwards, 'but, of course, you couldn't have done it without my help. I was blocking for you.'

Perhaps he had 'blocked', but I knew from observation that the others had been too spent for organised pursuit. With or without his help, I would still have won.

He was seeking reward and I forked out 10,000 francs, a third of my winnings. Of course I knew I was being taken for a ride, but I had no wish to make an enemy or acquire a reputation for not playing the game – baksheesh being customary in cycle racing. Above all, I couldn't face being harangued for an hour from the passenger seat on the subject of sporting ethics. Needless to say, I never again gave him a lift.

Transistor radios were in their infancy. Ours was one of the first. We had clubbed together to buy it from Pierre's wholesale outlet at a discount price of 25,000 francs (perhaps £400 in today's money!). It was a wild concession to luxury. In appearance, with its slender feminine carrying strap, it resembled a cute little make-up bag in pretty pastel shades of coral pink and grey. Nevertheless, though unencumbered by old-fashioned valves, with its solid wooden case and jumbo battery it was a dumbbell in disguise. Never mind the weight, it performed brilliantly and, even this far south and without a proper aerial, was our lifeline to the BBC. More importantly now, we kept in touch with the Tour via live commentary on *Europe Numero Un.*

Somewhat alarmingly, we had heard nothing of Vic since Bordeaux. But Sunday, 5th July, Stage 10, the race entered the Pyrenees and Alan and I tuned in just as riders were attacking the giant 2,113-metre high Col du Tourmalet. The background roar of motorbikes made it doubly difficult for me to interpret the animated commentary. It seemed a group of elite climbers had formed and the commentator was enunciating a crackly recitation – *Anquetil, Gaul, Bahamontes, Bobet.* He paused as if to check a number and fumble with an unfamiliar foreign name –'*et le petit Britannique, S-oo-tun.'* As one we leapt and punched the air as if our team had scored a cup final goal. Not just a survivor, Vic was climbing with the aces!

Tour de France, 1959. Vic Sutton leads Jacques Anquetil
on the Col du Tourmalet.

High summer and suffocating heat. We were glad of the chestnuts' umbrella shade. The nearby village pump clanked an early morning alarm call to breakfast. It was mainly housewives who stood in line carrying galvanised pails, sometimes a pair balanced on shiny wooden yokes across their shoulders. It was a centuries-old domestic ritual fulfilling a double need: first for water but also to cement the communal bonds with gossip. They chattered even as they swung the flesh-polished iron handle, drawing up a cold limy gush from deep down, and splashing their faces and arms with cooling liquid before tramping home up the baking high street.

So it had been for centuries, but things were changing. One day the far-sighted mayor told me of his hopes and fears for modernisation. In his eyes every so-called boon sowed a corresponding deficit. Take electricity: its arrival had ended the tyranny of candles and oil lamps, but disfigured the landscape with an ugly jumble of criss-crossing cables. And television: there were some half dozen sets already in the village providing splendid home entertainment for the better off, but would universal provision lead to increased social division and a decline in community participation? Piped water scheduled to arrive next year would save labour at the pump, – but at what cost to the meeting of minds? And this new 'supermarket' idea – might it not close down all the local shops and export jobs to the cities? It was bad enough now with youngsters being beguiled by 'jet-setting' images and emigrating to where work was better paid and more plentiful. No small community could survive without its young people, and Saint Claud was no different. The rural life-blood was being sucked away, leaving behind a tide-line of derelict farmhouses and ghost hamlets. The one bright cloud was that this new 'Common Market' might forestall impending catastrophe by providing agricultural subsidies. His eyes gleamed. To save *La Belle France*, farmers must be paid to work the land. What else?

His great dream is to build an abattoir for local employment. Meanwhile, the village must remain attractive to young and old alike. This is where his *Comité des Fêtes* comes in, organising social functions and fund-raising entertainments such as *bals musette* and the *Criterium Cycliste de Saint Claud*.

Why is he telling me all this? Reading between the lines I divine our small part in the scheme of things. It is more than simply to inspire and encourage the tiny group of youngsters who make up the village cycling club, *le C.C. St Claudais*. Our racing success will reflect publicity back onto the community as a place of rural enterprise and encourage investment. We help the community and the community helps us. Like our deal with the BCR it is intended to be mutually beneficial.

Alan and I train early morning to avoid the afternoon's heat. But first, after breakfast, comes another task of routine importance. Rats have nibbled a gothic arch through the bottom plank of a weathered oak door set in the opposing boundary wall. My entrance into this stinking communal loo lofts storms of indignant flies. I must buffet them out with strips of newspaper before dropping my pants and wriggling over a flesh-polished hole in the pine board. These earth closets, Lucien says, once served as safety deposit boxes in times of war. Wrapped in linen and canvas under a covering of malodorous slime, the family jewelry and silver was hidden away from prying eyes and the clutches of marauding soldiers. When the coast was clear all would be resurrected, the precious silver plate and cutlery cleaned and put back to domestic use – organic or what?

A fat spider springs from its web in the rafters to observe me. Crammed into crevices of the rough-hewn walls are intricately woven bird-nests and in one I can see tiny heads frozen in silhouette, the anxious parent birds fluttering and nagging outside the door. A torn newspaper headline catches my eye: something about De Gaulle struggling to bring order to the chaos of Algeria. Fierce sunlight is already striking the wall outside, but in here the night air still hangs cool. It is a rare, refreshing moment of peace and privacy in a life of perpetual struggle. Yet I must dismiss the temptation to sit and read. I have an uneasy feeling something akin to a Loch Ness Rat may be stirring in the depths of the cesspit, enraged by my dumped insults. My exposed hangings begin to creep and with a little shiver of horror I leap up – newspaper to hand, working-class bog-roll, slippery and non-absorbent but satisfyingly cheap.

So here's to you, Nessy! Nibble on my leavings and welcome.

As I exit, flies and birds rush in to reclaim their kingdoms.

We train at easy pace through the lanes of rolling Charente. My exit from the Tour still rankles, but talking it through with Alan helps me get matters into perspective. I recall my parents coming to terms with life's disappointments by saying: 'It was never meant to be!' – as if their fate was in more powerful hands than their own. I was mocking then, yet now their meek philosophy holds me in sway. From May onwards, mishap followed mishap, as if predestined: flu, bronchitis, allied loss of form, the mishandled crash at Charleroi and the day-long chase to Roubaix. No time for recuperation before that exhausting 286 kilometres from Rouen to Rennes when my depleted reserves ran out and I fell to the bottom of Ducazeaux's pecking order. Fate decreed I should become the sacrificial victim on the La Rochelle stage. Given good health, how differently it all might have turned out. But it was not meant to be. So best forget it.

But I can't. A dishonourable thought still rankles. Just suppose Retwig welcomed that puncture, even staged it? On a dry day and smooth highway – so easy to loosen a tyre-valve and let air dribble out in its own good time. Stranger things have happened to demoralised riders looking for an easy exit. And he was quick to abandon. This scenario is almost too awful to contemplate. If true, my pointless sacrifice was doubly pointless.

Meanwhile the Tour continues in the midst of a heat wave with midday temperatures in the high thirties. Each afternoon after lunch, legs still tingling from the morning's effort, we stretch out in the green submarine shade and sip delicious iced lemon tea (the ice from Raymond's brand-new refrigerator) as the drama unfolds on radio. There has been a massacre. The year's hottest day coincides with a switchback stage over the rocky spine of France from Albi to Aurillac when seven riders abandon and eight more are eliminated. Even ace climber Charly Gaul falls victim to the heat, losing twenty minutes, and is fined for accepting pushes on the Col de Montsalvy, where leather-jacketed Goddet, looking like some Hell's Angel on official motorbike *numero un*, punches a spectator for offering assistance. The papers carry a photo of the Angel of the Mountains, dismounted, his head in a fountain, behaving like some humble water-carrier – *Oh quel joli image!*

Nothing seems to trouble our Brian, 4th at Aurillac in the Anglade-Anquetil-Bahamontes group, and now 9th on general classification, just 12 minutes behind the Belgian leader, Hoevenaers. But with only five Internationals remaining, Brian pays the price next day for belonging to a weak team when he punctures in the Alpine foothills. The team car has gone AWOL and, though Shay is at hand to offer a wheel, Brian loses 35 minutes. Shay is eliminated and for a while Brian looks to be going the same way. But, at the last minute, under some obscure rule protecting the first ten riders on GC, Goddet reprieves him. Now he is 25th, 44 minutes back, and the team is down to four members.

Vic continues to amaze. From being near *lanterne rouge* at Bordeaux he has winged his way up the classification. In the mountain time-trial on the Puy de Dome, he finishes 16th, not far behind winner, Bahamontes, who climbs at an incredible average speed of 12 mph. In the Alps, at Grenoble, Aosta and Annecy, he figures regularly in the top twenty. For a neophyte, it is an astonishing performance that wins praise from the media, their only criticism being he is a poor descender. Alan and I conclude he must feel on cloud nine. '*Il faut sortir!*' French riders keep telling us: success depends on standing out from the crowd. Well, he's certainly done that, and the media attention should guarantee him a good flow of post-Tour contracts.

Yet, despite its high rate of elimination and abandonment, the race goes down as the least combative in recent history. The stars mark one another rather than launching those murderous attacks the public craves. Race leader Bahamontes is isolated inside a weakened team and vulnerable to a determined onslaught by the French, who have a stranglehold on the Challenge Martini. But Anquetil of Helyet-Leroux and Rivière of Geminiani Cycles hold off, more concerned with the threat from second-placed Anglade of the Centre-Midi, for whom victory would translate into a publicity coup for Liberia Cycles and the pick of post-Tour appearance contracts. Although it makes financial sense to Anquetil and Rivière for the Spaniard Bahamontes to win, such naked triumph of commercial over national interest scandalises the patriotic French public, and hostile crowds boo the two French stars, with cries of 'Treason!' and 'Traitors!' signalling the death-knell of the national team concept favoured by Goddet. The end of his reign as race director in the 1960s will mark its demise.

Meanwhile, en route to Chalons-sur Saone, Robinson has taken advantage of the truce to chalk up the second stage victory of his career. A soporific peloton, dubbed 'a bunch of sheep' by the hypercritical press, fails to react as he races off alone to win by 20 minutes.

But here something else occurs to steal Brian's limelight. Little blue-eyed veteran Robic has fought his gutsy way through the Pyrenees and Alps with a fractured wrist strapped-up from a fall way back in Roubaix. One can imagine his pain from pulling on the bars uphill and the fracture vibrating on rough descents. He is a heroic survivor of the old school, cycling's elfin-eared answer to Piaf, until today that is, when he finishes outside the time limit and is eliminated. Only two stages remain and he pleads his case for reinstatement, arguing that one is a time-trial and the other a triumphal procession to Paris, neither subject to elimination. To exclude him now would be cruel and unreasonable. An exception has been made for the foreigner Robinson, so why not for him, a Frenchman and glorious victor of the 1947 Tour? But patriotism and palmarés no longer cut ice with an appeals committee sick to death of hearing 'special' pleading and, despite some powerful behind-scenes lobbying, they show their independence and kick him out. There it might have ended but for tearful Madame Robic, Jean's wife. She phones Goddet. 'Think of me, Monsieur, if not of Jean,' she sobs. 'Haven't I already purchased my new dress for the *Parc des Princes*?' Goddet listens unmoved. Unfortunately for madame, this tough leather-jacketed race director is no dedicated follower of female fashion.

23

*Once upon a time in Périgueux, we awake after midnight to hear
Victor screaming, 'I'll have the bastards!'*

Bastille Day. We race at Saint Junien, between Confolens and
Limoges on the RN 141. Traffic has been diverted to allow us to
pack the start across the highway. But first, *La Marseillaise*. As the
town band strikes up with *'Allons enfants de la patrie'*, spectators
behind the barriers stiffen. Sombre parents grip their children tight
and handkerchiefs dab away the tears. Why such grief on a day of
public celebration?

Thirteen kilometres separate us from Oradour-sur-Glane – once
a thriving populous little town, but now a war memorial, deserted
and in ruins, exactly as the Das Reich S.S left it in June 1944. It is
just fifteen years since that infamous day when almost its entire
population was massacred – 642 men, women and children herded
together into the church and burned alive or dynamited to death.
Why Oradour? No one can be sure. S.S. battalion commander Adolf
Diekmann, acting without recourse to higher authority, gave the
order for this act of barbarism, but was himself killed in action
some weeks later, taking his secret with him to the grave. The best
guess is that it was to avenge the assassination of brother S.S. officer,
Sturmbannfuhrer Kampfe, ambushed by partisans on this same
N141 near Limoges as he returned home from bloodily suppressing
an uprising in Guéret following the Allied D Day landings.

The precise facts remain a matter for argument and conjecture, but
there is an alleged cycling connection. Some coureurs from Limoges
are said to have stumbled across the aftermath of the massacre on
a training ride. It was to be their last. They were arrested and next
day, after the S.S. had departed to the Normandy bridgehead, their
cycles were discovered stacked outside a barn, water still in their
feeding bottles, a racing cap perched jauntily on a handlebar, as if
the owners had simply made a café-stop. Inside on the reddened
earth lay their bullet-riddled bodies.

Buried under the seeming placid flow of everyday life, lies horror
still too raw to forget. Raymond, who, during the war, hid in the

forests and fought with the *Maquis*, tells bloody tales of collaboration and vengeance – girls, heads shaven, paraded through the streets after liberation, cursed and spat upon, their 'crime' to have loved an enemy soldier, whilst others in the Pyrenees, condemned by kangaroo courts, were taken outside and shot. He recalls a local butcher, collaborator, trapped inside his shop after the German retreat, tied on a chopping block and hacked to death with the sharpened tools of his trade.

No wonder they weep. What can we understand of this great burden of grief, hatred and guilt? We were never occupied, humiliated, betrayed by our politicians, and our smug unofficial anthem, 'Rule Britannia', redolent of victory, boasts of a nation that never shall be slaves. Here, heads thrust high, the French sing 'La Marseillaise' with tears of torrid defiance. It is a call to arms against an enemy long gone, yet still perceived pressing at the gate of memory.

The anthem ends and the race begins, many laps of a hilly two-kilometre circuit – top gear down the highway, bisected by barriers, past tricolore-decked bars and shops, only to climb back to our point of departure via a parallel side street. Time and again the Speaker's throbbing voice pursues us through this loop, the climb harder at each repetition. There is no successful breakaway. The survivors contest the sprint and I come 4th, richer by 13,000 francs plus primes and appearance money.

'*Toucher de l'argent*' as the French say. Cash is good. An old guy with an official armband sits behind a table in the café-bar, dripping fag ash over a stack of manilla envelopes. *Toucher* – *what* a tactile word! In return for my race number and signature, he hands me envelopes. I break them open and coins and banknotes slip into my hand, the wages of sweated effort. How deliciously tactile!

'*Alors, tu as touché tes primes,*' Raymond remarks. Lucien is there too. Their broad smiles express pleasure and admiration and I enjoy that inner glow of satisfaction from a job well done. I join them on a bar stool alongside Alan. For once the drinks will be on me.

The Tour has ended in stalemate and victory for Bahamontes. From 120 starters in a 'slow' race, only 65 have reached Paris, including three Internationals: Brian 19th, Christian 41st and Vic 37th (to date the fourth highest British ranking, beating Boardman's 39th). At the Parc des Princes his anxious but proud parents, on a special *Cycling* excursion, are there to greet him, his mum typically bearing a change of underwear for her son. As the crowd of 30,000 roars its approval, a besuited Fausto Coppi steps forth to acknowledge his achievement with a handshake, a memory cherished for the rest of his days.

There is no hero's welcome when he returns to Saint Claud, no flags flown in his honour, no official reception, for he is not a true French son of the village. But some of the younger inhabitants cross the street to grip his hand, and from the close attention paid to his every movement in public you can tell he has garnered himself huge respect. He has completed a Tour de France, raced with courage, and that, in the eyes of the French, singles him out as a rare human being.

But this is not the same man who left the village eight weeks before. Never exactly plump, he is now a walking skeleton, gaunt-faced and skinny-ribbed, with sunken, staring eyes like a concentration camp survivor, blonde hair bleached white by the sun. He has paid a prince's ransom in kilos. At bedtime, unveiled, the mismatch of lily-white torso and burnt-sienna limbs shocks the eye. He has gone through the flames and been recast – not just physically but as a person: cockier, more assertive, impatient and less willing to compromise. He has grown meaner. Living cheek by jowl, as we must do, this doesn't bode well for relationships. Already Alan and he are bickering, their comments barbed with venom – and for some reason I begin calling him Victor.

Lucien's promise of racing aplenty now came true. With the criterium season in full swing, we could race every day if we wished, twice even, by fitting the odd nocturne into our itinerary. But we must travel great distances, spend hours each day at the wheel, and become racing machines. During the next eight weeks we rarely touch our caravan base, averaging four races per week, criss-crossing central and western France as far north as Brittany and Normandy. It is an exhausting routine made tougher by the need to economise on expenses. For this reason we lunch on a diet of homemade sandwiches and stay at only the cheapest, flea-bitten back-street hotels, hiding our faces under the bed-sheets from prowling mosquitoes and next morning scratching the inflamed rings on our bellies and backs where the arrogant fleas have held court. Once upon a time in Perigueux, we awake after midnight to hear Victor screaming, 'I'll have the bastards!' In the clammy darkness it seems like a bad dream, until the naked dangling light bulb illuminates Victor beating his bed. Alan and I follow suit, throwing our sheets and blankets onto the oak-stain floorboards, shaking them out in search of our tormentors. But the crafty blighters have leapt off, deep into their mattress dens – all but for one slowcoach. Victor has it between finger and thumb, a hard pellet of vermin that he squashes on the glass-ringed bedside cupboard. Blood spurts out. 'The little thieving swine!' he exclaims. 'That's *my* blood!'

24

Even from a distance, the tall thin man, pulling on his cycling shoes, looked familiar. Suddenly there was a groundswell of sound like a rustling prayer – 'Il Campionissimo!' – and people hurried from everywhere until a small crowd engulfed the car. It was Fausto Coppi.

With so many races on a tight schedule, we hardly had chance to pause and catch breath. Life became all rushing hither and thither, and time of the essence. Rosy was partly to blame for our permanent state of exhaustion and tempers becoming frayed. We needed a fast reliable motor vehicle to whisk us to far-flung destinations with a minimum of stress and effort. But what had we got? Rosy! Dear old Rosy, like a lumbering, aged, over-fed Labrador, leash in mouth, always having to be chivvied along to keep up with our aspirations.

Motor vehicles play a starring role in this account of cycle racing. I make no apology for that. The car with upturned bicycles toe-strapped to the roof-rack, wheels a-spin and a-glitter in the onrushing wind, was the emblem of the racing cyclist and a vital accessory. Without transport in the rural Southwest, you might as well tear up your racing licence.

Le problème Rosy came to a head in the Corrèze at the start of our eight-week travelling marathon. It was Alan's turn to drive, on dangerously twisting forested roads bordering a precipice, with a deep ravine and river far below. Imagine playing a game of table soccer blindfold. That was like steering Rosy towards its goal. The decrepit steering mechanism engaged at extremely odd points of the compass, rarely the same twice over, a touching eccentricity that we believed had something to do with Wolseley, the motor company, beginning life DownUnder as a manufacturer of sheep-shearing machines. On bends, with the precipice at Alan's elbow, she strove to creep sidewards like a disoriented suicidal crab. The driver needed to exercise his powers of intuition and concentration undisturbed, but one passenger kept interrupting.

'We're late!' Victor announced. 'Can't you get a move on?'

He'd been annoying Alan by winding his window up and down

and fiddling with his shirt collar to adjust the interior draughts that substituted for air-conditioning. Now Alan, in an absolute rage, pitched up on some ground beside a five hundred feet drop and I wondered if he might be about to throw himself or Victor over the edge.

'Go on then, smart arse! See what you can do!'

Victor could do no better, though he tried to give the impression of speed by a jerky operation of the clutch, which flung us to and fro in our seats.

'Jung!' Alan exclaimed at each resulting lurch. 'Jung! Jung!'

We'd already missed the coureurs' free lunch, typically a communal al fresco affair at long wooden tables – local pâté and sweet tomatoes, ham from the Auvergne, bread baked in a wood oven, soup that the riders tinged with a dash of red wine and drank straight from the bowl, juicy Charentais melon dipped in salt to enhance its flavour – good, honest, delicious country food. No, forget that little perk, we made do with a sandwich in the car, arriving with barely five minutes to spare as the *speaker* called over the tannoy for riders to assemble. Whilst Alan and Victor unstrapped the bikes, I rushed off to find the *café permanence,* miraculously still doling out numbers. I signed on for us all, left 300 francs deposit and ran back. We stripped off in the street, treating gawping bystanders to a speeded-up Keystone Cops routine. The weather was close. Soaked in sticky sweat, we had trouble pulling on our woollen racing jerseys and shorts. We half-inflated our tyres, stuffed food in our pockets and tore off, turning back immediately. We'd forgotten our feeding bottles. The organisers delayed the start, but we met with black looks and a slow handclap from the assembled, who were singing a version of La Marseillaise approximating to 'Why are we waiting?' It began, *'Alors enfin arrivent les Anglais!'* This was no way to run a whelk stall.

Raymond commiserated with us on our return to Saint Claud. 'Concerning Rosy,' he said, 'she's like those cars you see in the old gangster movies.'

'Yes,' I said, 'No need to rub it in, Raymond, we know – walnut dashboard, leather seats and a place for mobsters to stand and machinegun the cops.'

'Exactly! I mean no insult, but she really belongs…'

'…in Al Capone's museum.' He'd said it so often I could finish the sentence for him. But he was right. No insult was too gross to satisfy the way we felt about Rosy. She was a museum piece and totally unsuited to our hectic life-style. When, not if, she blew up again, it might happen in some god-forsaken spot in the Corrèze, miles from a telephone. Then, without transport, we'd be in serious trouble, unable to fulfil our lucrative contracts.

'You need a powerful, reliable, modern car,' Raymond continued, 'roomy enough to carry all of you plus the bikes. Monsieur Lacouture has the very thing up at his garage, a lovely Renault Frégate, the sort Anquetil drives, though his has been sprayed an exotic shade of strawberry. Why not take a look?' We did and, after a test drive, bought it on the spot.

'Rosy'

The Renault Frégate

Compared with Rosy, the Frégate was heaven. It had a neat little steering-column gear-stick, snazzy, white-wall tyres and gleaming chrome bumpers. It was roomy and comfortable. It was swept back and aerodynamic, unlike the box-like Wolseley, and its powerful 2000 cc engine speeded effortlessly up to 160 kph. No wonder it was Anquetil's's car of choice. After some haggling, Victor and I got the price down to 400,000 francs, which we split between us. Alan, whose curiosity for continental racing was just about sated, opted not to contribute. He was unlikely to return next year, and who could blame him, given the murderous schedule we had set for ourselves?

During one fourteen-day period we raced on ten occasions, sprinting between venues in South West and Central France. Without the Frégate this would have been impossible. Even so, fatigue was our constant companion and sometimes our legs ached so much, we could barely lift them over the saddle. The pull of contracts and generous expenses kept us going whenever the temptation came to take a day off. Victor might receive start money in the range of 15-25,000 francs from the Paris-based Piel agency, Alan and I somewhat less. It all added up to a good income while it lasted. But there was a flip-side to every contract. You were expected to put on a decent show. Exhaustion was no excuse. The bigger the contract, the stronger the moral pressure not to abandon and disappoint the public.

It was August 17th when we fulfilled our contracts to race at Castillon-la-Bataille, a small town on the Dordogne in the great wine region of St Émilion. Banners strung across the highway proclaimed an international cycle race as we drove in past the ranked vineyards. Unusually, the word 'International' was highlighted in red. As most criteriums included Belgians, Dutch, Swiss, Spaniards and Italians, we wondered what made this one so especially 'international', surely not our presence?

We parked close to a tree-lined square. Large numbers of spectators milled around the pavement cafés and there was a special buzz of expectancy at the *permanence* where new arrivals were scrutinised and stars, like Gérard Saint (9th in the Tour), hounded by autograph hunters. But for us, largely ignored, it seemed just another day at the office.

Then, an unassuming black car edged its way into the square and two men got out. One was already dressed for competition and the other, his aide, began checking his glittering bicycle. Even from a distance, the tall thin man, pulling on his cycling shoes, looked familiar. Suddenly there was a groundswell of sound like a rustling prayer – '*Il Campionissimo!*' – and people hurried from everywhere until a small crowd engulfed the car. It was Fausto Coppi.

Coppi was in the twilight of his career and his criterium appearances outside of Italy were becoming rare. I had never seen my boyhood hero in the flesh until then, and didn't know quite what to expect: something fabulous, I suppose, justifying his fame: a luxury sports car, police escort, army of minders, fanfare, choir of angels! But, no, there was nothing, just these two men and a modest black car with the crowd swarming around them. Yet so powerful was the Coppi mystique that this humble presentation seemed merely to enhance his glamour.

Some 1950s stars enjoyed an aura of almost religious veneration. Today the scene is different. When big money poured in from *extra-sportif* sources during the seventies, eighties and nineties everything was to change. No mystique could survive that constant glare of publicity and commercialisation. Today's stars – the likes of Armstrong, Ullrich and the late Pantani, dollar millionaires with large fan clubs, – face having their lives shaped, picked over and recycled in a frenzy of instantaneous speculative media coverage, whilst they and their hard-nosed agents are also jealously manipulative of image. They are necessarily a part-manufactured product with no space left vacant around them for the myth to take root and grow. Unlike the stars of old, and especially Coppi, they are admired, but not revered.

The quasi-religious atmosphere surrounding cycling pre-war and for two decades after is hard for our cynical age to understand. Journalist Tim Hilton put it succinctly (*The Guardian* 30th June 1989) when he pointed to 'the great years of the Tour – between 1947 and 1967 – and the ritualistic and sacrificial nature of this annual summer festival.'

All of old Catholic Europe was drawn to France as though to a circumbulatory shrine. The route was a procession, the riders seen as heroic in their martyrdom. It was the people's religion, all the more so because nobody in the Tour, from the bunch or the caravan, could be cast as a priest. In the primitive, darker Catholicism of Franco's Spain, religious symbolism was overt. Federico Bahamontes, 'The Eagle of Toledo' as the press always called him, won the Tour in 1959. His yellow jersey is now preserved as a holy relic in the cathedral of his native city: a spare jersey was ripped into tiny pieces and thrown to the mob.

Hilton enlarged upon this religious connection by pointing to the cult of Coppi: '...with those long, thin arms and legs, sunken cheeks, aquiline nose and deep brooding eyes he resembled an icon. Was he not, of all cyclists, the one who seemed most to resemble Christ crucified?'

Indeed, Coppi was already legendary during his lifetime. Even the sexual scandal of the so-called 'woman in white' and his tumultuous rivalry with Gino Bartali, fought over in the Italian press, barely diminished his majestical aura.

And here he was now, on the square at Castillon-la-Bataille in the twilight of his career, making a rare appearance; and I watched as people crowded in around him, reaching out to touch his car or his bicycle or brush against him as they might do to a religious icon or medieval king from whom they sought a blessing.

Something strange had happened. Despite four consecutive days of racing, I was in remission from fatigue. My confidence had returned following the Tour fiasco, and after a second place in a criterium at Bergerac here I was hunting again at the front of the pack.

Mid-way through the race I jumped away to take a prime. A gap opened and I kept going alone, until in a swish and rush of displaced air I was joined by three other riders. Gérard Saint was followed by Victor. The third man was Coppi. I tagged on, positioning myself between Saint and Fausto, as diminutive Victor offered poor shelter. For lap after lap our lead was no more than two hundred yards, and under my arm I glimpsed other riders sprinting from the bunch and dying of exposure in the gap.

This company was the most exalted breakaway of my career: Saint, the 'new Anquetil', was an up-and-coming time trial ace of immense promise; Fausto, a former World Hour Record-holder and Tour winner. We each blasted through in turn, performed a few pedal revolutions, and fell back. Victor, never a natural *rouleur*, was bouncing in his saddle at each pedal thrust. Veteran Coppi too was gasping, and drops of perspiration dangled from that aquiline nose and chin, the 'brooding' eyes pinched to slits. Saint was the real strength and it was as much as I could do to hold his wheel and get past as he swung over.

Long before the finish we imposed ourselves over our pursuers, and the bunch was comfortably out of sight. It was a well-organised and disciplined break, and we shared the remaining primes. As the town loomed into view for the last time, and the switching and jockeying for position began, Saint made a half-hearted attack on the single hill, which was quickly countered.

It was decision time. We manoeuvred, standing out of the saddle, an eye for each other and one behind in case someone was sneaking up to take us by surprise.

I had Saint marked in my book as clear favourite. But I reckoned he would discount Victor and me and focus on Coppi; though the old maestro was visibly tired, his reputation still commanded immense respect. My best chance, I thought, was to go early and leave these two to debate who would close me down.

I stationed myself last, slipped into top gear and jumped with 300 yards remaining. For a short time I had a sense of space opening up behind, and the sight of the chequered flag and spectators straining at the barriers gave me hope. Then Coppi came sizzling past dragging Saint, only for Saint to take him on the line. I was 3rd and Victor 4th.

From the crowd's reaction you would have thought the victor was not Saint but Coppi. I wanted to seal my delight at finishing third by shaking his hand, but he was hidden by a mob of spectators and I couldn't get close. Saint, sipping at his bottle, was watching and I saw him give a little respectful flick of the head as if to say, 'Well, would you believe it!'

I consoled myself. There would be other opportunities and surely *Il Campionissimo* would remember the rare English coureur who had challenged him so courageously. Saint, tall, blonde and handsome, a great French star in the making, was still standing beside his machine. So I pedalled across and shook his hand instead.

It was well I did so. This would be my last chance. Within a few short months, both these men, now smiling and signing autographs, would be dead.

25

'Yes, Lucien, I know of Simpson. He takes no prisoners. For him it's victory or death.'
'Like Napoleon then,' said Lucien, seeing everything through a French prism. 'C'est moi qui gagne!'

Driving northeast from Castillon, I collected my prime prize of twelve bottles of cabernet sauvignon from a classic St Émilion vineyard. In Périgueux, 'truffle town' as every restaurant proclaimed, we resisted the temptation to dine exotically on our winnings and settled for the usual cheap meal in a cheap hotel. For once it was bug-free and despite the sweaty heat we slept well.

Then into the heart of the Corrèze for the Grand Prix d'Uzerche, a race typical of this beautiful region of gorges and boulder-strewn mountains, its sweeping climbs rarely steep enough to suit the pure *grimpeur*. At the halfway point, following a long forested ascent, we would drop through the gorge and back into town. I was ensconced in the lead group and going well. With some twenty plus riders, I cleared the summit and began descending through a double wall of spectators.

Suddenly, from the right, came a tirade of barking and a brown and white terrier thrust through the legs of the crowd. It halted briefly before plunging into the bunch. One rider tumbled, then another. I slammed into the pile-up full tilt with hardly chance to touch my brakes. We were doing well over 40 mph and the impact ripped me from the toe straps and propelled me through space like a human cannonball. Like someone facing execution, I had time to reflect upon my impending fate as the ground passed beneath. Still in mid-air I thought: this is going to hurt. Let it not be my head!

I wore only a cotton cap. But it was my right knee struck the ground first, then my gloved hands, forearms and chin. I slapped down and skidded, gravel ripping flesh. I stopped and rolled over, momentarily numbed. I was staring up at the sun, which pulsed in and out of vision like a faulty neon sign. Then the pain began. It was excruciating, as though someone was driving red-hot spikes into my leg. There was blood everywhere: dripping down my chin, my arms, gushing from the shredded remnants of my knee. My thick leather mitts were grated, but my hands spared.

A group of farm-workers in denim overalls stood over me. They observed my agony with due solemnity. I am reminded now of a dream sequence from one of those Italian *nouvelle vague* films where the 'deceased' gazes upwards from the grave into the curiously unmoved eyes of mourners scattering earth. '*Au secours! A l'hôpital!*' I pleaded, squirming. No one responded. I might just as well have been that 'corpse'.

An age later, as the acute pain subsided into throbbing misery, a siren signalled the arrival of the *sapeurs-pompiers* from Uzerche. There were no ambulances in country districts. Rescue and first-aid were the duty of the fire brigade. In full uniform under the blazing sun, two burly chaps roughly bandaged me up and I was chair-lifted onto a wooden bench seat at the rear of their vehicle. The other walking wounded joined me, one with a nasty head gash.

There was to be no hospital treatment. Instead I was deposited in town at a doctor's surgery. As soon as the man lit his bunsen burner, I knew he had something fiendish in mind. Having cleaned up the earthwork that was once my kneecap using scream-inducing spirit, he produced an array of pincers and metal staples. He heated each staple in the bunsen flame – for sterilisation, he explained, and to pinch tight on cooling – then, without anaesthetic, clamped it across the wound. It was the French version of stitching. Each application of a red-hot staple was another ratchet on the rack, which had me jumping and moaning. '*Bravo!*' he kept repeating. '*Bravo!*'

'*C'est nécessaire, tout ça?*'

The good doctor gave me an injured look. '*Bien sur! C'est absolument normale!*'

It might have been normal for him. For me it ranked with *ventouses* and blunt hypodermics as yet another example of the French Inquisition practising under the name of medicine. I scanned his shelves for sight of a mallet and chisel. Praise be I hadn't fallen on my head and required delicate brain surgery.

'Don't worry,' Lucien said, trying to cheer me up, 'the dog is fully insured. You can sue the owner for damages.'

I was stretched out on the same bed in the room above Raymond's hairdressing salon where I'd suffered from flu back in May. My knee was elephantine; I had to keep loosening the bandage to relieve the pressure of swelling. Two days after the crash, it still throbbed like an angry planet and was locked solid. I feared I might never be able to bend it again.

'It could be worse,' Lucien continued. 'I phoned the doctor in Uzerche. He was surprised you'd got off so lightly.'

'Lightly!' I fumed. 'My season wrecked and maybe I'll never race again. You call that getting off lightly?'

'The doctor's words, not mine. He said you could have ended up in a wheel-chair or worse.'

'Worse? How worse?'

'Put it this way,' said Lucien, joining his hands in a thankful gesture. 'You still have a pretty face.'

More consolation came in the shape of a visit from Victor.

'The contracts are pouring in,' he informed me. 'Shame you're going to miss all the races. But maybe the rest will do you good. Just think of us, flogging our guts out.'

There was no polite answer to that.

At least, now I'd time to read. Lucien brought me some books and recent copies of *L'Équipe*.

'Who is this English Sam-per-son? Do you know him? He's with Rapha-Geminiani and doing well.'

'Simpson. Tommy Simpson.'

'*Ah oui, Sim-per-son.*'

Word had already arrived on the bush telegraph from Britanny about this young Englishman who'd fled his native country to avoid national service. He *was* doing well. Wins in prestigious amateur races like the Fougères–Rennes time trial, Grand Prix de Marboue, Circuit de L'Armel, a stage win in the Route de France and in L'Essor Breton had made him the man to watch.

Lucien had been talking with a local rider fresh from a racing trip to Britanny. '*Il est fou!*' the rider said. 'Every race he attacks from the start. Attack, attack! That's all he understands. He'll burn himself out.'

Knowing Tommy, I wasn't so sure. We first bumped into each other in 1956 on a training ride in the Peak. I recognised him from photos in *Cycling* – he was just a fresh-faced kid then, but had already won a place in the track pursuit team for the Melbourne Olympics. I remembered how he'd quizzed me about the Warsaw–Berlin–Prague, desperate to squeeze out every detail of what it was like to race abroad. It struck me as odd that his interest was with road racing when most of his previous experience had been in time trials and on the track. 'I intend to turn professional,' he said. 'I want to go abroad, ride in the Tour and all the big classics. Britain is a waste of time.' This sounded like so much teenage bullshit. Race abroad? How? When? Surely it was just a fantasy he would grow out of?

But there was a gleam in his eye that left me wondering.

Now, like us, he'd broken from England and the Raphas had snapped him up, recognising his huge talent. He should have won the Tour de L'Ouest that year after taking two stages and holding the leader's jersey. But on the final stage he made a naïve error and allowed close rivals, including team-mate Jo Morvan, to escape in a breakaway that was never caught. Morvan was overall winner and Tommy dropped down to 18th on GC and afterwards was bitter. His team had refused to work for him. *His* team? Why should they: wasn't Morvan also a Rapha in the lead, and, more to the point, a local boy, born and bred, a veteran at the end of his career? They knew this victory meant more to him than it ever could to a cheeky young incomer like Simpson, whom they guessed correctly, was destined for many more big paydays.

'Yes, Lucien, I know of Simpson. He takes no prisoners. For him it's victory or death.'

'Like Napoleon then,' said Lucien, seeing everything through a French prism. '*C'est moi qui gagne!*'

There were many expressions of sympathy for *le jeune coureur cycliste anglais* from customers in the hairdressing salon. When at last I arose from my sick bed and stumped stiff-legged downstairs and out onto the main street, I felt hidden eyes observing me. Turning a corner, I encountered an old crone in black widow's weeds, propped breathless against a house wall.

'*Bonjour, madame.*'

'*M'sieur.*' She visibly crumpled with compassion. Ayiyi! So young, so lame!

But removing the bandage in the caravan, I saw the wound was clean and beginning to knit together. Had I been too quick to condemn the French way of doing things? After eight days, with deft twists of his pincers, the village doctor removed the staples and I felt unbound. From there it was a short step to bending the knee, degree by degree, gingerly and with bated breath for fear of popping the thin bond of skin.

Each day I progressed with bending and walking, till at last I was confident enough to lean my bike against the caravan, hoist my good leg over the crossbar, squirm into the saddle and begin slowly to back-pedal. Two days later I did my first lurching ride, pedalling in fits and starts as if with oval chain-rings. Then, as the knee-joint progressively freed itself, I went from 25 to 50 to 75 to 100 kilometres of training. I was back.

Eighteen days after my crash I raced again, at Limoges. I felt strong, won several primes and a place on the podium. Astonishing! I could hardly believe it. Victor had been right: the rest had done me no harm.

But back in the old regime of racing and commuting, fatigue returned with implacable vengeance and I won no more big prizes that year. My knee resembled an alien transplant, its contours permanently rearranged. A once smooth escarpment had become a deep cleft between two mushroom-shaped kops of bone. Now I would be a strong contender in any Butlin's Knobbly Knee competition.

October. Come the first strong wind, bursting chestnuts were primed to fall onto our aluminium roof in a thudding reminder of childhood. Back home, lads would already be ravaging the trees, as I once did, throwing sticks to dislodge their green-cased treasures. But here there was no tradition for conkers. Instead, with country boys of all ages, some grey-bearded, the all-absorbing passion was for *La Chasse*, a lifetime pursuit so fundamental to their existence that it rivalled food and sex. Early Sunday mornings, you might glimpse small guerrilla bands of men lurking in the fields and woods, with all their shoulder-slung paraphernalia of shotguns, bandoliers and leather game-bags, whistling their ecstatic dogs to heel and signing each other to advance, retire or encircle. They employed the grand strategy of outflanking the enemy with pincer movements. It was the French equivalent of playing at soldiers, but with a real and bloody outcome. You could be forgiven for thinking it was total war against some deadly cunning and formidable foe and not just hunting puny little rabbits through the undergrowth. Most hunters wore heavy boots and stiff gaiters to guard against snakebite, concerning which the French were utterly paranoid, ignoring the much greater risk – swigging cognac out of their pewter hip-flasks and blasting each others' heads off in an alcoholic haze! '*Attention*

Vipères!' Thus red-paint placards were posted at field boundaries, and in the far future became a war cry against CAP set-aside policy as farmers hyped up the risk of their uncultivated lands becoming 'deserts of vipers'.

Raymond, a passionate hunter, was convinced the English Spaniel made the best gundog and Victor had promised to return with one next year. As a city dweller, this mass slaughter of wildlife made me feel a bit queasy, but at least, unlike our fox hunting, the product ended up in the cooking pot. Anyway, it was so deeply embedded in rural French culture that it seemed wise to keep one's mouth shut in favour of *l'entente cordiale*. We were, after all, guests in someone else's country and reliant on goodwill.

Whilst men hunted for game, their womenfolk, with similar passion, hunted for mushrooms, and Raymond's wife Huguette once presented us with a bagful of woodland *ceps* and *chanterelles* the size of pramwheels. She was astonished to hear we didn't eat these in England, preferring the smaller common variety of field mushroom, and even more astonished when I told her that our folk back home, with walking sticks, thick mittens and suitable receptacles, would now be exploring the hedgerows for blackberries. 'Blackberries!' she scoffed. 'Food for birds!'

Even in mid-October the sun could still burn your skin after the valley mist dispersed from the River Son, and you rarely needed arm-warmers to train or race. But there was the smell of autumn in the air, wet grass and golden leaves, and with all this foraging for food going on, you got the sense of heat leaving the land and something ending. It was time to go home.

We were professional to the last. Even our return journey to England was made the occasion for a race. Paris–Tours, the 'Blue Riband' of the French racing calendar, with its big field and rapid flat course usually ended in a huge bunch sprint. But as none of us was a twitchy-legged sprinter-roadman, horses-for-courses we opted instead for the 80 miles overflow support race on a circuit round Tours. This served as a crowd-puller for the Blue Riband, using the same wide uphill boulevard *arrivée* as for the classic itself. It also produced a bunch finish, but I just managed to scrape into the prize-list, no bad way to end my season.

The powerful Frégate lacked a tow bar, so Rosy still had to pull the caravan and our progress towards the Channel ports was consequently slow, with many a stop to cool a steaming radiator.

Alan, Victor and I took turnabout with the Frégate, but I was at Rosy's wheel the day she went dramatically out of control down a hill in Northern France.

Even before the hill, the caravan had begun to pendulum in a stiff side-wind. With brakes about as useful as a chocolate monocle at a beauty contest, I stamped on the pedal to no avail. In fact, the harder I pressed, the further the pendulum swung, until at the end of each arc one wheel of the caravan was being jerked off the ground before crashing down again with a terrifying thud. Thud! Thud! It seemed we were about to jack-knife and overturn in a mess of blazing fuel. It was like being strapped to a dungeon table in some old horror movie, helpless to prevent that penduluming razor-sharp blade scything ever closer to your face. Alan in the passenger seat had a look of stark terror and was clinging to the dashboard.

'For fuck's sake!' he yelled. 'Stop!'

'I can't! She won't have the brakes!'

Brakeless, our screaming engine striving to tear itself free of its retaining bolts, we raced at 55 mph through a 40 kph sign, the boundary marker for Saint Something or Other that sat in the bottom of this Big Dipper U. It was a case of letting rip and saying our prayers. Touching 60 mph, a record for Rosy, we flashed past the first houses, streaks of paint-pealed stucco, smudges of doors and shutters. Then the village square hove into view below, where, to my dismay, market stalls formed a narrowing alleyway of wood and canvas. Our route lay between buckets, brooms, crockery and clothing on tottering racks, all converging to an apex in my line of vision, where safety beckoned in the form of deceleration up the opposing slope. Thud! Thud! Wrestling with a steering mechanism designed for shearing sheep, something said to me this was no place to overturn. I took careful aim somewhere between north-east and south west as my brain registered potential hazards: a woman stepping backwards from an egg stall, farmers haggling over a restless cow, a backing van puffing exhaust, skipping children, a dog roaming the gutter, all blissfully unaware of the approaching mechanical catastrophe that was Rosy and the caravan gone mad. There was nothing else for it. I pressed my hand on the horn and held it there as we tore through like a banshee Flying Scotsman, our drunken bar-room brawler of a caravan flaying wildly behind.

I dared not look back. Expecting at any moment to hear a police siren, I kept going up the incline out of the village, uneasily aware that our GB badge must have been remarked upon and that *l'entente cordiale* would now be minus a *cordiale* or two and maybe even the entire schmaltzy *l'entente*. Victor, following at safe distance in the Charente-number-plated Frégate, had tried to convince himself and everyone else that he was a French national and whatever transpired was of no consequence whatsoever to him.

That was to be the last time the caravan and Rosy had their wicked way with us. Both were sold within a fortnight of our return. Though the caravan never occupied the ambulance's special place in my heart, I'd grown quite fond of quirky Rosy and was pleased when Victor, our sales negotiator, informed me she'd gone somewhere she would not feel out of place – to a scrap yard, for a price equivalent to the cost of a decent pair of sheep shears.

26

It never occurred to me I was pushing my body too hard – Racing and resting were famine and feast.

Finding temporary winter employment was easy. The jobs vacant section of the local paper offered a wide choice. Milk roundsman sounded ideal. Beginning early morning, I could be finished by lunchtime, leaving me with the rest of the day to do as I pleased.

As ever the interview was cursory, no awkward questions asked about my time spent abroad or future plans. In fact, it was all too easy and should have served as a warning for what followed. I was set to partner a prickly old-timer on the edge of retirement with a view to becoming his full-time replacement. A know-all bigot with extreme political and religious tendencies, even after a lifetime in the job, Jim had never been promoted beyond rounds-man. It was hardly wise, working for the Cooperative Society in the Socialist Republic of South Yorkshire, to profess to being an arch-Tory. Jim, an early model for Alf Garnett, viewed youngsters like me with profound distaste. I was 'wet behind t'ears' and 'wouldn't last five minutes in t'job.' (Right there!) When I complained the pay was low, he labelled me a Trotskyite. He believed his working class customers needed 'a bit o'stirring-up' and to this end, through the grimy proletarian streets of Darnall and Brightside, he carried a large picture of Winston Churchill, complete with plutocratic cigar, on the front of his milk float. There he happily engaged with his unionised miner and steelworker customers along the lines of 't' bloody unions is bringing t'country to its knees!'

A mare exhibiting signs of being as ancient and stubborn as Jim himself drew our float. Unless Sally sensed the imminent conjunction of her mouth with a carrot, nothing could persuade her to a trot. She knew the round so well that Jim's direction was superfluous and for all his jerking of reins and gee-upping she conducted herself throughout at the same dignified plod. Sally was beloved of children and pensioners, the latter because the copious steaming golden presents she deposited on the cobbled streets could be swept up and redistributed on some backyard cabbage patch in the sure and certain knowledge 'It's reight good fert gardins!' Some folk attended her daily arrival with tit-bits and if one of her regulars was missing, Sally would refuse to budge unless Jim produced a morsel of apple or carrot from his own bag. Jim was philosophical: 'Nowt yer can do! She were unionised before I 'ad 'er!'

After a few weeks, I gave notice. Sally's lethargy added an hour to each shift. Worse, I'd begun to dread Jim's non-stop chuntering. He criticised my every movement and this came to a head one icy November morning when some empties were frozen to the doorstep. As I tried to kick them free, one shattered. Jim accused me of 'wilful sabotage' and later complained to management 'he's wreckin' t' round'. I declined their kind offer of another partner. The joys of early rising had diminished somewhat at the prospect of alternate soaking and freezing as winter took hold.

Now I looked for a nice easy desk job indoors and found it with the local gas board. Again the interview was conducted in a timeless vacuum. The fact that my previous employment had lasted but a few weeks wasn't questioned. There was no queue for this ill-paid, dead-end post, which had to be filled because it was there and vacant. Did I want it? OK, then sign here.

It turned out I was 'ghosting'. There was no real work to do. At least, under-employment afforded me plenty of time to review the past racing season. I have always been a record-keeping anorak. My notebooks detail every cycle ride I ever took, every date, place, race and distance. The analysis of my 1959 season was composed sitting at my desk in the office; and as it consisted of a list of facts and figures, a casual observer could be fooled into believing it was lawful employment in the gas board's name.

Time spent abroad: 34 weeks
Pro race prize money: 250,000 French francs
Pro race contracts and expenses: 210,000 Ff
Inde/amateur race prize money: 200,000 Ff
Inde/amateur contracts and expenses: 70,000 Ff
Total earnings: 730,000 Ff or 21,470 Ff per week

I started out with 80,000 Ff and finished with 180,000 plus a half share of 200,000 in the Renault Frégate and 12,500 in our radio. The cost of living, including food, accommodation and motoring expenses, totalled 405,000Ff or 11,900 per week, leaving a weekly surplus of over 9,500 francs. To put this into a British context: the currency exchange rate was then around £1 sterling = 1,300 Ff and the average weekly wage in Britain about £8, equivalent to 10,500 Ff. Though I'd earned double the weekly wage, expenses had gobbled up over half my earnings, much down to the trials and tribulations with Rosy. But there was clearly room for improvement and our investment in a good reliable car ought to show dividends.

These earnings were far higher than my former civil service salary and would have been still higher without the blank weeks of illness and accident. There was a good living to be had from cycle racing and with luck and good health I was convinced I could double or treble my earnings in 1960. The clinching factor would be to win a professional contract, have my season organised with access to the classics and the lucrative criterium contracts that went with being in the public eye. My form around the time of the Tour de L'Ariège had convinced me I was capable of high achievement. I was barely 25 with time to improve. Perhaps I could never become a star, but I reasoned there was no harm in setting myself difficult targets even if eventually I had to settle for something less. After all, I'd surprised myself by becoming National Junior Champion and winning the Tour of Britain. The future was unpredictable and every glittering prize up for grabs. I had to keep thinking positively.

I continued writing my analysis of 'What the 1959 season has taught me'. Two things in particular were of concern. Out of 75 races ridden (48 professional, 27 independent), an average of more than two a week, I'd abandoned in no fewer than 23. This no longer surprises, given my indifferent health and the exhausting repetition of race piled on race. Yet, in the uncompromising jargon of the time, a race abandoned was a prize lost. It was unforgivable weakness and I put it down to attitude. I wrote:

I must foster a proper attitude to racing, and ride each race, big or small, to win. Much better perish in an ill-fated breakaway than spend a race sitting in the peloton too timid to move. Not every break will fail and it is only by having the courage to attack and, like Anglade, ride to my maximum that I will achieve success.

Anglade's second place in the Tour was widely reported as being the fruit of aggressiveness and courage.

178

'Never abandon,' I continued, 'and have courage.' I suppose by this stern reprimand I was doing for myself what any good coach now does for his protégées as a matter of morale-boosting routine.

The other thing bothering me was my guaranteed annual collapse of health. Over the years bronchitis had cost me dear, but what could I do about it? I made a number of suggestions: get more rest; go to bed earlier; avoid too many long, tiring journeys; do breathing and other yoga exercises; take garlic capsules.

Garlic was first brought to my attention as protection against chest infections and the common vampire in Bill Shillibeer's coaching column published in *The Leaguer*. It was hard to obtain in Britain. Mine came in capsule form from a high out-of-reach shelf in Boots. Today's alternative-medicine phenomenon is quite recent and signals our loss of confidence in doctors and hospitals. But in the 50s, vegetarians, garlic and yoghurt-eaters and people frequenting herbalists were all lumped together as sandal-wearing Liberal-voting cranks. Recently I'd let my attachment to garlic lapse and put my faith in yoga breathing exercises.

It never occurred to me I was pushing my body too hard. I did, in fact, take it easier that winter: I had nine days off the bike on my return to England, and some weeks during November, December and January I cycled only once. All in all during this winter break I covered 1,300 kilometres in twelve weeks; but even this meagre total exceeded the previous winter by 200 kilometres. Racing and resting were famine and feast. To ease right off wasn't a conscious decision; it was an instinctive response to the call of weariness, both physical and psychological.

27

Sidling up to me in the peloton, grasping my shoulder, he would take
tow and say, 'Alors, Tony, have you had your English breakfast?
The bacon and eggs and a little of the pudding of Yorkshire?'

That winter I did a lot of serious thinking. 1960 marked the beginning
of a new decade, a signpost in time, but that alone couldn't account
for my New Year resolution that it would be my make-or-break
year in cycling. When I looked back on my career, it was with some
dissatisfaction, and when I looked forward I contemplated change.
I was still young, but felt old beyond my years.

My stay-at-home friends were marrying off. Steady jobs and
serious relationships knitted them ever closer into their communities
whilst I, living abroad, grew apart. It seemed they would dedicate
the rest of their lives to working hard in a single career and bringing
up their families. That is how it was then for the vast majority of
folk, who by and large accepted their destiny, lived for the day and
were as content as mortals can be.

But some major life-changing events had contributed to my
feeling of restlessness: national service in the RAF broke the
childhood link with home; living abroad had given me a whole
new perspective on culture, beliefs and politics, whilst the frenetic,
nomadic existence of the professional racing cyclist had normalised
my *expectation* of change. The professional's life of constant flux, on
and off the bike, made for a restless routine. Even the sport itself
took place through a minute-by-minute reformation of landscape
that both determined the nature and outcome of competition, and
provided its actual stadium. Time and motion were thrust to the
heart of being.

And, of course, I knew cycling wasn't a life-long career. Bartali,
Il Vechio ('The Old One') had been exceptional, still pounding the
roads at forty-five, by which time most coureurs were in their
rocking chairs, dangling their grandchildren. By the early thirties, it
was generally agreed, you were on the way down. Some said peak
performance declined past 26 and I was unsure whether I'd peaked
or was on a plateau. Perhaps some amazing transformation was in

the pipeline to rocket me to fame? As the clock ticked on, one had to believe in such miracles.

Then something happened to bring all my uncertainty and restlessness into sharper focus. It was one morning in January and I was preparing to go to work, when an item of news on radio stopped me in my tracks.

'It is reported from Italy that the racing cyclist and former Tour de France winner, Fausto Coppi, has died in hospital at Tortona. He had been ill following a safari trip with friends to Africa.'

That was all, a bald statement of fact, a few grudging words recognising the seismic shockwave sweeping over Europe – momentous if only for the fact that Auntie had deigned to feature an item of cycling on her prime-time news.

Coppi dead, and in mysterious circumstances! All that week, and for long after, I couldn't remove that thought from my mind. It seemed inconceivable. The images of *Il Campionissimo* were still fresh before my eyes from the criterium at Castillon a few short weeks before. Then he had been strong and vigorous. Now he was dead. It was natural for those old past caring to expire in the fullness of time, but there was something sickeningly heart-stopping about this happening to a great champion before his race was run.

And he was more than just a champion. In some mystical, quasi-religious way he had become a worldwide ambassador, a pope of cycling, with his *soigneur*, Cavanna, like some blind soothsayer of ancient Rome, adding to the reverential aura that surrounded him.

I felt personally affected. Coppi had been my boyhood hero; racing with him at Castillon had converted that immature image into real live flesh and blood. Together we had shared an endeavour, and who could have guessed on that golden day, as he disappeared amongst the mob of autograph hunters, that *Il Campionissimo* was about to quit the stage forever?

Coppi's sudden death was not the only circumstance to move me in this strange spine-tingling way, as though the first sod had been turned on my own grave. The previous autumn, as the leaves browned and tumbled, news came of the death of Eugene Tamburlini. 'Tambour' ('the Drum') was, like me, a former Tour of Britain winner (1954), a coincidence that helped to bond us in joky comradeship. With his shock of black hair and Italianate good looks, this star of Troyes had graced many races in Champagne. He was a formidable opponent, strong, resourceful and aggressive, always drumming up the vanguard of action. Together we shared a long-running joke based on his first-hand experiences of execrable British food-fare. Sidling up to me in the peloton, grasping my shoulder, he would take tow and say, '*Alors*, Tony, have you had your English breakfast? The bacon and eggs and a little of the pudding of Yorkshire?' His olive-skinned vivacious *commedia dell' arte* face grinned devil-may-care.

I imagined his death had been from an accident, as with 'Chocolat' Moizan, an equally popular coureur from Charente, killed by collision with a police motorcycle outrider. But meeting up with one of his team-mates, I learned the sad truth. It was suicide. He had gassed himself in some wild Latinate gesture of revenge or despair. I wondered how, of all people, a champion athlete in his prime could have so chosen to dishonour his own body?

'*Il s'est suicide pour une femme!*'

It had been about love and rejection. These words from his close friend expressed a sense of disbelief, disgust and even betrayal. I too felt sick to the heart.

I dug out a newspaper with a recent photo of Tambour snapped at some unguarded moment in the aftermath of a race. I had been utterly wrong about him. A joyless, abstracted face with blank eyes stared out from the crowd, not the carefree champion I thought I knew, but someone battling up a col of spiritual *défaillance* that only he could name, and was destined never to surmount.

28

Our enterprise in being the first British riders ever to have the bare-faced cheek to darken their threshold must have perversely ennobled us in their eyes, for as we knelt in supplication they tipped our shoulders with one of their precious chain-wheel sets. Arise Sir Tony! Arise Sir Victor!

For a bike-racer, these were bad vibes. I was becoming too serious and introspective. Some of the histrionics and frenzied ego-building associated with the bike game were beginning to grate, whilst reading books like *The Hidden Teaching Behind Yoga* by Paul Brunton had brought my orthodox religious beliefs into question. Also, reading novels and stories was spurring my imagination. And the last thing a racing cyclist needs is a powerful imagination.

Whatever image he presents to the public, the ambitious coureur needs to preserve an internal self-image that is assured and cocky to the point of dominance. In the heat of competition, he must no more empathise with opponents than does the warrior on the battlefield. Opponents are there to be beaten, and there can be no space in his heart or mind for a sympathetic Court of Human Rights. Above all, treasonable imagination must be expunged. In the ramrod rush of rocks and trees on some precipitous mountain descent, leaning into each treacherous bend, concentrating to find the right line, he must remain blinkered to the possibility that only two razor-thin strips of rubber separate him from eternity, or lose ground to the opposition. In the barging, elbow-to-elbow bunch sprint, weaving and chopping savagely for position, fear must be edited out and only Raymond's parody of Napoleon admitted, *'C'est moi qui gagne!'* – Simpson's unwritten motto.

Our long-standing problem of accommodation was resolved. Word came through from Saint Claud that rooms had been found for us in the village to be paid for out of community funds. This gesture of welcome was recognition that our presence had been a credit to the community. We'd done our best to mix with the populace and, perhaps more importantly as far as local sentiment was concerned, attracted the right sort of attention and not made a nuisance of ourselves.

Our financial position was now transformed. We were absolved from the expense of purchasing and towing a caravan and though fixed accommodation tied us down to Charente, it was a region rich in racing where we knew we could earn a good living.

Mid-January I met up with Victor in Thorne to fix a departure date and agree our travel agenda. His latest acquisition, the Spaniel pup Charley, our gift to Raymond, rushed out to greet me, tail rotor-wagging.

Disposing of the caravan meant that space for all our belongings was now at a premium and we discussed how best to divide bikes, spares and luggage between the Renault's roof rack, boot and back seats. Adding to the crush was Charley – and two football whistles.

Raymond, and his charming wife Huguette, had been the souls of generosity. At the drop of a hat, Raymond closed his hairdressing salon to ferry us to races, and they had given me bed and board to recuperate from flu and my injuries at Uzerche. Nothing had been too much trouble, and now we considered it was time for us to show our appreciation.

Charley was our gift to Raymond. Before we departed for England in October, our friend had talked of little else. The English Spaniel associated with King Charles was considered *de rigueur* amongst French huntsmen, and swanking off blue-blooded Charley was bound to earn him no end of Brownie points amongst his cronies. Something else *de rigueur*, apparently, was the Made-in-Britain football whistle. According to Raymond's rugby refereeing *copain*, it commanded respect and authority like no other. One blast with that inimitable keynote of British self-control would stop the burliest, boot-in-face thugs dead in their tracks – so he believed. Keen to export our gentlemanly reputation for being good sports, I gifted not one but a pair of Acme thunderers.

I enquired of Victor where he had located Charley.

'From a bloke in Thorne who knows about hunting.'

'Not the same bloke who knows about cars and sold us Rosy?'

There was an offended silence.

We fixed on 2nd February as our departure date. It was time for me to give notice at the gas board.

In fact, we left three days late due to a quirk of fate that put Victor on collision course with a geographically challenged bus-driver who assumed *priorité à droite* from a side road. Many people might have waived their right of way over a bus in the cheery spirit of hail-fellow-well-met, but not Victor, who drove much as he raced, letting into line only friends and team-mates. The resulting thud ker-rip delayed us several days whilst the dent in the Renault's wing was knocked out and re-sprayed at the Transport Department's expense.

This time we weren't heading straight down to Nice. First we had business to attend to in London and Paris before dropping off Charley and the football whistles in Saint Claud.

French Simplex and Italian Campagnolo were rival giants of the cycle components industry. Simplex front and rear gear mechanisms and Stronglight chainwheels and cranks were standard equipment on many new lightweight cycles. Their advertisements in the cycling press boasted of many professionals enjoying their sponsorship. In fact, this widespread largesse gave the impression Simplex possessed a stranglehold over the sport outside of Italy. A man named Merody ran their London office and I arranged a meeting with him to enquire, in the light of our success, if some sponsorship crumbs might be cast our way. He was charming but non-committal. Such requests must be addressed directly to company headquarters in Saint Étienne. But why not drop in there on our way south? He typed us a letter of introduction to the managing director, Monsieur Perroux.

Quitting the midnight ferry at Dunkirk, we were halted at immigration and customs control. Charley, concealed under a blanket, thumped his tail joyously, perhaps registering this stop to mean 'walkies'. Unsure how French law stood on animal importation, we held our breath. I left the engine running to pass off the thumping tail as a big-end knock. But the official gave no sign of hearing anything untoward and merely asked the purpose of our journey.

'Coureurs cyclistes, Monsieur.'

He checked the roof rack and waved us through. Gallic bureaucracy was best avoided, for once set in train it could last as long as a term on Devil's Island.

Bleary-eyed, we drove on to Paris for a reunion with team manager Ducazeaux in his apartment above a brasserie on Faubourg Montmartre. Ducazeaux was from Biarritz, a well-presented man in his late forties. In common with most team-managers, he had been

185

a 1930s professional and had contacts right across the sport, a good guy to know. Now he slipped Victor a jumbo envelope containing his cut of Tour prize money and expenses. Victor was so touched he said thank you in French. We were further encouraged by news that he was negotiating for British teams to participate in Genoa–Rome and the Grand Prix Cyclomotoriste. These were big races. Inch by inch, it seemed, the door to our recognition was creaking open. With this welcome morale booster, we shrugged off travel weariness and headed south to discharge Charley in Saint Claud, where we arrived long after dark. Wined and dined chez Helion, we staggered whoozily across the road to inspect our new lodgings above the village pharmacy.

Its solid oak door would have graced a dungeon and an iron key the size of a small canon tipped the tumblers of its gargantuan lock. Dusty stairs conducted us to rooms of rough-hewn floorboards and flaky distempered walls, damp, long empty and unloved, something from Hugo's *Les Misérables*. A modern-day estate agent might have described it thus: 'unspoiled, with many period features, ripe for conversion' i.e. in a primitive state of disrepair from a War on Want brochure. Furniture and fittings were basic and minimal: a couple of iron beds and plywood wardrobes, kitchen cupboard, sink, table, rickety chairs, a rusting iron stove. No running water, of course. This had to be drawn from a pump in the backyard and lugged upstairs. The pump needed priming, impossible now in pitch blackness, so it was back to the Helions with our bucket.

Outside, a cruel east wind skinned the flesh. The stars shone with glacial purity. Charente in winter could be as cold as the Scottish Highlands. We stuffed the stove with paper and a few old sticks and created a blaze, but it was like trying to melt permafrost with prayer. The rooms were icy and, despite piling every available blanket on top of all our clothes, we slept little.

Next morning the lashing Siberian wind was a real gooly-freezer, little cushions of ice spotting the pavement outside the bar where last evening's clientele had spat after exiting. We bade the Helions farewell, sobered by news that Charley had passed the night alone, whimpering in the kitchen. Overcome by alien smells, people and language, he had crapped all over the floor, not exactly endearing himself to his new owners. Not for the last time, Victor and I wondered whether we had made the right choice of gift.

Arriving in Saint Étienne after dark, too late to contact Simplex, we found a city-centre hotel and, at reception, surrendered our passports to a frosty clerk. This was the custom at French hotels as was the completion of an autobiography-length *fiche*. It felt a bit humiliating, like being taken hostage, but was the law, so one had to grudgingly submit. After all, France was at war, sort of, and this was Saint Étienne, a centre of arms as well as bicycle manufacture. It was winter and off the tourist trail, and my passport bore those incriminating hammer and sickle franks from the Warsaw–Berlin–Prague. We could be terrorists or saboteurs and why wouldn't a bored bomber want to inject a thrill into his otherwise dull existence by flaunting an incriminating passport? I lay in bed thinking it over. That sharp-eyed receptionist, she had phoned her suspicions through to the Ministry of Interior. Come the dawn, Inspector Himmler and his gun-toting heavies would thud up the stairs and splinter our bedroom door from its hinges, thus affording me a second chance to confound Froggy paranoia with righteous British indignation. It would have made a great story – but sadly for this tale, it never happened.

Instead, next morning, we duly presented ourselves in the mundane offices of Simplex/Stronglight or Stronglight/Simplex with Merody's letter of introduction and I began arguing our case for sponsorship with Messieurs Perrin/Perroux or Perroux/Perrin, two rapid patter artists whose names and mannerisms put me in mind of a music hall comedy duo. But it was no go; the buck stopped there. They politely affirmed that they dealt only with team managers and agents, never individuals (and certainly not *coureurs anglais!*). However, our enterprise in being the first British riders ever to have the bare-faced cheek to darken their threshold must have perversely ennobled us in their eyes, for as we knelt in supplication they tipped our shoulders with one of their precious chain-wheel sets. Arise Sir Tony! Arise Sir Victor!

So, another cul-de-sac on the long road to recognition! Victor and I totted up the value of the chainwheel sets against our petrol and hotel costs and reckoned we'd just about broken even.

Jock was already in Nice, staying at his own expense in the Castel Breton hotel with his Mercier team-mates. It was proving a drain on his pocket, so he jumped at the chance to link up again with us, just like old times, and together we toured the letting agencies looking to rent a villa. Even in winter, prices on the coast were high, so we hunted inland with an eye for economy but without sinking to the degradation of a Peymeinade-type hovel. Eventually we plumped for a farmhouse on the lofty plateau of St Pancrace overlooking Nice.

Go to St Pancrace today and you can dine luxuriously at a three-star *Rôtisserie*, where glasses clink to vibrations from the nearby A8 motorway. In 1960 there were no motorways, hotels or coachloads of tourists, just tranquil isolation, accessible by narrow roads or stony tracks, the haunt of birds of prey. Our villa garden enjoyed stunning views over the Bay of Angels, and what was then just a large farmhouse is now likely to be some millionaire soccer star's much improved mountain eyrie.

Negotiating just out of chain-range of the North African owner's demented throat-ripping dog, I haggled over the rent of a suite of rooms. Haggling then was considered in Britain to be 'foreign' and distasteful (now, in the competitive post-Thatcher era, we are up-front and in-yer-face to the point of rudeness) and some years previously I might have instantly succumbed to his first offer. But selling-jobs and living in France, where money wasn't a dirty word, had toughened me up, or so I imagined. Fancying my chances, I started low. But I was up against a man from Morocco where haggling was a sworn ancestral duty. This man, capable of haggling a dowry for his blind, deaf and toothless nonogerian grandfather, caught every bullet of my haggle between his teeth and spat it back. Oh dear! He was a Jacques Anquetil of haggling. I suppose our flashy car and the knowledge we were bike pros lent an impression of opulence. At any rate, ignoring my haggles, he banged on about his poverty and the land hereabouts being unworkable for a smallholder like himself. And anyway, he was a sick man: he enumerated finger by finger his multiple afflictions and hinted that we should be ashamed expecting a man of his age (he was fortyish) and condition to do heavy manual labour, as if the land's barrenness was our fault. Last year's lettings were down, his wife pregnant with their first child, the dog needed to see a vet (psychiatrist, more like.) and so on. He became so distressed by this lamentation that he momentarily lost the power of speech and turned away to wipe his eyes. This should have been my cue to have him by the short and curlies, but strangely it worked the opposite way and I found myself settling for his original offer. Something in my eyes must have told him I'd just read *The Grapes of Wrath, Down and Out in Paris and London* and *The Hidden Teaching Behind Yoga*.

My spineless capitulation disgusted Victor. 'Wish I could speak bloomin' French. He ought to be paying us to live up here.'

Still we demurred over paying the extra premium for central heating, a decision I was to regret. The reason was partly our natural stinginess, a precautionary habit, since we no longer had to count every sou. At root, I believe, was the unspoken fear of 'going soft'. None of us had grown up with central heating. We were the wartime generation of make-do-and-mend and had been further toughened by National Service. Our sport was one that championed hardship. We instinctively distrusted any step down the slippery slope to 'luxury' and being 'corrupted' by ease. Absurd as that now may seem, I think it offers insight into the 'man's world' zeitgeist of that epoch.

A temperate climate and access to good early season races accounted for the Côte d'Azur's popularity amongst professionals. You could usually rely on days of unbroken sunshine, balmy temperatures and sea air rich with ozone, enough for training to become at times pleasurable. If you sought a challenge, the mountains were close at hand. For an 'easy' day, you could pedal the flat coastal road to Cannes or St Tropez – two abreast, for there was little traffic to disturb companionable progress, and drivers, unlike back home, were considerate and gave space. As for races, there was the usual litany – Grand Prix Sigrande, Ville de Nice, Ville de Cannes and so on – to the tune of maybe two per week with a stage race (The Tour du Var) thrown in at the end. The Paris–Nice ('Race to the Sun') was the culmination and Milan–San Remo followed soon after. It was an annual pilgrimage for racing cyclists from all over the continent.

But 1960 was different. The weather was atrocious: overcast, wet and cold. At elevation 1,000 feet, we rose shivering to the sight of hoar frost or snow whitening the scrubby garden. In its kennel at dawn the dog rattled its chain and its fitful barking resounded across the empty, frozen hills like canon-fire, until the cursing owner flung some mollifying food scraps through his bedroom window. We sympathised with the poor beast, feeling equally deceived. It was not supposed to be like this. We could have stayed in England at no expense to enjoy the cold. Despite wearing gloves and innumerable sweaters, it took all our willpower to launch forth each morning and freewheel down the long icy descent into Nice. Overshoes had not been invented and our feet froze in the blast. We began to regret our penny-pinching choice of a mountain training camp. It says much for our determination and professionalism that by March 19th, when we left for Charente, our total of 2,400 kilometres in five weeks roughly matched with previous years.

Despite the dire weather we trained most days, putting in several rides of 100+ miles, often with a couple of cols thrown in. Braus, Brouis, Tanneron and St-Sylvestre all figure in my training record. Zigzag stacking on zigzag signalled the temporary suspension of our two-abreast chumminess and the pace gradually screwed up to the incline as one or other of us demonstrated his climbing prowess. Oddly, it was not always ace-climber Victor who led the assault. Jock was very competitive and hated to be beaten, even in training, whilst I too had my good days. That is until illness struck again.

What started as a sniffle caught from Jock turned into bronchitis. Jock's cold got better and, after two days' rest, he resumed training. I took four days' rest and became bronchitic. That was the difference; the old childhood curse of strong-heart-weak-lungs acerbated through being reared in the most heavily polluted city on planet Earth hadn't gone away. I was in the same dilemma as after the Tour de L'Ariège with no guarantee of a cure even with prolonged rest. A return to fitness zero was what I most feared, and so I determined to train on in the hope the bacteria might die of boredom and leave me in peace.

Abandoning garlic for yoga had not paid off. Classic poses such as the Lotus, Perfect, Fish and Twist, practised daily, served more to raise my comrades' spirits (they laughed like drains at my contortions) than improve my health. Switching on the central heating was the obvious remedy, but instead I stupidly chose to stand on my head and breathe deeply of the cold, dank atmosphere.

29

A confirmed masochist, his idea of fun, as I later learned, was to have his batman beat him until his buttocks bled, a delight, had he only known, that Flemish cobbles, rain and a hard saddle could have improved upon without the need for a tip.

It was not all cycling. Once or twice we enjoyed a cinema matinée in Nice. 'South Pacific' was showing along with 'Le Soleil Aussi se Leve' and 'Dieu Crea la Femme'. The fêted and hounded sex-goddess Brigitte Bardot was in her prime, and the press always seemed to be running some new 'exclusive' on her or Piaf or Jean Paul Belmondo. Britain's own press was then restrained in its coverage of celebrity. Of course, it has since more than made up ground and raised lying and intrusion into privacy to new art forms justified by the so-called 'public's right to know'.

Books were another source of distraction. We discovered the English–American Library housed in some rooms close to the Anglican church on Rue Buffa. Nice had once been a British colony in all but name. But the war had bankrupted Britain and our aristocrats had mostly sold up their great country houses to live in gentile poverty. When the British holiday boom came, Spain, not Nice, would profit. The library was now a sad, lonely outpost of a dying Empire, patronised by a bunch of eccentrics straight off the set of an Ealing comedy or 'Sanders of the River'. In super-chic Nice, their dress code – creased leather-patched blazers, crumpled hacking jackets, soup-stained cravates and baggy flannels (and that was only the women) – denoted their determination to continue flying the flag in the face of Froggy *haute-couture*. Living out their last years in the sun, these ageing ex-colonials, some subsisting on meagre pensions, remained irredeemably British, addressing one another formally as 'Colonel' or 'Mrs Jackson-Prudhoe' or 'Lady Bent'. Many were ex-army or 'trade in Bombay', quitting after India gained independence. One couple claimed to be 'artistes'. A uniformed, bearded ex-sea captain caught my attention as he scanned the bookshelves, proclaiming loudly, 'We must sting!'

I imagined this stirring battle cry must refer to some glorious World War Two naval exploit, until the librarian disabused me. 'Oh no,' she whispered. 'It's just the captain's way of saying how damned awful life is in this land of the rich. He misses not having a Roller parked outside. That's what stings.'

No one seemed surprised to hear we earned our living by cycle racing. Fellow eccentrics, we were welcomed into their coterie of eccentricity with open arms.

The librarian recommended me to read T.E.Lawrence's *The Seven Pillars of Wisdom*: ('A great book by a great man!') Knowing nothing much of Lawrence of Arabia's WW1 desert campaign, I took the 'wisdom' too much at face value, hoping it might go further than *The Hidden Teaching Behind Yoga* to reveal the true meaning of life (and everything). But for that I was disappointed. It was more about death: blowing people up (preferably enemy Turks) and standing by helpless as one's wily yet faithful Arab servants expired yelling the praises of Allah. I suppose the many references to heat, thirst and long exhausting journeys did have points of contact with cycling. But for the meaning of life I had to await Douglas Adam's 1979 *Hitch Hiker's Guide to the Galaxy* where it was revealed as a number in the low forties.

And yet, if cycle racing ever needs a secular patron saint, Lawrence of Arabia is your man. Multilingual, he once commented to a friend, *'Pour être content il faut souffrir.'* (To be content one must suffer.) A confirmed masochist, his idea of fun, as I later learned, was to have his batman beat him until his buttocks bled, a delight, had he only known, that Flemish cobbles, rain and a hard saddle could have improved upon without the need for a tip. In fact, in his youth he possessed a racing cycle and claimed to have raced it *on sand* over a measured distance at 40 mph, – flying with the fairies even for champion sprinter Harris. Though, like Hassenforder, he was a master of tall stories and self-advertisement, his unique training method deserves mention in the common-man's coaching manual. To strengthen his willpower and render journeys more arduous, he cycled uphill but walked down, thus depriving himself of any pleasure earned from previous exertion (which puts Armstrong's 'dedication' firmly into perspective – let's see *him* walk down Ventoux and Alpe D'Huez!) As I say, such exquisite sacrifice and self-torture will ring bells with racing cyclists everywhere and should rank him highly amongst hair-shirt regimists such as Robic, Briek

Schotte, Van Steenbergen and Cavalla. I pondered injecting backbone into my own training by walking downhill into Nice and sprinting back up, but refleced it might wear out my shoe plates long before it stiffened my will.

I abandoned Lawrence for Neville Shute's *On the Beach*, a cheerful novel about man's last days on earth as atomic fall-out annihilates the human race. Yet, before handing back that battered library-copy of *Seven Pillars*, maybe I should have checked its publication date. A first edition recently sold for £750,000 at auction in New York. With that sort of money, who needs to know the meaning of life?

To cheer me up, a 65,000 francs postal order arrived from St Claud, my insurance payout from the dog-induced crash at Uzerche, with my earnings assessed at 32,500 francs (£25) per week. It took no account of pain, stress, loss of morale and fitness, nursing costs and so on, but was better than a poke in the eye with a bent stick. Then came bad news from Ducazeaux, who had failed to persuade the Italian organisers of Genoa–Rome and Grand Prix Cyclomotoriste to accept British teams.

Gloom descended. Bronchitis was again sapping my energy and for the first time I failed to finish a single race, the closest being in the Grand Prix d'Aix-Thermal, where I managed 150 of 208 kilometres. En route to Aix we gave a lift to a French rider from Lorraine, who took it upon himself to commentate, refreshingly non-stop, on my driving skills and map-reading ability. It was he who recommended a hotel, where Robinson and Simpson were also booked in, and Coe and Geddes camped outside in their van. Ominous was the absence of French riders, the reason soon apparent: indifferent food and accommodation at inflated prices.

Over dinner, Simpson boorishly bombarded everyone with bread, then kicked it under the sideboard. And next morning he was still clowning around in the background as Robbo brandished the exorbitant bill and put on a fearsome show of outrage, gesticulating and shouting in his execrable bikie's patois. The equally outraged proprietor shouted back and threatened to call the police, but when Tom began his Chaplinesque baton-whirling, moustache-twirling parody of a gendarme arriving to beat us all up, it was too much and his face cracked. With a flourish, he reduced the bill and honour all round was satisfied. All this time our man from Lorraine hovered, bemused. Why hadn't we asked *him* about the hotel? He'd known it for rubbish as soon as he saw the net curtains, sure sign of an establishment that shunned transparency. Secretive hotels were invariably rip-offs, as every good Frenchman knew. If only we'd asked.

'But we did, we chose the hotel on your recommendation!'

'*Bien sûr!* But that was before I saw with my own eyes.'

Oh shurrup! There was no arguing with idiots.

It added to my gloom when Tommy, Robbo, Jock and Victor, all exuding robust health and primed with energy, finished well up on race classification, whilst I was roared off and abandoned yet again. Returning to Nice more determined than ever to rediscover my form, I doubled the number of yoga repetitions, especially those involving standing on my head.

Late one night there was a hammering at our door. It was the proprietor, perspiring and in a fair old panic. His pregnant wife! The waters had just broken and she needed immediate hospital confinement. He had no car. Could we help?

How could we refuse? There might be some sort of full uniform *sapeurs-pompiers* service out of Nice, but would it reach this remote spot on the mountain plateau in time? Even the dog was in a panic-stricken frenzy, tearing at its chain. We all piled into the Frégate, the woman on her husband's arm, clutching at her swollen belly. He sat her upon a towel, to us lads an ominous sign that something indeed was about to happen.

The man directed me down a boulder-strewn track, which, he said, was a short cut. We bounced up and down to the spring-stops and swerved round craters. Thrown about in the back, I feared the poor woman might be induced to give birth. What then? Would he run off in fright and leave us to it? Our expertise was more in handling spanners than babies' heads. Then, oh my God, it began to rain and with rain came mist and a smeared windscreen, the headlights forming an impenetrable curtain into which I drove blind. Whenever I slowed, there came a yell from the back. '*Plus vite! C'est un cas d'urgence!*' I prayed he'd done a haggle with the Allah of Blindfold Driving and come up with a good deal. I bashed on and eventually we reached tarmac and the hospital hove into view. We left the couple on the steps and drove back to St-Pancrace the long way round.

Early next morning the proprietor was hammering on our door again. There he stood with glasses and a bottle of sparkling *Lys*. '*J'ai un fils!'* he declared, his eyes brimming. He came into the kitchen and popped the cork. The child had been born during the night and mother and baby were doing well. *'Santé!'* We drank their health, and then the man raised his glass to us.

'Vous êtes tous heros!' Tears ran down his plump cheeks.

'What's he say?' asked Victor.

'He says we're heroes.'

'Bloody hell! Quick, ask him to knock something off the rent.'

Eventually, succumbing to the freezing weather, we abandoned ourselves to heedless hedonism. From a *quincaillerie* in Nice we bought a bottle of butagaz and the largest radiator we could find. It was painful parting with so much money just to burn, but it had one immediate benefit: we became more sociable. Instead of gobbling our evening meal, washing up and rushing off to our warm beds as the temperature plummeted, we lingered over the table in newly found ambiance and talked.

'What was that book like,' said Jock, 'that Seven Pillars thing you were reading?'

'A bit boring. All about war in the desert and feuding Arabs.'

'You should have had a gangster book like me,' said Victor. *'No Orchids for Miss Blandish.* Brilliant.'

'I thought with "wisdom" in the title it might teach me something.'

'Like what?'

'The meaning of life?'

Victor guffawed.

'I thought you went to church to discover that,' Jock commented tartly.

'Why don't you pray for your bronchitis to get better?' asked Victor, ever the soul of polite circumspection. There was an uncomfortable silence whilst I thought of an answer.

'It doesn't work that way. God might know what's best for you and you don't always get what you pray for.'

'Can't see the point, then.'

I, too, was becoming a sceptic and thought he might be right.

30

The pressure of competition and a stressful life-style created the right conditions for selfishness and unreasonable behaviour, and sometimes tempers were on a short fuse.

It was proving to be one of the coldest, wettest and most depressing winters in the living memory of Provence. A pall of mist obscured the Bay of Angels. One night a violent thunderstorm cut the electricity. As hailstones beat down and lightning arced over the mountaintops, the villa shuddered in a tempestuous blast of wind and the primitive-hued Moorish tapestries jiggled eerily on their hangings. It was the last straw and, two weeks earlier than planned, we packed up and headed west. If there were to be rain, it would be cheaper getting soaked in Charente.

Our new friend, the proprietor, handkerchief at the ready, waved us off, whilst his wife cradled the precious bundle he sentimentally averred was a by-product of our heroism. His unrequited hound paced in front of its kennel. Haggling was for humans. It had contemptuously rebuffed all our attempted tit-bit bribes, and it now cocked its head quizzically, sensing ultimate triumph.

Jock was making his own way direct to St Claud, whilst our destination was Bordeaux for the annual 170-kilometre minor classic Bordeaux–Saintes. En route we halted in Barsac, home of the eponymous dessert wine. It was a mark of our growing reputation that Max Desarnault had kept on trying to inveigle us to join his Velo Club Barsac, of which he was President. Now, in the club's headquarters, he tempted us yet again with a delicious repast of tenderloin steaks sizzled to perfection over blazing vine twigs. It was apparently a speciality of the region, cooked in our honour, hinting at richer rewards to follow in return for our signatures on the membership form. A festive evening followed and the French indulged in what they do so well, conjuring a celebration out of something and nothing. The incense of smouldering vines and roasted meat was bewitching, but we held firm, promising merely 'to think it over'. Really our roots lay in St Claud where we now had free accommodation and the ties were already too strong for us to break.

Next morning we trailed a Danish rider, Lynge, his pretty blonde wife and baby son into Bordeaux and parked on a city-centre boulevard, donning our race strip in full view of fascinated churchgoers. As ever, we were late, everything last minute rush. We dashed off with our bags to collect our numbers beside the *ligne de départ*.

At the *l'appel* was one Raymond Poulidor, not yet a celebrity, but soon to rise from the Independent ranks to become Anquetil's chief rival. A strong headwind faced down early attacks and the peloton remained compact until the final kilometres. There in open country with a crosswind the race exploded. We ended up in the second group at Saintes. But there was consolation in decent weather. At long last, I'd finished a race, won two early primes even, and above all my lungs weren't sore.

Returning on Monday to Bordeaux, we discovered our car had acquired a parking ticket. I explained to a traffic warden that we'd been away competing in Bordeaux–Saintes, and he tore up the ticket, yet another example of that sweet Gallic reasonableness in affairs of the heart, cycle racing being one.

A surprise awaited us at St Claud. Jock's friend Bill Rowe, with wife and child, was installed in a caravan on our old spot beside the village pump. He, too, wanted to give bike racing a go. No problem in that except that no one had sought the mayor's permission and as this was not a municipal camping ground I was concerned he might think his English friends were taking too much for granted. I wanted nothing to threaten our special relationship with the community: playing host to three foreigners was one thing, an ever-expanding colony of bicycling immigrants something else. As it turned out, subsequent events would prove my fears, but for a reason none of us could have then predicted.

In a quirk of climate, the Charente weather was better than on the Côte d'Azur. Rising temperatures were helping my lungs to heal and I was in high spirits when, the Sunday after Bordeaux–Saintes, I came second in the Grand Prix de Civray. Victor was third. And yet it wasn't an unrelieved success. A spat with Victor was to cast a shadow over our relationship for the remainder of our time in France.

Despite once being dubbed by the press '*Les trois bagarreurs britanniques*' (The three battling Brits) as tribute to our combative approach to racing, we had managed to live together cooperatively, even in the elbow-scraping confines of our ambulance and caravan. We shared domestic chores, assisted one another in races, split expenses and occasionally, by agreement, even shared prize money, whenever it was clearly won by means of an equal share of effort. Cooperation and compromise had kept us on an even keel. A golden rule had been never to attack each other in races.

At Civray Victor broke this rule. I was doing my pull at the front in the break, when he attacked from behind. It was on a steep hill, the group split and I clawed back only with difficulty. Victor could have chosen to launch his attack when a French rider was taking the wind, but he chose me. I was angered by this act of selfishness and I told him so in no uncertain terms.

The next race was at Laguirande, a long drive from St Claud. It made sense for us to pile into the Frégate and pool expenses, but Victor was not agreeable to Bill and Jock sharing space in our car. There was another heated row and I ended up with the other two in Jock's Simca, whilst Victor, alone in the Frégate, had to persuade Raymond to accompany him as guide.

Tit followed tat. Up to now, as the French speaker, I'd accepted responsibility for shopping and keeping accounts. Most expenses came initially out of my pocket, the others paying their dues at later intervals. Now, in a fit of pique, I unilaterally pulled out of this arrangement and henceforward we all went our own separate domestic ways.

It was all unspeakably petty, akin to bickering between rival siblings. None of us came out of it well. At its root was the change in Victor's character. Since his brilliant performance in the mountains of the 1959 Tour, he had acquired more self-confidence and become more self-assertive. The pressure of competition and a stressful life-style created the right conditions for selfishness and unreasonable behaviour, and sometimes tempers were on a short fuse. Victor bore a long-held grudge against Jock for disparaging him as an uncouth Northerner. Now he was getting his revenge.

But he got no sympathy from Raymond, who lectured him on the virtues of cooperation, something I would have loved to witness as neither spoke the other's language. To Victor's credit, he recognised his behaviour had veered beyond the pale and apologised that evening. We all made up, but too late. Victor had acquired the badge of meanness. Harsh words had thrust discontent into the open and the row bubbled on beneath the surface to the end of the season.

The Sharpeville massacre, 21st March 1960, coincided with our return to St Claud. World news wasn't instantaneous then, and some days elapsed before the full horror of what had happened in far off Africa percolated through to us on radio. South African police had opened fire on a defenceless black crowd demonstrating against the hated pass laws, killing 69 people and wounding 180. It marked the beginning of the end of Apartheid thirty years later. Eyewitness accounts of this bloodletting moved us to comment and our opinions were split, typifying British society at large. Jock and Victor believed it was none of our business, whilst Bill and I thought that respect for natural justice demanded intervention from the civilised world, though we weren't sure what form it should take. At any rate, it put our own petty squabbles into perspective.

I was developing a social and political conscience. Growing up in a settled, working-class community post 1945, with the coming to power of a reforming Labour government, I was deluded into believing equal opportunities were at hand, whereas, in fact, every aspect of society remained dominated by the rich and powerful from public school backgrounds. Rather than envying or despising 'toffs', I pitied them as comic Lord Snooties, the politics of 'Dandy' and 'Beano'. In common with most of my contemporaries, I accepted things as they were and got on with my own life. But enforced National Service awoke me to the reality of a society divided by social class into officers and gentlemen versus squaddies. It stirred up feelings of anarchy and resentment and created space for radical thoughts. The 1956 Suez Crisis proved to be another focus of dissent: my NAB office colleagues were, by and large, gung-ho, but I felt uneasy about the British and French imposing their will by force over a weak impoverished nation like Egypt, something our government had decried when Mussolini's fascists invaded Abyssinia in 1935. I was becoming aware of politicians' hypocrisy and double standards.

I wasn't alone in thinking this way. Throughout the 1960s young people in democracies across the western world would rebel against the Old Order. Later, as a university student, I too became radicalised, joining the Anti-Apartheid Movement and demonstrating against

America's Vietnam War, marching across London with Tariq Ali, Cohn Bendit and Jack Straw, and the polyglot thousands who chanted:

Ho, Ho, Ho Chi Minh!
London, Paris and Berlin!
We shall fight and we shall win!

Change was blowing in the wind and even De Gaulle's conservative France wouldn't be immune, rocked by the student riots of Paris 1968. Those heady days were still before me, but already I was embarked on a different path from my companions at St Claud. Reading had planted seeds of change in my mind and increasingly cycle racing would be unable to satisfy a growing need for deeper personal development.

31

Such bullying behaviour in the workplace, like sexual harassment,
wasn't taken seriously. Nowadays, both are matters for employment
tribunals. In the normal world, that is. Cycling, of course, has never
been the normal world.

Just then a justice closer to home was on our minds. With the round
of regional races came good cash contracts. On successive days we
raced at Chef Boutonne and Saumur, where I tumbled on a patch of
sand and reopened the scars on my knee. Over the Easter weekend
came Bourcfranc and St Claud. Our contract at Bourcefranc was for
a decent 15,000 francs each, but there was no mention of any *prime*
de départ for St Claud and we were becoming increasingly concerned
that maybe we were expected in our home village to put in a free
appearance.

For the duration of the criterium, Saint Claud would be cordoned
off, blanketed ticket booths creating ticket-only admission to the
village. By 10.00 a.m. small queues had formed and the temporary
scaffolding stand erected on the square in front of a fairground
carousel was beginning to fill with spectators. 'Speaker' Marroneaud
began warming up the crowd.

The 'speaker' at a criterium was no job for an amateur. It
combined the roles of commentator, comedian, singer, raconteur
and general *chef d'orchestre,* entertaining the crowds, whipping up
enthusiasm for the race and encouraging the donation of prime
prizes, from which he claimed a percentage for himself. Marroneaud
was thoroughly professional, one of the best, and in full flow a sight
to behold. He occupied a small stage opposite the *ligne de départ* from
where he introduced the riders and commentated on the action as
each lap unrolled. Between times, he joked, clowned and sang, his
voice swelling eerily and echoing at your back as you raced into the
emptiness of the surrounding countryside. Microphone in hand,
'Monsieur Quinze Pour-cent' danced and jollied the race away, a live-
wire performance that in high summer left him gasping, like the
athletes themselves, his sweat-patched shirt stuck to his skin. It was
Marroneaud who raised the 3,000 francs prime that I took sprinting

uphill into the village before Graczyc made his solo race-winning bid.

Jock, Victor and I sulked for three days, convinced we'd been overlooked in the dispensation of *primes de départ*, but on Wednesday morning good old Raymond rolled up with three manilla envelopes, explaining the committee had needed time to square its accounts – 10,000 francs each, a small but welcome token of recognition.

The call-over before the St Claud Criterium –
the riders are introduced to the crowd.

Early one April morning as we breakfasted before training, Lucien stumped up our stairs bearing a letter. He was beaming from ear to ear. 'Good news! It's from Liberia-Grammont. They're building a team and they've invited you and Totor to join them.'

'What's he say?' asked Victor, hearing mention of his name. I was too dumbfounded to reply at once. Instead I read the letter for myself. There was no mistaking: it was there in black and white, an offer from Liberia-Grammont and signed by *directeur sportif* Pierre Brambilla himself. I could hardly believe my eyes. Already anticipating our acceptance, he was asking for frame dimensions and jersey sizes, with instructions to join the team at Sancerre on Saturday April 23rd. Our first race in Liberia colours was to be the Tour du Cher, 250 kilometres through the vineyards of the Loire.

The news came as a total joyful surprise. Jock's acquisition of his Mercier contract had convinced us that to emulate him we would need to star in some important stage race. Victor had done just that in the mountains of the 1959 Tour. Yet no offer of a contract had followed. It had been a huge disappointment and his hopes of advancement were dashed. We were both resigned to putting our dreams on hold until the pack was reshuffled after the 1960 Tour.

So what had happened to change the picture?

For some years, Liberia had been a cycle manufacturer with modest ambitions centred on a coterie of good Independents representing them in the Tour and classics. In no sense were they serious rivals to the big teams. But now they had linked up with Grammont, an expanding TV and radio manufacturer profiting from a boom in the TV market and eager to boost their public image. What better way than by sponsoring a professional cycling team with French hero Henri Anglade as its leader? It was an early example of the *extra-sportif* sponsorship that we nowadays take for granted. But funding was not to be a bottomless pit and Grammont proceeded with caution. Anglade apart, there would be no other established stars to make extravagant demands on the corporate purse. Instead, the likes of agent Roger Piel and Sauveur Ducazeaux were consulted for the names of promising young Independents who, like us, would jump at the chance of signing up to regular top-flight competiton, cheaply, *à la musette*.

I translated the letter for Victor.

'That changes everything!' he said.

He was right, it did.

'*Alors!*' demanded Lucien. 'Shall I say you accept?'

We were on tenterhooks at our first meeting with Brambilla. It was in the lugubrious setting of an empty barracks at Sancerre. This was our team 'hotel'! Iron bunks, barred windows, scratched paintwork and crumbling plaster provided stark evidence of generations of military servitude. 'Are you sure we've not signed up for the Foreign Legion!' Victor cracked.

I remembered other lifetime firsts: school, work, reporting for National Service at bleak RAF Padgate – always encountering something new and alien with both excitement and trepidation, as control over aspects of my life was temporarily forfeited.

From the go, it was a teacher-pupil encounter. Business-like Brambilla dished out our new bikes (standard off-the-peg frames and equipment) and clothing, everything but for a saddle (each rider's racing saddle was unique, its leather having been removed, trimmed, 'doctored' to suit personal anatomical shape then re-rivetted and broken in by months of wear). Shorts, jerseys, caps and tracksuits emblazoned with 'Liberia-Grammont', all fitting to a tee, we did a twirl for our new boss's approval.

'*Ça va bien.*'

Next he announced our racing programme. It was somewhat alarming to discover he already had us pigeon-holed: Victor as *grimpeur* and I as *rouleur*. Victor was assigned to the mountainous Tour du Sud-Est and Tour de Suisse, I to the undulating Tour de Champagne and Four Days of Dunkirk. We would have preferred to make our major stage race debuts together, for companionship and mutual support. Victor, speaking little French, would be isolated in a francophone team. I could have acted as interpreter and, dammit, wasn't I also a decent climber, bred in the Peak District and more suited to mountains than Brambilla gave me credit for? But it was a case of fait accompli, Hobson's choice.

To be fair to Brambilla, there was nothing especially oddball about his dictatorial behaviour. Aged only forty and just retired from an outstanding professional career (victor of the 1946 Tour de L'Ouest, 3rd in the 1947 Tour de France and bearer of the coveted yellow jersey), he was a new-boy on the *directeur-sportif* scene and so that much closer to his riders than the old guard. Only much later did I learn of his masochism. Having a bad day in a race, he was rumoured to beat himself over the head with his pump, crying, 'You must try harder!' afterwards putting his bike to bed whilst he himself slept on the hard floor. When he surrendered his yellow jersey to the Robic break on the very last day of the 1947 Tour, an awesome feat of incompetence, he is reputed, in a fit of pique, to have buried his bicycle at the bottom of his garden. Asked why, he replied sarcastically, 'To grow bamboo.' (Rims were made of bamboo.)

'It's a good job you didn't plant your bottles then,' said the journalist, 'otherwise you'd have grown a pharmacy!' – reference to his addiction to stimulants.

Yet many of his senior colleagues from the harsh Thirties school of racing were notoriously far more disciplinarian, acting towards their riders like distant paterfamilias. This was the age of the big B Boss. Contemporary football managers were even worse. The 'Busby Babes', for example, were forced to live in cheap digs near Old Trafford, and when Duncan Edwards bought himself a bike from his £15 a match wage and was prosecuted for riding without lights, Busby fined him £30 for bringing the club into disrepute. Try that on one of today's pampered £50,000 per week diamond-studded soccer stars. To bring his club into disrepute and incur a savage tap on the wrist, he would need to drive his spare Ferrari, blind drunk, over a whole club-run of cyclists.

'Sorry, Boss, didn't see them!'

'Not to worry! S'long you're not injured for Saturday.'

According to Jock, Mercier boss Magne ruled his outfit with a rod of iron. At meal times he would circle the table, scraping excess butter off their bread, cutting fat from their steaks and confiscating anything else he deemed bad for them. They were treated like naughty schoolboys. Such bullying behaviour in the workplace, like sexual harassment, wasn't taken seriously. Nowadays, both are matters for employment tribunals. In the normal world, that is. Cycling, of course, has never been and never will be the normal world.

So it was for *domestiques;* only stardom might earn the boss's reluctant deference. Brambilla, in fact, was on the liberal wing of *directeurs-sportifs.*

Next day I showed my face in a break, which was hauled back, and Victor and I ended well placed in the peloton. Brambilla seemed as relieved as we were. To complete a 250-kilometre race alongside top professionals without falling off or being 'roared' is solid achievement, and never to be taken for granted.

After breaking the ice with the Liberia team, we slept easier. But repose wasn't written into our contracts. Early next morning we were on the road again, this time to Boussac for the 130—kilometre Circuit Boussaquin. Graczyk, animator of the Tour du Cher and victor at Saint Claud, screamed past us in his brand-new Peugeot 403, and we in turn overtook a GB caravan being towed by Messrs Harry Reynolds, Stan Brittain and Owen Blower, who were bidding to follow in our footsteps and gain a toe-hold on the continent.

At Boussac, Tom Simpson was in attacking form, as ever. Again, I got into a break and again it was brought back, leaving me empty for the sprint – with empty pockets too. Then the long drive home, arriving in St Claud well after midnight, utterly shattered.

32

After one dance, I made some excuse about Brambilla clocking us all back into the hotel with his stop-watch. I reckoned being on this brazen teenager's hit list was, like the gravel corner, another disaster waiting to happen.

Something was bugging Jock, who was suffering from a serious loss of form, the underlying cause, he said, being some as yet unidentified illness. Always a hypochondriac, quick to interpret a mere sniffle as the onset of pneumonia, a plain old stomach rumble as symptomatic of appendicitis, he'd got to sticking out his tongue at me and spreading his eyes. 'Look, my eyes are yellow as guineas and I've got cat's breath. I reckon it's *mal au foie.*' Then he would emphasise the point by pinching and dragging his cheeks into the face of a cadaver. I thought he looked absolutely OK and would tell him so. But he remained unconvinced.

The French were a nation of hypochondriacs and there was something comical in the way they blamed *Mal au foie* (sickness of the liver) for every ill under the sun. Pharmacy shelves groaned from the weight of pills, potions and suppositories produced exclusively to combat this fearsome malady, supposed cause of depression, nervous agitation, ague, impotence, loss of appetite, compulsion to binge, diarrhoea, constipation, bankruptcy and anything else you care to mention. The profits from *Mal au foie* alone must have supported the top executives of Franco-Swiss pharmaceuticals in their opulent Riviera life-style. It was a billion franc money-spinner and catch-all scapegoat par excellence, a long-running 'Mousetrap' in the theatre of hypochondria. With French bike riders, *Mal au foie* was second only to *Je n'ai plus de morale* as excuse for loss of form. Not for nothing had Jock shared lodgings with the Mercier boys.

And yet, something *was* plainly wrong with him. A shadow of his 1958 firecracker self, he was concerned that recent modest results had placed him top of Antonin Magne's hit list and he became short-tempered, snappy and morose. Yet, strangely, I couldn't help noticing that whenever he met up with Tiny, Bill Rowe's wife, a cloud seemed to lift and together, out of earshot, they would hold long intimate conversations. He was a frequent visitor to the Rowe's caravan – perhaps unsurprisingly since Bill and he were old friends. Indeed, once, when Bill and Victor stayed away overnight after a race, he slept there in the spare bunk, explaining, 'Tiny is too terrified to be left alone.' The sharp-eyed villagers, pumping water nearby, missed nothing of these goings on and their tongues started to wag. Word got back to Victor and me via Raymond and the gossip in his barbershop, and we too began to wonder if *Mal au foie* was the only explanation for his loss of form.

Happier times. A jokey Andrews in the Mercier jersey during the Tour du Nord, 1958.

To maximise our earnings, we competed whenever and wherever we could. Any sort of race was grist for our mill, the big ones – Tour du Cher, Circuit Boussaquin and Boucles du Bas Limousin – and the small – Grand Prix Asnières, Poitiers-Saumur-Poitiers and Les Salles Lavaguyon. Even in provincial races pride, reputation and cash vied to raise the stakes and no one ever gave us an easy ride. As Tour de France riders we were marked men and the opposition took advantage, looking to us to take the initiative in a chase. Often it was like trench warfare. You waited for General Exhaustion to triumph and resistance crumble before unleashing your Big Push. Sometimes this waiting game worked, sometimes not. There were more ways than one to win a race and confound strength and talent.

The South West was notorious for its combines. These operated undercover, like a dealers' 'ring' at an antiques auction. In practice, a breakaway would form around one strong rider, usually a powerful sprinter virtually assured of winning prime prizes and the final dash to the line. Since the chasing pack included other favourites with no official ties to this sprinter, there appeared to be no problem – until you tried to organise a chase, whereupon many *costauds* would sit up and grin, inviting you to get on with it. Nothing could tempt them to take a real pull at the front. The race was fixed. They had entered into a backdoor deal to share their winnings and by placing a fellow conspirator in the break could enjoy a 'rest' day yet still end up with a wage packet.

It was infuriating. If unaided you reeled in the break, you took the mafia with you, wasting energy, since at point of contact another break with another placeman was sure to sprint away, leaving you back where you started, only more tired and demoralised.

'*Le coup*' (the fix) was illegal and unsporting and with good riders not privy to it especially unpopular. They would loudly denounce '*ce diable de mafia*' with all its works and pomps. But proving the fix was nigh on impossible and officials shrugged off protests, remarking, '*Qu'est-ce-que tu veux? C'est la politique du sport!*' It had always gone on and always would. As 'untrustworthy' foreigners we were never invited to participate in an organised *coup*.

To be honest, I find it hard to condemn cycling's version of 'Spanish practices'. For good Independents, who'd never quite made it to the top, and perhaps didn't seek the disruption to family life that a full professional career would entail, racing was a main source of income for six months of each year. Often they relied on it to support a wife and family. Three or four gruelling races a week was a relentlessly debilitating way to put bread into their loved ones' mouths. No one could possibly maintain winning form over such a long period. They needed 'rest' days and the fix was their means of guaranteeing themselves a sort of quasi-unemployment benefit or 'income support'.

In early May I competed four times in five days, 570 racing kilometres, before motoring up to Rheims on my 'day off' to join the Liberia-Grammont team for the five-stage Tour de Champagne. Fourth and fifth places at Poitiers and Lavaguyon had lifted my confidence. Was I clawing back to form? I was looking forward to linking up with old friends in Champagne and checking myself out against some quality opposition in a 'proper' race, in which a surplus of stars rendered a provincial-style *coup* impossible.

It was a monotonous nine hours' drive to Rheims – no in-car entertainment and no companion. So I wasn't unhappy to pick up a hitchhiker near Châteauroux. Amazingly, he was English! Amazingly, he had thumbed down a Brit in a French car, a very rare event indeed. He was a student at RADA doing his bohemian bit in France 'for the hell of it' and I was the first compatriot he'd met outside of Monaco. We fell to discussing our respective occupations and he was enthralled by my description of the continental bike scene.

'What a strange way to earn a living,' he said. 'It's rather like acting. I think you'd feel very much at home on the stage.'

'How do you mean?'

'Well, cycle-racing sounds to be more like show-biz than show-biz.'

Even provincial races were hotly contested – here Andrews 3rd; Hewson 7th.

I thought about it. He was right. And a year later, with no drama background, never having trod the boards or spouted the Bard, I used it as an argument for admission to a drama course at a teacher training college, where I took to acting like a duck to water.

But I risk getting ahead of my story. Liberia-Grammont was lodged at Hotel Cristal opposite the offices of *L'Union* newspaper. Over dinner I was expecting Brambilla to outline a strategy for the race, but he said very little. In Anglade's absence, André Foucher from Mayenne (6th in the 1964 Tour) had been annointed as team leader, but that apart it seemed to be a case of every man for himself. Next morning Brambilla's instructions were concise: 'Don't do anything stupid!' I remember thinking 'as if I would!'

All began well. I did my share of attacking and fetching and carrying, won some primes and was placed mid-point on GC after two stages. I detected a growing tone of respect in Brambilla's demeanour towards me. Before dinner in Charleville, we were whisked away to our Grammont sponsor's HQ for a team photograph. I can remember feeling immensely proud posing in my brand-new kit. It had taken an age, but at long last here I was competing in a top team.

I decided there and then that the 245-kilometre stage from Charleville in the Ardennes to Chalons was going to be my day. I would show them, Brambilla, Foucher and all the rest. A cross wind was blowing, no break had succeeded, and approaching Chalons the bunch was in echelons. I fought and fought to keep a forward position before unleashing my attack.

The race map indicated a ninety degrees right turn off the main road with one kilometre to go. I knew being first at this point would be crucial, so I jumped early, hugging the right-hand verge. At once I saw my error. The angle of my approach was too acute. To maintain speed round the corner, I needed to swing out left, but that risked sacrificing my lead. There was nothing else for it but to brake hard at the very last second and lean the bike over. I could see a marshal waving a large red flag amidst spectators on tiptoe, presumably warning of the corner. Indeed, it was a warning. That side road had just been thoughtfully resurfaced in loose gravel an inch or so deep. Banking too steeply, my wheels slipped and I slid on my side, scattering the crowd. The gravel ripped my arms and legs and I could hear the thud and smash of riders piling up behind. It had been the wrong place to throw caution to the winds.

211

I limped to the finish amongst the stragglers, a shattered front wheel rubbing both forks. I was shaken, hurting and despondent. My best efforts had come to nothing. Then, as if that wasn't bad enough, Brambilla rolled up, fuming, and began laying in to me.

Everything had gone wrong for the team: crashes and punctures galore, all our spare wheels used up. And now this had to happen in sight of the line. It was the very last straw! No use me apologising! Hadn't I realised Foucher was on my wheel for a lead-out? The team leader down, equipment wrecked and all *my* fault! Was I colour-blind? Did a red flag mean danger or sprint like an idiot? Hadn't he warned us not to do anything stupid?

He was as black as thunder the whole evening and the team took its cue from him. My bid for glory had ended in disaster. I was now their bogeyman and a *cordon sanitaire* was drawn around me at the dinner table. No one would look me in the eye and I felt completely isolated. How quickly I had gone from pride to despair.

Brambilla was in better mood next morning. The team mechanic had worked into the night and bought in some spare wheels. We were back in business. But after yesterday's harsh words, he had nothing new to say to me, and I was left feeling guilty and resentful, blamed for a gravel-strewn corner and an accident waiting to happen. In my eyes it was down to bad luck and I was being singled out as scapegoat for all the team's misfortunes.

The next stage, 212 kilometres to Troyes, was agony. To add to painful cuts and bruises were saddle-boils. My right leg ached intolerably from a bent pedal-spindle that had escaped the mechanic's notice. I was also in excruciating misery from an in-growing toenail, which rubbed the toe-clip at every pedal revolution. Despite all these woes, I gave of my best for the team, but it was all I could do just to finish in the peloton and the following day, on the road to Rheims, I climbed into the sag-wagon after 150 kilometres. The problem wasn't fatigue but a combination of ailments that translated the act of pedalling into self-torture. Brambilla didn't seem surprised. He must have realised that struggling on in such pain just to finish would be a useless gesture.

In Rheims curiosity took me to revisit *Le Bal du Tour de Champagne*. In '58 and '59 Jock, Victor and I had attended this post-race celebration as gauche observers until some French girls took pity and dragged us onto the floor. We made a surprisingly good fist of *la java*, a brisk, hopping dance to the lively music of an accordion band – something as traditionally French as *Gitanes* or lamping for snails. Now I met up again with Louise, Victor's former dancing partner. In full war paint and under the hall's smoky diffused light, she looked about eighteen, but as a pupil at the *Lycée,* was probably much younger. Victor must have made a big impression. Her face fell when I explained he was absent at another race. Then she brightened up. *'Ça ne fait rien!'* she said, leading me onto the floor. *'Vous êtes ici a sa place.'* From the sidelines, her friends observed to see if she was about to claim another English scalp. My priority was to avoid having my sore toe trodden on in the gallumphing melée. I confess that getting on to *tutoyer* terms with her had crossed my mind, but wiser counsel prevailed and, after one dance, I made some excuse about Brambilla clocking us all back into the hotel with his stop-watch. I reckoned being on this brazen teenager's hit list was like the gravel corner, another disaster waiting to happen.

33

Perhaps, heaven forbid, this bicycling flasher prefigured something more sinister – some dastardly assault? Rape! Even murder! Or was it all a bit of harmless fun, a hoax that had got out of hand?

Back at St Claud I had five days to mull things over before I was due to rejoin the team for Les Quatre Jours de Dunquerque. I was in a deeply negative frame of mind after the fiasco of the Tour de Champagne and wasn't looking forward to the race or meeting up again with Brambilla and my *co-équipiers*. In hindsight it's clear I should have excused myself on the grounds of injury. But ducking out seemed to be the coward's way and I resolved to see it through.

With Victor and I now operating on different race schedules, shared use of the car was becoming a problem. I had driven to Rheims, and it was now my turn to travel by train, allowing Victor to drive to the Tour du Sud-Est. But I was due in Dunkirk no later than 5.00 pm and there was no suitable rail-link from Charente to make that possible. The agreed solution was for me to drive to Paris and park the car for Victor to collect the next day. It was a complicated and unwieldy arrangement, but would have to do.

That evening Bill came round asking for a lift. 'I just want to visit the folks back home and sort out some family business,' he said. But I knew there was more to it than that. During my week in Champagne, the bust-up between Bill and Jock over Tiny had come to a head in a shouting match, which Victor reported blow by blow as his major item of news. There was nothing either of us could do except stand by as the emotional pot boiled over and matters took their course. Now it seemed Bill had had enough of being cuckolded and was set to quit the field.

When at 6.00 am I tapped on the caravan door, there was no response. I would have welcomed his companionship and hearing his side of the story, but time pressed and I left without him. Reaching Paris late, I parked the car on Rue Blondel, left the keys with the concierge at Hotel L'Escale and raced to the station, arriving just before the train pulled out. I was soaked in sweat. This was no way to relax before a big race. Whirly-gigging through my head as the train jogged me towards Dunkirk was the accordion music of the *java* and Piaf's frenzied song *'La Foule'*. Like her, I felt myself being buffeted by events out of my control. Life had become a mad round of racing, training and travelling. For years I'd dreamed of becoming a top professional. But here was the reality. I was running close to mental and physical empty and looking for a way out.

The small hotel stood close by the sea front. From the window of my room I could see grey, wind-whipped waves breaking over the promenade. More rain was forecast. Four days of Flanders and rain, my idea of purgatory.

I was introduced over dinner to the great man himself, Henri Anglade. He greeted me perfunctorily before resuming his conversation with the others. I sat there and tried to follow the talk as they gabbled away in argot, assimilating each topic in arrears and unable to contribute. Ignored, I gave up and got on quietly with taking sustenance on board. I suppose Brambilla assumed my reticence, like Victor's, was the norm for a stiff-lipped Englishman, a typical 'cold fish'. He addressed me only once, to ask how was the bike. I gave him no idea of how depressed I was feeling.

Next morning, assembling on the town square, freezing rain was tipping onto us from leaden skies. To counter the cold, everyone had donned two jerseys or racing capes and arm-warmers. Behind barricades, gloomy spectators looked like guests at a funeral, frozen stiff under their brollies. It was Friday the 13th. I was utterly without enthusiasm for the combat ahead and as the downpour increased was on the point of turning round and retracing to the hotel. What am I doing here, I asked myself. I was prevented by the thought that such a public act of renunciation would damage Brambilla and affect team morale even before the race began. If I was going to abandon, I owed it to them to do it more discreetly.

The cobbles were glassy and with the race barely under way the Libertas team van, jockeying for position, skidded out of control, smashed into another vehicle and ended up on the pavement.

I got through unscathed, but every bend had to be treated with upright delicacy and my recent scars tingled in morbid anticipation of yet another fall. I considered the possibility that racing itself might shake me out of depression. Perhaps I ought to give events a chance to unfold and see what resulted? I rode towards the rear of the peloton in sight and sound of the caravan, making it deliberately hard. But by kilometre 20 my mind was made up. This wasn't what I wanted out of life. I fell back and dismounted. The team van pulled up and Brambilla leapt out, demanding *'Qu'est-ce-qui se passe?'*

'I'm giving up,' I said.

'But you can't do that, you've only just started!'

'I can and I am. I've decided to quit cycle racing for good.'

He stared at me in total disbelief as I unpinned my number.

'Tu dois être fou!'

At that I laughed and he had his proof. *'Absolument fou!'* The man known to beat himself with his pump, share his bed with a bike or bury it in the garden had just told me I was mad. He flung his arms in the air and drove off in a furious rage to catch up with the rest of the pedalling asylum.

That decision lifted a great weight off my shoulders. I knew I had done the right thing. I cycled back to Dunkirk, singing to myself, and, ironically, the rain ceased and there ahead of me, arching over the road, was a rainbow like some immense finishing banner in the sky.

Back at my hotel room I propped the bike against a chest of drawers with a letter of explanation for Brambilla, the precious saddle removed to my suitcase. The proprietor looked baffled when I signed out and headed towards the station, feeling like a prisoner out of jail. It was the first day of the rest of my life, a blank page on which I was now free to scribble whatever I wished.

Next day a newspaper cartoon showed Brambilla on the shoreline, staring out to sea and scratching his head. An arrow pointed towards *Angleterre*. And there I was perched on my Liberia, cycling westwards over the waves. Word had got around that my abandonment was due to homesickness and the proximity of my homeland.

The truth was much more complex, something I hardly understood myself. Powerful feelings rarely have a simple genesis and like tangled pondweed can remain submerged deep in the unconscious, with tiny bubbles of self-knowledge clinging. Then comes a crisis to shake them loose. For a long time I had felt dissatisfied and unfulfilled without knowing why and the crash at Chalons had brought all these feelings to the surface.

I had begun asking myself what it was I really sought from life. I was no longer content to be swept along by the old simplicities of ambition and self-glorification. Reading had stirred my intellectual curiosity. The pursuit of yoga as a means of physical improvement had led me to explore the spiritual beliefs that underpinned it. I'd read up on Buddhism and, though not totally converted, found the idea of self-enlightenment appealing. Cycle racing was an exciting way to earn a living, but it was not enough and had begun to pinch like an under-size shoe. I realised it was not my ultimate goal in life but a stagepost. I was growing beyond it and I needed time and space to discover myself anew.

In his hairdressing salon, Raymond, like Brambilla, was scratching his head. He didn't exactly ask if I was mad when I came to explain that I planned to quit cycling, but his grimace of someone swallowing a dinosaur's egg said it all.

'You were starting out on a promising career and you've given it up, *juste comme ça?*'

I confined myself to a nod of agreement. Expressing complicated ideas and emotions was hard enough in my own language, never mind attempting it in someone else's.

'What will you do? Will you go back to England?'

Curiously, up to that moment, I'd given little thought to the immediate future, but now I sprang to a decision.

'No, I'm going to stay here and see the season out.'

'*Bon!*' He sounded relieved. 'There are some good races coming up. Rich pickings! You don't have to race in a pro team to earn your living, eh!' He rubbed together his thumb and forefinger. 'Something else.' Now he lowered his voice as a client entered. 'Your comrades, all this coming and going, it's a bit disturbing, you understand. Not for me, of course, *mais pour les autres*. There are busybodies in the village who pretend to be scandalised. *Tu comprends?*'

He was referring to the goings-on in the caravan. First, Bill Rowe and his family had rolled up and parked themselves uninvited by the pump. Then Jock moved in and Bill moved out, returning to England. Now overnight Jock, Tiny and family had all disappeared, without explanation, leaving the caravan curtained and locked, a mystery that whetted more appetite for gossip. It was just a temporary exodus to Normandy for a race, but their sudden disappearance added to a local sense of unease. In close-knit rural communities such affairs were usually conducted with more tact and discretion. The rural French, on the surface at least, were a conservative and conventional people; in their eyes only one other clan might be more 'correct' than themselves and that was *les Anglais*. No wonder there was tittle-tattle. A cherished illusion had been dispelled – beneath that phlegmatic exterior, perhaps, *après tout*, English hearts beat with real passion?

My sudden abandonment of a professional cycling career coupled with '*l'affaire Andrews*' were earth-shakingly unpredictable, and scandal was added to when someone in the post office, who understood English, overheard Tiny's child addressing Jock as 'Daddy'.

It was all too much for *l'anonyme charitable* who dashed off a poison pen letter to our absentee landlord in Paris, accusing us of keeping *une maison de tolérance* (brothel). Scandalised, the landlord wrote to Lucien, who paid our rent, demanding our immediate eviction or he would descend on the village to kick us out in person. Only when Lucien explained that it was a mere domestic tiff and persuaded the parish priest to back him up with confirmation that village mores were not about to crumble into a riot of licentiousness and orgy did he relent.

It was not the only sexy tit-bit to enliven gossip that summer. One morning, Lucien toddled upstairs from the pharmacy waving a copy of the local paper and grinning broadly.

'*Ce n'est pas toi, j'espére!*' He indicated a paragraph headed '*L'Homme à la Rose!*'

It seemed that a cyclist on an old clanking pre-war bicycle had been observed riding through the dawn mists. Nothing strange in that, you may think – except that this cyclist was naked, utterly starkers – apart, that is, from knee-length wellingtons and a fresh-cut red rose gripped between his teeth. And yet more! According to eyewitnesses, another red rose at saddle rivet level concealed – or perhaps drew attention towards – the man's rudimentary essentials.

He always manifested himself in the dawn's half-light, and never twice in the same spot, making speculation rife. Was it a phantom or real flesh and blood or just the figment of some sexually frustrated female's wild imaginings? Perhaps, heaven forbid, this bicycling flasher prefigured something far more sinister – a dastardly assault? Rape! Murder even! Or was it all a bit of harmless fun, a hoax that had got out of hand?

There were plenty of suspects to fit the bill, old ruffians who slouched around the market, hacking and gobbing up phlegm, talking to themselves in accents strained through slurry, coathangers for tattered clothes the texture of jammy toast, so many Worzel Gummidges. Maybe they were just harmless gappy loners, but who could say? It was a mystery for some Gallic Miss Marple to get her false teeth into. True to her British counterpart, she would discount the obvious culprits in favour of a pillar of the community – teacher, priest or mayor – kicking over the traces of respectability.

Today's tabloids would have made a meal of it, but in sober Charente the story was just a seven days' wonder. *L'homme à la rose* disappeared. He must have abandoned his dewy intercourse with dawn – hardly surprising really, given the practical implications of this pastime. A symbolic red rose between the teeth is one thing, quite another between the naked thighs, its thorns in intimate proximity to the masculine appendages, as Victor and I observed, picturing the man lurching painfully down our bumpy country lanes on his sit-up-and-beg.

'Coo! It makes your bollocks creep just to think of it!' Victor commented succinctly.

Yes! Quite so! Ouch!

34

Victor was worst affected. Returning from the doctor one day, he displayed his armpits, where a legion of lice was visibly performing the Procreation Samba. I took a quick step back before offering my commiserations.

My bedroom window looked down the high street towards the valley of the Son, a potentially beautiful view, but compromised by an ugly crissing and crossing of telephone and power cables, one of those ambivalent marks of progress to dismay the mayor and delight the songbirds. These wires made handy choir-stalls cum play-swings and each dawn the birds gave cacophonous vent to their joy, whilst I, in bed, cursed and bunged up my ears with cottonwool.

An extended hump of back-filled trenches marked yet more progress, this time underground. Mains water had just arrived, though not every householder welcomed it. Some couldn't afford to modernise, others wouldn't. However convenient, they believed piped water was no match for what Nature provided free, and their own horny hands pumped, unfiltered out of the good Charente earth, the ancestral way. We had no choice: with the groundfloor unlet it didn't make economic sense for our absentee landlord to install even a stand-pipe, much less baths, showers, flush toilets and all the accoutrements of modern sanitation. So the pump in the backyard was all we had for drinking and washing. But this needed repair, a new washer maybe, and after stormy downpours, and sometimes even without that excuse, it would go on strike, the handle swinging limp in your hand. We kept a spare bucketful at the ready, not as a votive offering to the gods of Artesia or for personal use, but for priming. A gallon sloshed in the top coupled with some lusty heaves on the handle usually pampered it back into action.

We learned the hard way to treat drinking water with due respect. During a rambling, sweltering ride through the baking *acs* of Charente's rural infinity — Lézignac, Massignac, Sauvagnac, Cheronnac — we replenished our empty drinking bottles at a derelict cottage. A field of contemplative cows froze in mid chew as we kicked a passage through waist-high nettles to the garden pump.

Miraculously, at third pull, it spouted water. The cottage had been long abandoned: birds fluttered through gaping holes in its tumbled roof, the guttering sprouted bonsai and the walls sagged. But the pump performed as if still in daily use by ghosts of the former inhabitants, without priming, and we drank greedily, splashing water over our burning heads and arms.

Next day we paid the price in stomachaches. Well-water, however tasty and apparently sediment-free, could be un-well water if your guts weren't attuned to its particular bacterial recipe. It was a painful reminder to stick to our rule of drinking boiled water only. The silt-free water from our own pump looked very good, but with the pump and stinking leaky earth-closet barely a handshake apart, that gave us pause for thought.

But still there was no mains drainage. A pervasive stench signalled the sewage tanker was at work in the vicinity, pumping out a cesspit or septic tank. I chanced to be in Raymond's salon one morning as this vehicle rolled up outside. Shouting a battle cry of *bonjour*, two burly fellows in gumboots and waterproofs, liberally coated in mud and other nameless filth, burst through the door, dragging their obscene pipe after them. Across the immaculate, newly laid Italian terrazzo flooring of salon, dining room, and kitchen they lumbered, grunting like trolls, and out into the back yard, glowing with potted geraniums, where the cesspit was sited. Back they came to start the pump, then back again to check its progress, back and forth a dozen times, each time leaving footprints to delight a site-of-crime detective and seeming to tow the growing stench with them. It was ladies' morning at the salon and Huguette and her apprentice, Christiane, garbed in their spotless white coats like vestal virgins of the permanent wave, had left their client to gag under the hairdryer and put distance between themselves and the pipe. Backs to the wall, lips pursed, scissor-fingers twitching helplessly, they stood as in some charade of Beauty preserving its delicacy from the Beast that blundered to and fro doing its worst.

A leak at a pipe union was oozing some nasty brown effluent across the floor. Huguette took her gaze off this long enough to give me a quick smile. 'It smells, eh!' a rare example of French understatement. A whole swamp-full of methane strong enough to strip the paint off a battleship invested the salon, and I guessed if anyone had walked in that moment with a lighted cigarette, we'd all have been blown to blazes.

The men finished their work and dragged their dripping pipe back out through the front door, pausing only to nod a curt *au revoir*.

'*Au revoir et merci!*' cried Huguette, swiftly dispatching Christiane to find a bucket, mop and cloth, with added instructions to be sure to wipe all the door handles. The puddled floor, previously clean enough to eat off, now resembled a jungle path trodden by dinosaurs.

'Typical,' she said, 'They promised me this afternoon between shop hours.' (Anything to surprise you there?)

I noticed in this encounter something almost unique in French life. No one shook hands.

Without baths or showers (even in Paris only 15 per-cent of houses had bathrooms) we kept clean as best we could with water in a bowl and a soapy flannel. Sometimes, weary from training, I couldn't be bothered carrying water upstairs for a wash in the sink and so scrubbed myself down with eau de cologne, paying special attention to the saddle area. The French were very big on eau de cologne, less so on soap, consumption being the lowest of any country in Europe. This wasn't necessarily unhygienic. A good scrubdown with astringent eau de cologne cleansed the pores, though Jock would remark afterwards that my room 'niffed like a Nanking tart's boudoir'.

Despite doing our level best to hold the bugs at bay, it was never enough. An itchy orange-coloured rash began to sprout on my upper body. Its zigzag borders moved up and down like temperature contours on a weather map and, despite treatment with a garlic paste prescribed by Lucien, only surrendered to the cooler climes of autumn. The main problem lay with sweating into our wool-rich training togs, an ideal breeding ground for bacteria. It was simply impracticable to hand-wash and dry them every day after use. Victor was worst affected. Returning from the doctor, he displayed his armpits, where a legion of lice was visibly performing the Procreation Samba. I took a quick step back before offering my commiserations. I was reminded of my father in 1917 coming home on leave from the trenches. Mother, then his fiancée, saw him scratching on the station platform. She withheld her embrace and banished the poor bloke to walk on the other side of the road to his lodgings, protesting her undying love for him nonetheless. She waited outside until he scrubbed himself down and dumped his uniform in the yard for the washerwoman to deal with. Friendship, even love, has its limits.

As for keeping our ancient apartment clean, the best we could do was to rearrange the dust of centuries from room to room. The more we swept, the more it seemed to proliferate. Nature abhors a vacuum, and so does dust. Unfortunately, we had only the primitive brush and pan and it was a hopeless struggle, even for ex-squaddies like us, trained in 'bull' and barrack-room hygiene. Shafts of sunlight heated the plank floor and mini duststorms swirled up on thermals. For a while they sparkled like the Milky Way, then cooled and drifted back down. Every level surface was coated with a furry powder. Food could only be stored safely in airtight tins and we tended to buy fresh on a daily basis.

As we sat to dine at the kitchen table, quizzical mice popped their heads through cavernous holes in the skirting before racing in to pick up crumbs from around our feet. Cheek doesn't begin to describe these Gallic rodents. Stamping a foot only served to make them run in circles, like recalcitrant missiles, before homing in again on their original target. Victor set traps, but it was no use. I disapproved of this slaughter and anyway increasing lack of competition only seemed to encourage the remaining few, like Battle of Britain pilots, to greater feats of daring. When a couple set up home in my empty Tour de France cardboard suitcase, squeezing in and out through a minuscule gap in the lid, I took pity and let them stay until the kids were big enough to leave home. Well, I mean, live and let live! I was going through my Buddhist phase. Naturally, I didn't inform Victor, who continued valiantly to trap, remarking, 'These bloody mice! Somebody must be breeding them!'

35

'Tu est chez toi!'

There was no collapse of morale following my decision to give up cycle racing. On the contrary, with two wins, several seconds and thirds, I was rarely placed out of the top six. This was good news because I was hoping to amass a goodly cache of money by the end of the season. I needed to tide myself over for the period in England when I returned without employment, and also I had a very special reason to buy out Victor's share of the Frégate. My English fiancée Katie and I were contemplating an October marriage in Saint Claud and honeymoon in Spain, a country still under fascist dictator Franco's thumb from the civil war. It would be a wonderful opportunity for us to see with our own eyes this romantic, primitive and cruelly repressed land, so vividly described in Hemingway's *For Whom the Bell Tolls*, before it disappeared for ever under the tide of modernity.

There was no collapse of morale...winner at Ste. Sulpice.

Romantic Spain, romantic honeymoon. But my long romance with cycling had come to an end, worn away by the unremitting drip-drip of training, travelling, competition and the frustration of recurrent illness. It had become like any other 9-to-5 job with a few perks and consolations thrown in to make it bearable. Many ordinary professionals that I spoke to more or less shared this view. '*Bien sûr!*' they still loved the sport, or so they said, whilst hedging this confirmation with phrases like 'It's served me well – It's what I do best – I earn a good living from it – It's a tough life, but better than working on the farm.' They spoke from real experience and left the gush of passion to dilettantes and armchair aficionados. Pain, perspiration and many a setback and disappointment had contributed to this laconic philosophy. A few still nurtured ambitions of a high-flying career, but short of a miracle, most accepted their lot as journeymen. Having reached a plateau of modest achievement by their late twenties, there was nowhere to go but down: no amount of training, racing or doping would ever alchemise their base metal into the gold of a Rivière, Anquetil, Van Steenbergen or Darrigade. One day their joints would glue up and the hills become steeper. What then? '*C'est la vie!*' They would retire in the hope of something else turning up. There was no racing for veterans.

Still I had some ambition and there was one race I really wanted to do well in. It was the three-day Tour de Charente based on St Claud. It was my home patch and I felt I owed it to the community to put up a good performance.

Any realistic chance of winning overall disappeared when I struggled just to stick with the peloton on that first day of ferocious heat. It had been a strange summer across the Southwest, periods of unseasonable cold and rain alternating with violent storms and heat waves. Now, in late June, the thermometer burst through the 90s, each day hotter than the last. The second stage was 176 kilometres from Angoulême to the shellfish port of Bourcefranc. Local riders forecast a refreshing breeze off the sea, but it never materialised and we raced without relief over the coastal plain of Charente-Maritime, pitilessly exposed to a scorching sun under a sky of burnished metal, the land a locked-tight oven. Eyes pricked and ached from squinting through the dust clouds kicked up by forward motorcycle marshalls. Tepid feeding bottles failed to slake a thirst that only something fresher could satisfy. Ahead, there was water a-plenty, great blue lakes of it glinting in the middle distance, yet these chimeras always retreated as we advanced. These were cycling's dog days when riders lost all self-discipline, plunging their throbbing bodies into wayside fountains or canals, plundering cafés for refreshment, like Simpson before Ventoux, anything for momentary distraction from the shrivelling heat.

A single roadside tree and the bunch would switch into its brief shade, whilst every shadowy village became an oasis, with sometimes the added blessing of a hosepipe or bucket of water flung in the face, terrifying if it caught you off balance.

At least on this stage I ended up in the front group, but it was nothing to shout home about. That night the marsh-arab mosquitoes shrilled in my ears as I flopped out, sweaty limbs sticking to the bedsheets, feeling like a bag of nails.

There was one stage left, the return leg of 186 kilometres to St Claud, my last chance to shine. An early break drifted off and stuck with a lead of around three minutes but there was little enthusiasm amongst pursuers or pursued to race. The heat swelling towards noon seemed to weigh in our veins like molten lead.

I conserved my energy until we entered the hilly region of west Charente, and then made my move. Two strong riders joined me, Bayle and Mesnard, and together we quickly caught and dropped the exhausted breakaways. Climbing through the Forest of Ruffec, with 40 kilometres left, Mesnard collapsed into a ditch and had to be resuscitated by the race doctor. He was suffering from heat stroke. But, unaccountably, I was enjoying a volte-face of form and felt reinvigorated, as though this were day one, not the end of day three. Bayle and I had the bit between our teeth and relayed each other smoothly, assured of being lost from sight in the high-hedged lanes approaching St Claud. Our lead steadily augmented.

Soon we were racing down the main street and out again, down a bank between cottages under the sneering stone gargoyles of the medieval church. Spectators clapped and yelled support for me through cupped hands. One lap of the Criterium circuit remained, five kilometres, before we re-entered the village from the Chasseneuil direction for an uphill finish. Short of an accident, I was certain of at least second place.

Even at speed, I was trying to compose myself. Concentrate, I thought, and don't do anything stupid. Watch for gravelly corners and check your opponent's every move. I tested him by accelerating hard up a short steep climb, but he was rock-solid and the only result of my effort was to bring on an attack of cramp, not what I'd had in mind.

He rode up beside me. *'Qu'est-ce-que tu veux faire? Tu veux gagner?'*

It seemed like a daft question. Of course I wanted to win! It was my hometown.

'Tu veux gagner, tu me payes dix milles.'

What? Did I hear him right? He wanted a ten thousand francs bung to fix the sprint in my favour. How unsporting! He was proposing a blatant cheat. Not how we British behaved! I was utterly disgusted and made my feelings clear.

'OK!'

He was a wily old bird, a top sprinter and odds-on to win. Anyway, I had cramp.

'Bon! Je te mène jusque cent mètres et puis tu me passes et tu gagnes par la demie-roue.'

He had the plan word perfect. Why not? It was routine business in Mafia-land. But it still had to be made to look right, and even as he led he kept glancing back and urging me on. I passed him fifty metres before the line. The crowd was ecstatic at my victory.

I didn't stop but rode straight through to our backyard and there lay beneath the pump whilst someone swung the handle. I can tell you, there is no feeling on earth to match your parched, aching body being soaked in icy water and you arising from it born again to the human race. It's better than sex. Only then did I return to receive the plaudits, address the crowd and do my tour of honour, waving my bouquet.

But there was no pulling the wool over the eyes of the cycling cognoscenti. Lucien sidled up and whispered in my ear, *'Il t'a laissé gagner?'* I nodded.

'Bon! C'est tout a fait normale. Tu est chez toi!'

He gave the deal with Bayle his stamp of moral approval. The Corinthian ideal of 'let-the-best-man-win' still dominated in Britain, but the continentals were more pragmatic. Here it was recognised that cycle racing was a *metier* and none tougher. You fared how best you could to earn your living.

I felt quite moved. Most of the village people had taken me to their hearts. French blood would never flow through my veins; I was irredeemably English, and yet they'd conferred on me the honour of unofficial citizenship. As long as I lived in Saint Claud I was *chez moi*.

36

'No need to go off course chasing down the peloton – just follow the trail of empty syringes and dope-wrappers!'

I'd grown pally with a number of local riders and several came to congratulate me at the finish of the Tour de Charente.

'Well done!' one remarked. 'Tell me, what are you on?'

'How do you mean "on"? I'm not "on"'anything.'

'Oh, come off it! To put in such a good performance and stick it out with a rider of Bayle's quality, you've got to be on something.'

It wasn't an accusation. Merely he was curious to know whether, as a foreigner, I had access to some new stimulant unavailable in France, my secret weapon.

'No, truly, I'm not.'

'Then you must be mad! You're putting yourself at a big disadvantage. Here,' – he borrowed paper and pen from a bystander and scribbled something down – 'Ask for that at the pharmacy.'

'But isn't it illegal?'

'Of course not! It's all quite normal. You can buy it without prescription. Everyone uses it. It's a tonic for nervous depression and such like. The only thing is, to cure their depression, bike racers need to take three or four times the normal dose.'

He winked.

The thorny topic of doping has punctuated almost every conversation about professional cycling that I have had in recent times. Was it widespread in your day, people ask? Did you get involved? The truth is as Erwan Mentheour admitted in court during the 2000 Festina doping trial: 'Doping in cycling is natural. It's sacred, it's part of the professional obligation. It's everywhere – in my whole career, I only came across a couple of riders who were not taking anything.' Those same words could equally have been spoken forty years ago. Jock, *domestique* to Bobet and in the know, would joke: 'No need to go off course chasing down the peloton – just follow the trail of empty syringes and dope-wrappers!' The near universality of doping was confirmed in a taped memoir left by the late Doctor Dumas (official Tour de France doctor from 1952) who attempted to curtail it, not on ethical grounds, but because of the health risk. Long before the Simpson affair, he had expressed his disquiet to the authorities that such virulent abuse might result in rider fatalities. How right he was!

So today's doping culture is not new in its extent, only in the way that modern medical science has 'improved' on the nature and power of the drugs administered compared with the crude stimulants and anaesthetics of yesteryear. What is new, however, is the media frenzy surrounding it and the fact that many other sports are involved, not just cycling. Each new exposé is fertile ground for the media to dig the dirt in a society that thrives on sensationalism. New, too, are the large sums of money up for grabs in modern-day sports. The incentive to cheat on this account is greater.

Of course, the continental sporting public and media of my day were not ignorant or stupid. When Mallejac collapsed foaming at the mouth on Ventoux in the 1955 Tour, it was clearly not due just to heat exhaustion or that extra breakfast cup of coffee. But attitudes to doping then, and the reasons for it being prevalent, were very different from today, whilst the money incentive was much less. Few riders made a fortune from cycling, though it was the hardest way to graft a living you could imagine. It was primarily to 'keep going' that riders 'took care of themselves'. French people advised me to stay clear of dope, not so much because they considered it cheating (then there was no tabloid finger-jabbing, no roadside banners proclaiming 'Drug Cheats Out!') but because, like smoking, it was bad for your health.

What did Mentheour mean by 'doping in cycling is natural'? To answer that, we must look to its early history as the supreme sport of physical endurance, besides which running marathons (of which I have much experience) pales into insignificance. In those first Tours, competitors might have to race for up to eighteen hours a day to the point of physical collapse, enabling organisers and sponsors to profit from the public perception that they were 'supermen'. How did these 'supermen' keep going? Amongst other things with sustenance from cocaine, morphine, ether and on occasions – heaven help us – strychnine and nitro-glycerine. They doped to survive. From there we arrive via an unbroken chain at the modern phenomenon of doping to win, a practice so long established that Mentheour labels it, with some justification, as 'natural' and 'sacred', a holy rite amongst professionals (though hara-kiri might be a better description in view of recent fatalities.)

Seen in this historical light, the ethical dimension begins to blur. 'Cheat' is hardly appropriate. We are talking not about individual transgressors but a whole culture that operated in ignorance, and until very recently, perceived itself as blameless. Dumas, clearly dismayed, comments: 'They told me everything, because they did not have the impression they were doing anything wrong.'

Put into a wider nineteenth and early twentieth century social and cultural context, the ethical argument is even further complicated. Some people speak as though doping was an invention of stupid, greedy racing cyclists in the twentieth century. But when cycle-racing first began in the 1860s, doping was already embedded in society as a means to enhance the sensations of living, or dull its pains. Laudanum, opium dissolved in alcohol, became the Victorian aspirin even as Britain cynically waged the Opium Wars against China to promote its commercial rights over the drug. Some writers (Coleridge with *Kubla Khan* and de Quincey with *Confessions of an Opium Eater*) employed laudanum to stimulate the imagination, thus acquiring a competitive advantage in the market for literature (Cheats?). Cocaine was also in widespread use. It formed the basis of a 'healthy tonic beverage' drunk by Queen Victoria, the matronly epitome of respectability. Well into the twentieth century cocaine tablets could be bought across the counter and were supplied to troops during World War One to mediate the appalling horrors of trench warfare. Even one of our greatest national heroes, Sir Ernest ('The Cheat'?) Shackleton, competitor in the race to the South Pole, was sponsored by Burroughs and Wellcome in 1909 to 'keep going' on its brand of cocaine tablets. The bottle was labelled, 'Allays hunger and prolongs the power of endurance — when undergoing continued mental strain or physical exertion.' Tailor-made for the Tour de France 1903 to 1967, you might say. Unsurprisingly, the humble *coureur cycliste* tuned in to this doping zeitgeist. What was good for a queen, an explorer knight of the realm, or an army in battle was surely good for him.

That was probably how doping first entered into cycling and why it went unchallenged for so many years. After World War Two, amphetamines began to replace cocaine as the number-one stimulant. 'Purple hearts', standard issue to keep bomber crews alert over target, leaked out into civilian society and even some football managers doctored their teams, according to a BBC expose (*Monkey Glands and Purple Hearts*, Radio 4 10/03/04). Caffeine and amphetamine pep-pills for social use could be bought in pharmacies without prescription across Europe during the 1950s and early 1960s. Full-strength caffeine in the form of bottles of strong black coffee was served up at feeding stations with official approval. In common with other riders, I drank plenty of it.

In William Fotheringham's *Put Me Back on the Bike* there is high drama when some shady Italian dealers arrive at Simpson's hotel during the Tour to sell him a cargo-load of the amphetamine Tonedron. The year was 1967 and the drug had been proscribed only in 1965. This illustrates the importance of context. When Simpson started out abroad in 1959, far from being banned, Tonedron was on open sale at any chemist's shop in France for a few hundred old francs as a nerve tonic, no prescription necessary, no questions asked – yes, a tonic: *un tonique qui stimule la force vitale.* Its status amongst racing cyclists wasn't unlike that of the modern sports drink, something to boost energy levels, and it was held in such familiar affection that in argot it acquired the pet diminutive of *Tonton.* Though cyclists doubled, tripled or even quadrupled the recommended dose, few would acknowledge it might be harmful or that taking it was cheating.

Even after its ban, Tonedron-use remained widespread and riders caught out at doping controls had a ready excuse. Commuting long distances by car in pursuit of their profession, several had been killed or injured in accidents attributable to falling asleep at the wheel, Koblet and Saint being amongst the more famous to impact with trees bordering the highway. These high-speed cross-country chases from race to race led to *Tonton* being used to stay alert whilst driving. It was, riders argued with some justification, like the wartime Purple Heart, a necessary ill. That 'necessary' highlights the chief mitigating factor in the 1950s' drugs debate. The cruel lifestyle necessitated for the professional in pursuit of his living virtually assured the promotion of doping.

From its earliest days cycling had identified with a cult of suffering. It was a badge of honour amongst British cyclists and when I began racing I was repeatedly told, 'You must learn to suffer' as if this alone guaranteed success. In the August 1957 edition of the BLRC monthly *The Racing Cyclist* a top amateur, Ron Beck, composed a paean to suffering in which he exorted: 'drive (yourself) beyond what is normally accepted as the limit of human endurance (to achieve) the fierce exultation of victory'. In a passage eerily reminiscent of Hitler's doctrinal Triumph of the Will, he confused the will to win with the necessity of suffering, something with which generations of sprinter-roadmen from Darrigade to Cippolini would profoundly disagree, since their objective is to get themselves into a winning position by means of guile and team-tactics with the absolute minimum of effort on their own part.

Although this cult of 'when you're shattered, attack' was not so eagerly embraced on the Continent, suffering was an inescapable by-product of the job. Indeed, if T. E. Lawrence was right (*pour être content il faut souffrir*), the professionals of forty years ago should have been the happiest people on earth, since their lives were an almost entirely unrelieved practice of suffering. At its heart lay the system of remuneration that forced riders onto a treadmill of fatigue. Only the stars were decently salaried – which remained the case for several decades until the intervention of wealthy *extra-sportif* sponsors provided cash for a proper salary structure throughout the ranks. For the rest, some benefited from small monthly retainers that barely covered the cost of their food and lodging, whilst the majority, like me, rode *à la musette:* for a bike, the sponsor's kit and a small winning bonus based on kilometres raced. Your living came from prize money, primes, travel and accommodation expenses and appearance contracts priced according to your publicity value as a crowd-puller. It was little different from the piece-rate wages forced on casual farm and factory workers. In theory, the more you raced, the more you earned. But it was not like filling so many grape baskets or machine-sewing so many garments. The coureur's marketable product was a display of pure energy and guts sufficient to delight the paying public whose expectation of a thrilling spectacle needed to be satisfied. He marketed himself with exhausting frequency, and rarely turned down the offer of a 'job' because he could not afford to, especially with a family to support. It was a debilitating penal treadmill, as I know from personal experience. Pain is the body's early-warning defence mechanism against harmful over-exertion. As the muscles exhaust their supply of glycogen and begin to burn fat reserves to maintain the same level of effort, so the pain increases. Exhaustion builds on exhaustion. In order to stifle nature's scream of pain, riders resorted to stimulants.

Two Paris-based agents, Daniel Dousset and Roger Piel, exerted a monopoly in France over the award of professional contracts (independents tended to negotiate their own deals with race promoters or via club secretaries). As these agents took 10 per-cent minimum of each contract, it was obviously in their interest to race-engage their clients to the maximum, irrespective of consequences to health. The best contracts went to the most successful riders and the agent was rewarded with a larger cut. Agents effectively took assembly-line control over a large part of each rider's programme and income. Literally, it did not pay to fall out with your agent or lose form and make yourself less marketable, for his hand was on the tiller of your career.

Drugs use thrived on the system of payment by appearances and results, with riders constantly being pressured to perform well by their agents or risk falling from the public gaze (though a smart self-publicist like Hassenforder always had an extra zany trick up his sleeve). Doping and the system of remuneration, partly dictated by a cartel of greedy agents, fed off each other. It was a culture. Today's stars, the Armstrongs and Ullrichs, limit their racing so as to reach peak form for the Tour de France, an impossibility in the Simpson era when the financial pressure was on to race, race, and race again. So is it surprising that old-time riders carried hypodermic needles blocked by wine corks to inject their tortured legs with morphine en route – bad practice by poorly educated 'country boys' (Dumas's words) who knew no better and for whom career alternatives were very few?

Put doping into its full context and the Simpson era emerges as radically different from today with many extenuating circumstances: it was a deep, historically ingrained culture; the peloton was involved 100 per-cent; the system imposed a penal lifestyle; agents exerted a stranglehold; riders perceived themselves as blameless and were ignorant of the damage to their health. To brand anyone from that era as a cheat is frankly absurd. Even Fotheringham is forced to confess: 'I cannot honestly say I would have acted differently in (Simpson's) position.' Nor, I suggest, can anyone else who was not there to experience it at first hand.

Of course doping is bad – bad for health, bad for sport. How much longer will sponsors risk having their names and logos dragged through the media mire and courts of law? Cycling's prestige is in free-fall. Unlike their forerunners, there is no excuse for today's well educated, salaried, rested and medically pampered riders to go down the doping path. If they cannot make a decent living without doping, they should, like Kimmage, give up and choose an alternative career. They dope by choice, not out of necessity but out of greed.

And yet, a whiff of double standards surrounds the current doping debate. Sport is not the only competitive arena in life in which celebrities have acquired an edge over the opposition by doping. Many other professionals, notably pop and film stars, rely on the fix. Not for them, though, the pejorative brand of 'cheat'. Theirs is more often referred to as 'a colourful lifestyle'. Nor are some cycling aficionados entirely free from the accusation of double standards. Whilst describing Simpson and Hoban as cheats, they will turn a blind eye to all their foreign contemporaries (If doping was 100 per-cent, who was cheating whom?). These are likely to be the same people whose shelves are weighted down with books and videos on the old-time stars of the Tour de France. Well, the honest thing would be to dump their whole collection on a bonfire. Burn one 'cheat', burn them all. Burn all the witches. Go on, be honest, I dare you.

37

'You'll have to wait. We're in the shower.' Again the door shook.'C'est moi, Roger Rivière!'
We grinned at each other. 'Yes,' I yelled back, 'and I'm the Pope.'

The crowd was beginning to drift off home and my obliging friend had also bid me farewell. I was staring at this scrap of paper in my hand. He had written just one word. 'Tonedron'. I was mildly disappointed. Is that all, I thought? I expected it to be some new revolutionary product, not the vitamin pill of the bunch. What sort of ignoramus did he take me for?

Post-race, in the queue to collect your expenses, you might overhear someone saying, *'Bien sûr qu' il a gagné, il était chargé jusqu' à là! Triomphe Tonton!'* ('Sure he won, he was drugged up to the eyes! Victory to Tonton.') It would be stated matter of factly without recrimination. The first time I heard this and naively asked who Tonton was, it provoked a ripple of laughter and the joke was passed all the way down the line.

We were 'clean', so how did awareness of not competing on a level playing field affect us? (Apparently, some top 1970s British riders turned their backs on the Continent, afraid of being corrupted.) By and large we shrugged it off. We trained hard, raced hard and hoped for the best. As Chris Boardman's Crédit Agricole team manager Legeay said in 1998, 'It doesn't matter what anyone else is doing. If you train hard and do your job properly, you will win races. Maybe not as many as you could, but you will win.' Hypochondriac Jock would say, 'I'm not putting that muck into my veins!' He argued his victories against professional opposition showed he didn't need it. As for me, I never brooded over the fact that a shot of something stronger than glucose-flavoured coffee might have won me the Tour du Var and Tour de L'Ariège. I was handicapped most by chronic bronchitis and no stimulant could overcome that.

As long as we three lived communally, there was no chance of us being dragged into the drug culture. But by 1960 we were going our own ways. Jock was domiciled with Tiny in Britanny; Victor and I had our separate rooms, and he was spending much time in the company of the Liberia-Grammont outfit I had just quit.

One day (diary date June 11th), crossing his room to the stairs, I caught him playing with something he'd purchased at the pharmacy. It was a syringe, which he was testing by pumping boiled water into and out of a cup.

'What's that for?' I asked.

'What do you think?' He looked up and grinned. 'Vitamins.'

Well, riders did inject vitamins. But the word was also a tongue-in-cheek euphemism for something with a more immediate kick. What did I know? A punishing schedule awaited him. Three days later he joined Liberia-Grammont for the Tour de Suisse, in which he finished fifth on general classification, an achievement few Britons have equalled. Then, without rest, he travelled straight to Lille to begin the Tour de France on June 26th. He certainly needed something to keep him going.

Eventually, some weeks after the Tour de Charente, curiosity overcame me and I decided to give *Tonton* a try. The small metal phial purchased from a pharmacy in Angoulême contained around twenty slim tablets the size of aspirin. The packaging described it as a nerve tonic and anti-depressant, maximum dosage two tablets daily, or as the doctor ordered.

In the next race I took two. The result was disappointing. A feeding bottle of black coffee would have done as well. I doubled the dose. Same result. So then I trebled it. Now I really did get a kick. I was imbued with a fierce energy that seemed bottomless and launched myself into one reckless and fruitless attack after another. I chased down every break, but when I missed the good one, the mafia closed the race down and I was left with nowhere to go. All it had done was to impair my judgment.

That night I sweated and rolled around in bed, sleepless, as images from the race spun before my eyes. At dawn my head still thundered, as if a volcano was about to burst through my skull. Aspro brought some relief, but it was late afternoon before I was fully recovered.

My French friend had told me about *Tonton*, the upper, but neglected to mention the downer, Pervitin (*'Tintin'*).

I didn't raise it with him again. It was a cautionary experience that I was in no hurry to repeat. In any case, for maximum effect, I would need to pulverise the tablets or inject from an ampoule. But what was the point? It was too late for drugs. In a few short weeks I was abandoning professional cycling for good, and it made no sense to risk my health. Three races had satisfied my curiosity. I knew for sure that if I'd stayed with Liberia and wanted to really shine, I would have had to go down the drugs trail alongside everyone else.

The half empty phial ended up in my Tour de France suitcase, where I came across it during a clear-out twenty years later. I chucked it in the bin.

Meanwhile, Jock and Tiny had quit the village under a black cloud. One day, without warning, they packed all their belongings into the caravan and drove off to St Brieuc in Brittany, leaving behind some bad debts. Lucien was fuming. Since he was liaising between the community and us, he had to account for Jock's debt and he was threatening legal action, which would have reflected badly on us all.

It was an oversight. Jock was no crook. Fortunately, just in time, Bill Rowe returned from England to occupy Jock's empty room in the apartment. Though still bitter at his betrayal, he had remained in communication with the runaway couple throughout this game of matrimonial musical chairs and was now able to resolve their debt problem.

Bill turned out to be a boon in more ways than one. With Victor away at the big Tours, I had been living alone in the ancient house with its creaking shadowy stairs and creepy locked rooms. At night I listened as the darkened building resonated to the scuttering and gnawing of mice and distant ghostly murmurings that seemed to emanate from the walls of those shuttered empty rooms. Bill's company was welcome. He was easy-going and, despite his recent marital catastrophe, possessed of a dry wit, quick to see the comic side of life. The British press, he reported, was highlighting a new social evil, the invasion of London by young people described as 'Bos' (bohemians). Forerunners of 1960s' hippies, these 'jobless scrounging layabouts' had seemingly taken to raiding Lyons Corner House cafés for sugar lumps, 'their sole source of nourishment'. 'So you see,' said Bill, 'if we can't make it as bikies we need never starve.' Sugar lumps figured large in the comic down-and-out life-after-cycling that we began to create for ourselves.

Bill and I hit it off at once. Of all my companions, he was the best. I admired his guts. He packed a decent sprint, trained hard, rarely abandoned and by the season's end had improved sufficiently to notch up a third at Civray (with Victor and I frustrating the chase) and a sixth at Châteauroux. This confirmed what I had long suspected about British cycling: a large pool of untapped talent existed among 'ordinary' riders, enough to mount a serious challenge to the continentals' supremacy. But it was no good sitting on their hands. They needed to abandon their homeland for the rigours of full time foreign competition, as we had done. The part-time circus back home was barely a taster for the real thing.

Having renounced my own place in the 1960 Tour, I followed the progress of Victor and Jock with fascination. The eight-man British team consisted of Andrews, Brittain, Kennedy, Reynolds, Robinson, Sheil, Simpson and Sutton. Both Victor and Tom had engendered pre-Tour press speculation, Tom for his explosive aggression and promise of a scintillating future– 'le dynamateur – le grand bonhomme de demain' – and Victor for his reputation as a climber, acquired in the1959 Tour and enhanced by the recent Tour de Suisse. If only he could descend as well as he climbs, commented *Miroir Sprint* in its special Tour edition. '*On cherche un successeur a Gaul – Sutton, peut y prétendre.*'

To be mentioned in the same breath as Charly Gaul was a wonderful boost to his ego on the eve of the Tour. If he really could take up the Luxembourger's mantle as 'Angel of the Mountains', he would be guaranteed a great career and an everlasting place in cycling's pantheon.

One by one, save for Robinson, Simpson and Sutton, British participants fell away – exhausted, out of time, injured (Reynolds fractured his collar bone) or sick. On stage 4 Sheil suffered a replica of my misfortune at Charleroi. Bent forks after a crash necessitated a change of bike, which, as for me, was bundled by the mechanic. He was stranded for five minutes. The spare bike had been intended for the much shorter Robinson, and brought on cramps during his 50 miles chase. By Caen, 30 minutes down, he was 55 seconds outside the time limit, but the organisers took pity and reprieved him.

It all sounded familiar, this story of a disorganised team with cobbled-together backup. Sheil was 'lucky' in that his chase lasted only 50 miles; mine had been double.

Meanwhile the French national team was squabbling again, Anglade versus Rivière, the two men supposedly cooperating as joint team leaders. By stage 6, St Malo-Lorient, Anglade had a firm grip on the yellow jersey – that is until Rivière pulled the rug by teaming up in a break with Junkermann, Adriaenssens and Nencini. Their stunning 15-minute lead handed the jersey to Adriaenssens and put climber Nencini, eventual Tour winner, into an almost unassailable position. Anglade was outraged and threatening to pack his bags. It required all of team manager Bidot's diplomacy to smooth things over.

But there was worse to come. No one could have forseen the real tragedy awaiting the French team on a gravel-strewn bend in the Cévennes.

Rivière was threatening Nencini's dominance. He had just embraced his spouse, Huguette, at the roadside in his home village. This was familiar territory with his partisan supporters roaring him on and he wanted to impress. Perhaps he was tempted to take one chance too many – or perhaps it was the amphetamines he later confessed to imbibing that impaired his judgment. Descending the Col de Perjuret, he misjudged a bend, plunged off the road and flew like a bird into a deep ravine. Dramatic pictures showed him being stretchered up into a helicopter, his back broken. This superb athlete would never walk again much less ride a bicycle during the remainder of his short life. Confined to a wheelchair, he died aged forty.

Brilliant time-trialist, Rivière rivalled Anquetil in every department and might not only have won the 1960 Tour but several more. His accident changed the profile of stardom and opened the way for Anquetil's lengthy dominance. I raced against him in the Tour de L'Ouest and many criteriums, including the criterium at St Claud. At the time, my impression of him was clouded by something that occurred after a criterium in 1959. Changing facilities were usually primitive; a washbasin back of a café was about as good as it got. But on this particular occasion, we Brits got wind of a shower room at a hotel and, hurrying over there, bolted ourselves inside. No point giving pushy French riders the chance to jump the queue. Hardly had we begun sluicing ourselves down, when the door started to shudder and rattle under a rain of blows and kicks.

'Open up at once!'

'You'll have to wait. We're in the shower.'

Again the door shook.'*C'est moi, Roger Rivière!*'

We grinned at each other. 'Yes,' I yelled back, 'and I'm the Pope.'

The slender bolt gave way and a rider in a Rapha jersey fell into the room, scattering his belongings into a puddle on the floor.

It *was* Roger Rivière, pop-eyed with rage and amphetamines, still living the combat. It didn't help that we laughed aloud. He stamped up and down, threw our towels around and called us some unspeakable names. But we were three to one and made him wait his turn.

All this is in sharp contrast to Jock's impression of him: 'When he wasn't psychotic on dope, he was a thoroughly nice guy. Generous. Once he invited us to his house for a meal and took us round the sights in his flash new car.' It has to be remembered that Jock was no ordinary rider, but a Mercier, pals with Bobet, and as such one of cycling's privileged inner circle.

Wild behaviour wasn't too uncommon in the doped . All it might take was for someone to feel aggrieved by a real or imagined insult or being chopped up. Tempers flared with screeches of *'Ta gueule!'* sometimes with the addition of *'ou je sauté dedans!* ('Shut your big gob – or I'll jump inside it!') If other riders felt endangered by this yelling, pushing and lashing out with bicycle pumps, threatening the peloton's concentration to stay upright, they also might intervene, spreading the quarrel. On rare occasions I saw riders stop and dismount for a roadside punch-up.

Jock's run of bad form continued and he abandoned with Kennedy in the Pyrenees. Victor, by contrast, seemed thoroughly in control and reached the Pyrenees unscathed. In the mountains his fortunes were mixed. On the Aubisque stage he suffered a seized-up leg muscle and fell back. Next day, up the cols of Tourmalet, Aspin and Peyresourde, he was with the leaders, finishing 13th, one place ahead of Rivière and outdistancing both Simpson and Robinson. Together they won the day's team prize. Into the Alps and he stormed up the Izoard, but only two days later, on an easy climb, lost contact and abandoned, according to journalists, 'suffering from a cold'. For him, there was to be no repeat of 1959.

But this was no cold. Hospitalised at Thonon-les-Bains, he was reported to have collapsed from total exhaustion. From the Swiss Alps, with barely a break in three weeks of racing, he had pedalled a personal *grande boucle* back round to the French Alps. There, it seemed, his body gave up.

A letter arrived from his hospital bed. The news was dire. Doctors had told him confidentially that he had a heart condition and must never race again. All of us – Lucien, Raymond, Bill and I, the entire village as the news spread – were stunned.

The Tour, like the fabled Hollywood show, went on, with Robinson and Simpson as our last representatives. Unusually, Brian bettered Tommy in the time trial. Both men survived to Paris, Robinson 26th overall, Simpson 29th.

Though I continued to race, I remained resolute to quit the sport at the season's end. What would I do then? I had no plan beyond a vague desire to further my education, possibly by doing a university degree in French. That wouldn't be easy. The élitist world of academia wasn't the open door it is now and, nationally, admitted only the top four per cent of ability. Two 'A' levels plus 'O' level Latin were the minimum entry requirement and I had only French and Latin. I realised I had some catching up to do. I started borrowing books from St Claud's part-time library and, besides reading Hemingway and other modern writers in French, I struggled to make sense of the classics: Racine, Molière, Stendahl, Flaubert – just picking books off the shelf at random and plodding through them, a dictionary at my elbow. There were many unfamiliar words and expressions, long out of common use or too literary to creep into everyday speech. It was hard going, even for a cyclist trained in endurance. To this I now added a correspondence course in Short Story Writing from the London School of Journalism. I borrowed Bill's typewriter and spent many absorbing afternoons concocting stories, which I rated as innovative and powerfully written examples of the genre. My tutor seemed to agree. His comments were supportive and encouraging and, I believed naively, totally honest. In fact, my tales were turgid second-hand regurgitations of Hemingway, all about rebellion and war in far-off lands, of which I had no first-hand knowledge. I even pinched my characters' names from *For Whom the Bell Tolls*, though the nearest I had been to Spain or the Spanish was in the redolent slipstream of Gil and Bahamontes. The characters spouted vainglorious clichés of patriotism and love, *Boy's Own* heroics.

My tutor suggested I should 'test the market' and so I sent these overblown concoctions to various popular magazines that gave space to the short story. I was surprised and a little offended when the rejection slips bounced back. Surely these people recognized burgeoning genius when they saw it? I had more success with *Cycling* and Jock Wadley's *Sporting Cyclist*. My cycling-related pieces were snapped up. It took me a while to learn the first rule of writing: to write about what you know best, or research your topic in imaginative depth.

These setbacks only made me more determined. I was like a convert in the process of swapping religions, with one foot still in cycling and another in a parallel universe. The physical competitive life still exerted its sway and always would. But increasingly for my satisfaction I was inclining towards the life of the intellect.

Lucien phoned the hospital at Thonon-les-Bains for news of Victor. He had improved, but the doctors were in no hurry to discharge him, and he was beginning to feel bored and restless – a good sign, I thought. He was torn two ways. With the Tour ending, he was champing at the bit to profit from the appearance contracts that would flow his way. On the other hand, here he was, a cycling hero, being fussed over by nurses and boarded and lodged in the equivalent of a rather nice hotel at the organisers' expense. Did he really want to rush back to our squalid apartment, back to cooking, shopping, lugging water, mousetrapping and generally doing for himself? It was a genuine dilemma.

Finally, eleven days into convalescence, he returned, looking pale and wan. It was the day Lucien took us sightseeing in Angoulême. Climbing the stairs of the Town Hall tower, he was forced to pause and catch his breath. It didn't look good. Nevertheless, ignoring medical advice, he resumed training and racing. Lucien put him in touch with a heart specialist, but by the time the test results came through, Victor was away racing in the east. Raymond dashed off a telegram to the organisers. 'Sutton must not race. Blood dangerously thin. Any cut fatal.' The telegram arrived too late. Maybe Victor would have ignored it anyway. 30,000 francs, three times your average British weekly wage, exerted a strong pull and he rightly expected to have some payback for all his blood, sweat and tears.

Despite the threat of haemophilia, he returned from his round of contracts 'cured'. A swollen wallet was cycling's equivalent of a trip to Lourdes and now, once more, he felt 'strong as a bull'. Sadly, his joy was short-lived. On the drive home, he crashed the Frégate, without injury to himself, but ensuring that a sizeable chunk of his earnings transferred itself to the even bulkier wallet of *garagiste* Monsieur La Couture to pay for knocking out the dents. This was a blow to his morale, which two subsequent victories in Charente could barely assuage. It must have been still bugging him when he sat down one day at the kitchen table with Bill and me to discuss the future.

'Can't seem to win at this game! There's always something. You bust a gut and think you've come out on top and then...' He shook his head in bewilderment, 'something happens – something always happens.'

'*C'est la vie!*' Bill smiled wryly. He had more cause to feel sorry for himself than the rest of us put together.

'That's one reason why I'm jacking it in,' I said. 'When the Big Fella in the Sky was dishing out health, I must have had the day off sick.' It was a joke I'd heard some place.

'What's the other reason?' Bill asked.

'We've made a living from bike racing and we could go on. Maybe you two will. But I just keep thinking how hard it is. All that effort – I mean, is it worth it? Anyway I'm getting married.'

There was silence. Victor stirred his tea and munched a biscuit. A gnawing sound started up behind the skirting. Bill stamped his foot and miaowed. The gnawing stopped. Then restarted.

'Those bloody mice *never* give up!' Victor said.

'They've got tiny mouse brains. What else do they know but to run round in the same old circles? I reckon I can put all that energy into something else and succeed. That's why I'm chucking it.'

'For what though?'

'I don't know – yet. But there's got to be something else out there.'

'Too right there has!' said Bill. 'We can always become "bos".'

Victor was silent. What I'd said was no surprise to him. It was a conversation we'd trotted around more than once since I quit Liberia-Grammont. I guessed he was still weighing up his own future.

A few days later the decision was made. He came into the kitchen as I was chewing through my evening meal. He was whistling between his teeth and studying his blurred reflection on the inside of a saucepan, always a sign he was about to make a pronouncement.

'Shirley and I are getting married'

'Congratulations! Over here?' I had visions of us booking a double wedding at the church in St Claud.

'No, back home. I'm quitting. You're right about what you said. All that effort – there's got to be something better.'

In a way I was surprised and in a way I wasn't. Now was his chance to make a good career from cycling. Aged only 25, with time to improve, he had potential as a climber that was of interest to several prominent *marques*. Ducazeaux could oil the wheels. He'd broken through, joined the élite brotherhood, cycling's equivalent of becoming a made man. He was better placed than Jock, whose Mercier contract had just been terminated, and who was riding *à la musette* for the much smaller Margnat-Coupry outfit. It didn't make complete sense for him to give up now. Was he holding something back? Had the health scare damaged his confidence? Was he worried about living alone in a foreign country and as member of a foreign team when he couldn't speak the lingo? Despite our spats, a bond existed between us of shared experience that he might miss when I was gone. We were both tykes.

The big question-mark came over his health. Though he claimed to be fully recovered, hanging over him was the threat of a repeat of his mysterious collapse in the Alps. Was it simply heat exhaustion or something else – an underlying cardiac problem, as suggested by his consultant? He might not know until it happened again, and then it could be too late.

Also I wondered if he was losing his nerve. He was a poor descender, his hands, like mine, too frequently in contact with the brakes. We had both learned the hard way that immortality was no longer the option it had once been. I had crashed badly; he had been there the day Rivière went over the drop. Saint, Coppi, Tamburlini, Moizan – where were they now?

'What about you, Bill? Are you coming back next year?'

'What? And live off sugar lumps? No, it's been good experience and I've satisfied my curiosity, but I reckon I'd be pushed to make a living at it.'

Shortly after saying that, Bill did his best ride ever, a third place at Civray. Afterwards, as we drove back through the falling dusk, a ghostly pale shape flitted from the forest across our path. There was a soft thump. Stopping to inspect, we discovered a barn owl lying limp on the road amidst a corona of broken headlight glass. It was still warm from flight. I lifted the beautiful dead creature and deposited it gently on the grass verge. 'Bang goes another 3,000 francs!' said Victor resignedly, toeing the orange-tinted shards. Though I'd bought him out and was now the Frégate's sole owner, we were sharing running costs to the season's end.

'This wise owl is a messenger of the gods,' joked Bill in his mock-portentous voice. 'It's an omen. If we were Romans, we'd read its entrails to see what the future held in store.' Turning the bird on its back and spreading its great white wings, he pretended to make an incision in its belly and peer inside.

'What forecasteth thou, O mighty Bilious?' I demanded.

'Verily, thou, Antonius, and I will come into great wealth and fortune and live off the fat of the land, whilst yon Victorius will end up on the dole.'

'Very funny!' said Victor. He returned to the car, whistling between his teeth. 'Does that mean I'm excused my share of the headlight?'

38

Already I was packing my bags with nostalgia, truffling through the memorabilia of a life that was passing me by and would never return.

It was October and I was alone in the old house. It was a time of waiting, a time for reflection. A solemn procession of black-garbed parishioners was passing beneath my bedroom window, advancing up the Confolens road, the mitred priest and his altar boys bearing a lofted crucifix. As was customary, the village had turned out in force to pay its last respects to a good friend and neighbour. In the distance, the pale sunlight glinted metallically off a line of stationary vehicles halted by a gendarme at the cemetery gates. They were passing familiar landmarks of my two years' stay: Helion's hairdressing salon, with its advertising slogan *'Exigez la Brilliantine FORVIL'* on the housewall, painted in huge pink letters ten feet tall; the sculptural stack of blue butagaz bottles at the door of the hardware store; Delpy's habadashery where women went to buy wool, ribbons and cloth to repair and replenish the family wardrobe; the tiny wasp-buzzing greengrocery of fermenting fruit, whose bowed old crone of a proprietor mumbled spells as she tapped her ancient scales to exactitude. On went the procession towards the gendarmerie, Lacouture's garage and the tumbledown farm where we purchased France's scarcest commodity, fresh milk, by the unpasteurised jugful, steaming from the udder.

In the other direction, the Chasseneuil road lay deserted in the soft autumn light – hotel, post office, Avia filling station, the square with its sentinel trees beside the war memorial, a scatter of parked cars and the scarce visible *ligne d'arrivée* towards which, four months previously, Bayle and I had 'raced'. Opposite, the blacksmiths, where once I had had a cracked frame rebrazed gratis, stood the mobile distillery under a canvas awning and flaming chestnuts, a hissing Heath Robinson alembic of wood-boiler and curling pipes on its annual pilgrimage through the *acs* to magic rough local wine into mind-embezzling brandy. Self-sufficiency was the name of the village.

St Claud: funeral procession.

St Claud: the mobile brandy still.

I recalled summer evenings, lying on my bed, legs pulsing from the afternoon's racing, listening to the clink of boules and the players' yelps of triumph and anguish from the dust patch outside, or waking at dawn to the squealing death-throes of a pig in the slaughterhouse near the butcher's shop. Squealing, too, from the honeymooners on the midnight of their *noces*, being forced-fed with *soupe à l'oignon* from a chamber pot, the traditional ribald send-off. And that earthquake – or so it seemed – the thunderous roaring and shaking that brought everyone to their bedroom windows as an entire armoured division – tanks and artillery on low-loaders – gear-crunched its hour-long negotiation of the bend en route south to confront the latest Algerian crisis – a show of force that inspired our mockery of French pomp and grandiloquence next day as we bestrode our bikes and launched forth, '*Allons y, enfants de la patrie!*' not onto the Queen's Highway, but '*sur la grand'route du Général de Gaulle*'.

Already I was packing my bags with nostalgia, truffling through the memorabilia of a life that was passing me by and would never return. My companions, Victor and Bill, had just departed, cramming all their bikes and belongings into Bill's (erstwhile Jock's) Simca. For some reason we all shook hands through the car window, solemnly, as though for the last time and with a formality of departure that was very French. With the cycling link broken, there might be no reason for us to meet again. Then they were gone, grinding through the gears up the high street and northwards towards Confolens and the Channel ports, leaving behind a haze of smoke and stench of burned oil.

And I was alone.

I was alone for a fortnight, awaiting the arrival from England of my bride to be. One small race remained to be raced and I continued my training, fifty to sixty miles per day. Old habits die hard, but when the Sunday morning dawned cold with rain pattering the window-pane and chuckling in the gutters, I turned over in bed, pulled the blankets over my head and went back to sleep. I felt like one of those Canadian log-rollers. Years of sheer spinning effort had kept me in physical and psychological equilibrium, but now I'd stepped off the log and was being swept downstream into some profoundly different future circumscribed by the unpredictabilities of marriage and a new career.

It was both exhilarating and sad. I had fine-tuned my body into a racing machine, touched my personal peak of athletic endeavour – and I realised this once-in-a-lifetime achievement would never, could never, be repeated. I was sloughing off an old skin to be reborn – in what new form I could only guess. Marriage would have a big say in what I was to become.

Katie and I had first met on the upper floor of a pub in grimy Castleford. It was late October 1958, the 21st birthday party of a mutual friend, and I was just back from France. I would never have dared approach this stunningly well-dressed and beautiful girl, who looked as if she'd just walked in off a film set, but for Gary's mother, doing the catering, who introduced us. The big brown eyes, long blonde hair and immediate warmth of someone who communicated easily put me in thrall. What she said she saw in me was this tall, lean handsome guy with a mop of chestnut hair, looking bronzed and healthy as sin in a cold climate (a description I'm prepared to accept!). Peggy Lee was singing 'Fever' from the record player. It must have been catching. On this enchanted evening we touched hands and danced and nearly fifty years on are still dancing and haven't found the cure.

Katie worked in the textile industry. It wasn't easy being the working girl friend of a professional racing cyclist who spent eight months of every year abroad. Communication had to be mainly by letter. Katie made the trip to France three times in two years, but travelling was prohibitively expensive and her annual holiday allowance small, and with the coureur having no summer holiday, the demands of training and racing got in the way of romance. It was an unsatisfactory state of affairs. It couldn't last and we both knew it.

In August 1960 Katie stayed with the Helions. They got on famously, despite speaking next to nothing of each other's language and it was Huguette who recommended *Le Moulin Enchanté,* an old watermill become restaurant on the banks of the Charente near Ruffec. Here Victor, our resident piscatory expert, had previously offered us a lesson in the art of angling. With an immense cast, he hooked himself to an overhead tree-branch and, as Bill and I fell about laughing, was forced to cut the line. Despite such comic association, a more romantic location than this ancient *moulin* at firefly dusk on the meandering river is hard to imagine. The giant honey-coloured wooden cogwheels made a backdrop to our candlelit table. Our sumptuous four-course meal included a platter of enormous blush-pink, pop-eyed langoustines, speciality of Charente Maritime, supposedly aphrodisiac, which we downed with a sharp white Sauvignon from Bordeaux. Later, over coffee and calvados, we reached agreement. We would marry in Saint Claud and honeymoon in Spain, a privilege few of our background and means could then afford.

Our St Claud friends were delighted – naturally, for it was they who had planted the seed of the idea, my Catholic credentials being confirmed when I became godparent to Lucien's son, Jean-Luc.

It took the best part of ten weeks to overcome all the hurdles of French bureaucracy and the Byzantine rules and regulations surrounding foreigners marrying in France. The twin civil and religious ceremonies meant Church and State each had a stake in the proceedings. But first, I had to 'regularise' my over-stay beyond the six months tourist limit. Testaments to my good character were sought from village worthies: gendarme, mayor and priest. Angoulême Townhall officials then debated the correct 'permission', whether *carte grise, carte de résidence* or *carte de séjour*. Each had its particular purpose to exercise the bureaucatic wit. The *grise* allowed for three months' settled residence, but couldn't simply be tagged on to an overstay. The *résidence,* valid for ten years and privileging me to pay French taxes, might, they debated, be over-egging the cake as I was soon to return to England with my bride. The *séjour* permitted you to work in France for up to six months. Technically, professional cycle racing was 'work', and we had all committed an offence by failing to apply back in February, something they now graciously overlooked. At long last, after much to-ing and fro-ing, a *carte de séjour* was issued.

That was just the beginning. Blood tests commissioned both sides of the Channel were required to certify us free from venereal disease before the civil ceremony could go ahead – there was to be no infecting France with congenital disorders. The Church demanded proof of our Catholic baptism and confirmation, with marriage banns to be posted in both countries. The priests of two nations had to be placated. Nowadays we might well have decided to live together as partners for a trial period, but this was not a real option in respectable 1960 society. Indeed, the French priest sternly lectured us on the duties and responsibilities of marriage and parenthood, an experience of clerical control-freakery that later turned me agnostic.

Lucien was my guide through this bureaucratic maze. When the final 'permission' had been slotted into place, he remarked, with a touch of irony, 'Well, that wasn't so bad now, was it?'

By contrast, the British end was a dream. A letter to the Bordeaux consulate quick-fired a reply with simple instructions on how to register our marriage, all accomplished with a minimum of effort.

On the day itself, after the civil ceremony in the mayor's office, we crossed to enter the ancient candlelit church of St Claud with its Romanesque origins that preceded even our medieval English Queen Eleanor of Aquitaine and her court of troubadors in Poitiers. Stepping down the flagstoned aisle, we were taken aback to see so many full pews. The reason became clear as we emerged from the nuptials and passed beneath an arch of bicycle wheels. C.C. St. Claudais had turned out en masse to witness my relinquishment of *la vie de garçon*. It was a complete surprise. We had been given no inkling of this moving tribute, nor of the reception arranged afterwards in the café/bar, with speeches in our honour and our health drunk in Pinot, that powerful Charentais liqueur notoriously '*très mauvais pour la santé et surtout le foie'*, but nonetheless quaffed in quantity.

At last we were released to Spain, clutching a gift of a plate and cake knife in Limoges porcelain, naturally of *fleur de lys* pattern. '*Gardez-les bien!'* they joked. 'They will serve to cut the cake on your Golden Wedding Anniversary.' We have them still.

39

Road racing is what really counts.

Three main protagonists have animated this tale: young men in pursuit of stardom, cycling itself and France. The years have passed, almost fifty, and much has changed for good and bad in the interim. When has fate ever dealt an equal hand?

The time I spent living in France was to affect me profoundly. I grew to love the country and especially *la vie française* for its spirit of community, close-knit family ties, *chic* and wonderful, wonderful food and wine. The French had many failings, but they knew how to live and to celebrate life. They had little time for contemporary British hang-ups over money, social class and sex. Despite their burdensome bureaucracy and recent enemy occupation, they evinced a spirit of personal freedom, perhaps never expressed better than by the colourful and anarchic cycle race.

And yet, there was much to deplore. Their disorderly governments seemed at war with themselves over Algeria, terrorism was at large, (our Irish troubles lay ahead) and there was a perpetual sense of crisis in newspaper headlines. The education system was stiflingly conservative. There was no *habeas corpus* and harsh Napoleonic penal law gave the police wide powers of search and arrest. This and compulsory identity cards suggested a government, with an eye on bloodstained history, fearful of its own citizens. By contrast with booming Britain, France was relatively impoverished. Outside city churches, you might well encounter beggars. (Imagine that, homeless people begging on the streets!) And there was a big question-mark over French competence. Whenever some disaster overtook them – the collapse of a building or a train smash – we three would share some grim joke about their lack of Anglo-Saxon savvy. They had sunshine and *joie de vivre,* but we had competence. They caved in to Hitler, whilst we held out, assisted by our bulldog grit, pragmatism, inventiveness and natural-born genius. Overall, our sums added up to a feeling of smug superiority.

But France was on the turn and, over four decades,underwent a remarkable transformation. Whilst our wartime victory made us feel complacent and self-satisfied and we clung to the past, they, out of their defeat, embraced their former enemies and worked in unison to reconstruct a new Europe along broadly socialist lines. Later, motivated by US and Thatcher-style individualism, we traded community values for tax cuts that chiefly favoured the rich, whilst they invested in their infrastructure, health service, social benefits and pensions in an effort to share out more equally their burgeoning prosperity. Today it is we, the English, who are suffering from an identity crisis in our me-me culture. Abroad, the former perception of us as warrior gentlemen is tainted with a reputation for impatience, rudeness and hooligan binge-drinking. At home, boasting of low taxation and being the fourth richest nation in the world, we insult our pensioners with means-tested 'charity' and a struggling, historically cash-starved health service. Despite computerisation, incompetence in public and private office is rife – and now, lo and behold, we have a 'Labour' government, with authoritarian instincts and wedded to bureaucracy and spin, that wins elections but appears unworthy of our trust. The French *Non* in the European constitution referendum was a vote against adopting our Blairite, Anglo-Saxon, market-driven, long-hours culture and for retaining their social subsidies. Unrealistic? Unfair? Maybe, but who can blame them? It is not just for the sunshine that thousands of Britons each year emigrate to live in France.

And what of cycle racing, the passion that invested my every waking hour for thirteen youthful years? Abroad, it remains alive and well, and despite football's global domination and the damage done by drugs scandals, holds its place in popular affection. Yet poor recruitment at grass roots bodes ill for its future. Young people no longer come forward in anything like the numbers of fifty years ago. C.C. Saint Claudais long since went to the wall, typical of many small clubs unable to retain a viable membership. Even the once mighty BCR, founded in the penny-farthing era, is increasingly reliant on ageing veterans for its continuance. 'Young people nowadays want the easy life,' Pierre remarked to me in 1996, shortly before his death. 'Cycling is too tough.' He was right. Youngsters, ever more sedentary, succumb to the allure of computer games, junk food and 'soft' sports that eschew the full-time dedication and quasi-monastic lifestyle of the serious athlete. Moreover, to achieve the peak of physical fitness they have further to climb: people of my generation grew naturally fit and lean out of labour-intensive employment and having only their own two legs to get them about. Tumbling time-trial records, you ask? These are deceptive. They owe much to aerodynamic state-of-art bicycle and sportswear technology. Put the exceptional Boardman on an ordinary bike and even he struggles to surpass the World Hour Record achieved by Eddy Mercx thirty years before. The true barometer of decline is in athletics where our best male track and road middle and long distance runners operate well below the standards of earlier decades. Though Africans chip away at the London Marathon record, ever fewer homebased athletes achieve the once three hours' target of the good club runner. Sedentary life-styles, bad diets and obesity in childhood cast long shadows over the quality and appeal of athletic competition in the developed world. Good news, perhaps, for golf, darts and snooker, but bad for cycling.

In fact, for road racing in Britain, the news has been remarkably bad for some years. The sport suffers not only from a low media profile and, consequently, poor recruitment, but riders face training and racing in a traffic-bound, life-threatening environment. Confusingly, whilst the bicycle is repeatedly voted the greatest of modern inventions and successive governments advocate its health rewards, little has been done to counter the strident and intolerant propaganda of motoring lobbyists and petrolheads integral to the threat. Simply put, they want the bicycle off *'their'* roads. From my observation, this highway war is a uniquely British disease, a nasty leftover from our class system and past failures to promote the sport. Continental motorists are much more respectful and tolerant of the velo. Why? Because over there the long tradition of cycle road racing has promoted the cyclist as an athlete, someone to be admired and entitled to his place on the highway, and not, as in Britain, an urban guerrilla or foolhardy pedal-pushing eccentric unable to afford a better mode of transport. Unsurprisingly, responsible parents think twice before encouraging their offspring to compete in such a hostile fearful climate.

It all looked so different in the optimistic, traffic-lite 50s. Writing in 1958 of Britons racing abroad, the late-lamented journalist, Jock Wadley, rosily prophesied:

'...the determination of our 'caravanners' and other enthusiasts will one day surely mean Britain's establishment as one of the top road-racing nations of the world.'

The omens then certainly looked good. Ian Steel with his 1952 Peace Race victory set a marker. The Hercules team, on a steep learning curve, did amazingly well and Brian Robinson later became the first Briton contracted to a French team, and first to win stages of the Tour de France. At the amateur level, Stan Brittain was 1956 Olympics road race silver medallist and twice came close to emulating Steel's victory in Warsaw–Berlin–Prague. Our own venture by ambulance showed that the DIY approach to continental racing was a viable option and strong performances by Jock, Victor and Simpson inspired imitators. The formation of the BCF in 1959 brought unity and promise of further improvement. British riders featured regularly in the Tour. Hoban became a stage and classics winner, Simpson, Graham Webb and Beryl Burton world champions. There was such talent in depth: Booty, Geddes, Holmes, Sheil, Blower, Alan Jackson, Bill Bradley, Alan Ramsbottom (16th in the 1963 Tour), Vin Denson, Derek Harrison, Sid Barras and a host of others challenging at the highest level. Above all, the racing calendar back home was expanding and provided for all riders, professional down to third-category amateur. Take, for example, a typical Sunday in July, 1954 when the BLRC handbook featured 21 road races and compare this with the weekend of 3rd July, 2005 where BC offered a mere 13. There was a base from which to build.

Of course, we did not live in a risk-obsessed society and litigation fears were not the barriers they are today in designing courses. Light traffic enabled use of the whole road network, including the mountains of the Lake District, Wales and Scotland. The Circuits of Britain sponsored by Quaker Oats (1954-56) were amongst the toughest amateur events in Europe and gave riders like me a taste of long-distance stage racing through mountainous terrain, which proved invaluable when I transferred to France, something that short circuit racing can never emulate. Above all, we had political-savvy officials, the likes of Charles Messenger, Bob Thom, Vic Humphrey, Eddie Lawton, Dick Aldridge, Bob Frood-Barclay, Percy Stallard and others, people driven by messianic zeal to promote their beloved sport on a shoestring. There was also, at first, the spur of competition with the NCU (one wonders if unity without competition risks creating remote monopolies, a charge that has been levelled at BC?).

Fifty years on and there is little of Wadley's optimism left. To develop our young talent beyond nursery level, we must still export it abroad to learn the trade, partly on charity, the worthy

Dave Rayner fund. At home, cycling generally rates in the public eye down alongside carpet bowls. To be fair, BC, formerly BCF, (one worries about an organisation in difficulty that suddenly severs the federal link with the past and rebrands itself as a monopoly. Why?) admits as much, but blames factors outside its control:

> The profile of the sport isn't high enough (to attract rich sponsors) because the Great British Public are basically only interested in established British sports like football and cricket, or sporting events that take place in Britain (e.g. Wimbledon), or in success at the Olympics. (BC President Brian Cookson, *LVRC newsletter* 2003)

True, but that begs the question why, after 140 years, cycling isn't already an 'established British sport' when there is a bike in every home? Is it right to blame it all on 'the Great British Public'?

On the question of profile, it is well worth considering the structure of road racing abroad. The Tour de France is the flagship event commanding worldwide media attention. But the Tour alone could never support a full-time professional class. The Tour is the beating heart that feeds other organs of body cycling and receives vital sustenance in return. All the various national Tours, the Giro, Vuelta and lesser regional stage races, contribute, and, to continue the analogy, so do the arteries, veins and capillaries of the single day classics and thousands upon thousands of minor road races across the Continent, both professional and amateur. All are mutually interdependent and play their part, large or small, in keeping the sport alive and in the public eye. Continental cycling grew organically from around 1865 and with it the prestige, respect and media attention that today guarantee its influence with public bodies, such as governments, local authorities and the police. Above all, it is interlocked with community. (I can imagine no situation on the continent where a road race promoter would be told by a local police superintendent, 'We will have you off the road in a few years time', as has happened over here. The community would not permit it.)

British road racing has no body. That is the problem: no permanent race structure to speak of on the continental model, just a series of stuttering starts and stops. With no bankable tradition, low prestige and low expectations are inevitable (where would tennis be without Wimbledon?). Consequently, it enjoys little respect or influence outside the sport. Two opportunities to create such a body have been lost. In the 1890s F. T. Bidlake and his cronies surrendered to the horse and carriage lobby and abandoned road racing in favour of time-trialing. They touched the forelock and admitted to their lowly place in society. They could not possibly have foreseen the dire consequences of that decision. At a stroke it severed us from the Continent and all the benefits for cycling and cyclists here that would have accrued. It thwarted the formation of a professional class with eye-catching potential for a homegrown Tour and classic offshoots. It ensured that a huge amount of energy and talent was diverted into the publicity-free zone of time-trialling, where much of it still resides to this day. So began fifty years of divorce from community and 'meddling in cycling's affairs', the foolish separatist philosophy that Dave Orford, a community-relations exponent, bitterly dubs 'cycling for cyclists'. Then came our second opportunity in 1942. We all know the story, how Stallard and company formed the BLRC precisely to put Britain back onto a footing with the Continent and create a body cycling we could all be proud of.

The BLRC had real passion for road racing and it is tempting to wonder whether the outcome would have been better if it had remained in sole control and not been forced into the 1958 shotgun wedding with the NCU under pressure from the Home Office (the threat was to end negotiations on the right to race on public roads enshrined in the 1960s Highways Act, thanks to the BLRC). Typical of the infectious NCU strand of early BCF thinking was promoting Britain's first ever stage of the Tour de France fourteen times up and down the wretched Plymouth by-pass: it was the mentality of the 1930s' closed circuit. The Tour of Britain's lost years, the demise of televised city centre criteriums and our World Cup Races have been damaging, whilst entrepreneurship (evinced by flagship race promoter Alan Rushton) seems, for whatever reason, to have run into the buffers. In 2003, the correspondence columns of *Cycling Weekly* were deluged with complaints of BC – publicly funded with a stream of salaried officials to do its bidding – turning its back on road racing and the grass roots.

Abroad, doughty Britons – Wegelius, Wiggins, Hayles, Hunt, Winn, the immensely talented Hammond and others – still fly the flag, but none since Robert Millar has looked likely to fill a top spot in the Tour or become points winner in the Vuelta (Malcolm Elliott 1989). We can all laud the splendid achievements of Yates, Boardman and David Millar, time-trial specialists who captured the yellow jersey. But the first two are now history, and Millar about to attempt a difficult come-back from a drugs scandal. And none was a great climber, for it is in the mountains where the Tour is won and lost. Out there somewhere in the general population, languishing undiscovered, may be our own all-round Ulrich or Armstrong. The question is whether he would ever be recruited into a sport like cycling with its lack-of-image problem.

BC claims to have the answer: to by-pass the road. It will focus on and recruit to the track, 'the more controllable and predictable environment'. It cites the example of Australia where 'currently successful road professionals O'Grady and McGee began their careers on their country's track squad' and it claims early success here 'in the form of (track stars) Bradley Wiggins and Rob Hayles – both now members of Division One pro road teams'. That was two years ago, and for two years, and the first time since 1955, Britain has had no representative in the Tour. But we must give it more time. Professional roadmen have to serve a demanding apprenticeship and we should not expect too much too soon.

There are obvious flaws in this plan. Track and road are very different disciplines and it does not follow that success on one leads to success on the other. Former track stars tend to do what you would expect: they win sprint finishes and points competitions (yes, that would be nice!), but not, as yet, big stage races, where the climbers see them off. Also, too narrow a focus on track and circuit racing risks neglecting those with different abilities. Vic Sutton's forte was as a climber. He was no track or circuit rider. If that was where he had had to prove himself, I doubt he would ever have been discovered, much less selected for a national squad.

And there is another danger in the track/circuit philosophy. What is to stop some future track-struck administration abandoning the road altogether? We no longer need it, they may say. Let's negotiate away our right to race on the traffic-congested highways in return for the promise of funding to build a string of purpose-built circuits. Fanciful? Not at all! The chairman of the League of Veteran Racing Cyclists, speaking personally in 2003, advanced a similar solution to the problem. Oh dear! Abandon our birthright for a string of Eastways? A petrolhead could not have put it better.

It may come to that, but I would rather hang on to the slim hope of a miracle changing the climate for cycling in our crowded isle. What would it need? Profile is, indeed, crucial. Simpson was once a media ikon, BBC Sports Personality of the Year. His fall from grace left a deep scar on the image of British cycling. Now we need a second coming, a whiter than white high profile ambassador for the media to latch onto (a male version of gutsy Nicole Cooke?). Whilst, importantly, Olympic track successes produced a golden rain of funding, the publicity value proved ephemeral. Road racing is what really counts. Nothing, but nothing, could possibly match the immense prestige and political patronage that would accrue from a Briton winning the Tour de France. Dream along with me. Just imagine the scene: Blair meeting Chirac on the steps of the Elysée Palace, milking our victory for all its worth. Observe the smirk on that man's face as he puts one over on the French! Another Agincourt! Another Trafalgar! And imagine the aftermath, the doors that would open to cycling in Britain. Titter ye may, but, sadly, in my opinion, a miracle is our best hope for the future: our third and probably last chance to create a body cycling.

EPILOGUE

'Oui, coureur cycliste anglais.' I bit my tongue. God knows where that had come from.

I still live in hope of witnessing that miracle. My French friends were extremely patriotic, but also fair-minded and would have rejoiced with me and laughed at Blair – 'would' because, alas, for Pierre, Eliane, Raymond and Lucien, it is too late. They are all deceased, though my godson estate agent Jean-Luc sells property in Charente to an ever-expanding clientele of British incomers, wooing them with tales of his cycling godfather.

As for the rest, none of us, fortunately, ever had to live off sugar lumps or the dole. Bill quickly remarried and went to live in prosperous Switzerland, his bride's homeland. Derek created a successful electrical business in Brighton. Alan never quite got France out of his blood and now resides in a converted mill in the Dordogne.

After his marriage to Shirley, Victor found his true metier in salesmanship, running a thriving jewelery shop in Cottingham. I became godfather to one of his children. He never lost interest in road racing and, after retirement, made a successful come-back in the 60+ veteran category, culminating in a fine ride in the 1999 *L'Étape du Tour*, a hilly 200 kilometres in the Auvergne which he covered at a rapid 25 kph. Sadly, two weeks later, he collapsed during a veterans' road race and died from a heart condition. He always cherished his memories of our years in France and the stardom he achieved there. He was laid to rest with the BCR's tricolore enamel badge pinned to his lapel.

I guess, when our time comes, all of us would choose Victor's way of going over Jock's, if we could: swift, painless, carefree, doing what we love, and if not actually racing then during a bike ride or at the café stop in the company of friends, head down into our favourite platter of nosh as the waitress rushes over with the bill and the blazing angel in the dark tunnel of Eternity waves the chequered flag.

Jock's way, by contrast, was bundled and painfully drawn out. When Victor and I quit, he continued racing alone in Normandy, living with Tiny and the children in Bill's caravan. But domestic pressures to care for his new family abroad proved overwhelming and he also quit and returned to England in 1961. He named his son Louison, in Bobet's honour, and eventually put his motoring and upholstery expertise to work on vintage cars. His skills were in great demand and his workshop in Wiltshire resembled a motoring museum, bulging with priceless old vehicles awaiting restoration.

But for him nothing could take the place of cycling: his true vocation, as he believed, to have been a sprinter-roadman of the quality of Hoban or Elliott. This was no impossible dream. He had the gutsy talent of one who stands on the podium and reaches for the sky. Only twelve professionals bettered him in a world championship race, most with the help of drugs he repudiated. Somewhere, somehow he went wrong, allowed his single-minded focus to slip and the opportunity passed him by. There was no way back.

Tape-recording his memories for this book, we reminisced together for hours. He was recovering from a tardy operation for bowel cancer, which had been originally misdiagnosed. Despite that, the prognosis was good. But then he phoned to say he had started with chest pains, a muscle strain according to his incompetent GP. In reality, the cancer had spread to his lungs and he underwent radiotherapy. It failed, and Christmas 1999 saw him occupying a hospital bed close to the exit. He was in a coma, apparently terminal. 'I was dreaming,' he told me, 'that I was on my bike – in a race, busting for a pee. I hopped off at the roadside and found myself wandering out of bed, trailing all these bloomin' tubes behind me. The staff rushed in to put me back. "You shouldn't be here," they said. I knew what they meant, but I'd been a bike rider and didn't give up that easy.'

He spoke optimistically of being in remission and booking himself a springtime holiday in Italy. He had a yearning to retrace the route of the 1959 Rome–Naples–Palermo, the part Vespa-paced race in which he had given his all to assist Bobet. But it was the morphine talking. He died at the end of March, just as the trees along the route were bursting green out of bud.

So, of us three comrades, only I remain to tell the tale. 'Follow your star to the bitter end...' advocated F. A. Mitchell-Hedge. Quitting cycle racing, I abandoned one star to pursue another: to get the best education I could and take my life forward. I accepted a temporary job and studied in my spare time by correspondence course to acquire the minimum qualifications for university entrance. It was a hard slog, but I gave myself up wholeheartedly, just as I had to cycling, and after eight months' study was in a position to apply for a place at Leeds to read French. There, bizarrely, my interview took a strangely familiar twist.

The gowned professor behind his desk flicked rather dismissively through my application form. He glanced up to ask what I had read.

'Some Racine, Molière, a Balzac or two' – I gave him a list of classic French authors. He looked sceptical, maybe assuming I had just dipped into an encyclopaedia.

'In the original?'

I nodded. His patronising manner was beginning to grate. As he continued reading, the gloomy book-lined walls seemed to be pressing inwards. From a niche shelf beside a model sailing dinghy, a bust of Voltaire peered mockingly over the professor's shoulder and in the breathless silence I imagined I could hear the tapping of his tropical fish on their aquarium glass.

At last he found another subject worthy of inquiry. He dabbed the page with an accusing finger, expressing incredulity.

'Racing cyclist?'

'Oui, coureur cycliste anglais.' I bit my tongue. God knows where that had come from. It had just slipped out.

He stared disapprovingly as I expanded on my life in France, cutting me short with an irritable gesture.

'Just how old are you?' he muttered, searching the pages.

At twenty-seven, I was probably far too old to match his ideal profile of the young sixth form student fresh from school. Eighteen was the tabla rasa age preferred. 'Mature' students were considered 'over the hill', even if they spoke French with a good accent, were well read and had actually lived the culture. It was evident he had made up his mind and he foreclosed with a metaphor from the then élitist world of yachting. 'I have to say you're way off your moorings.' The formal rejection slip followed in the post.

I had felt sure my experience would have counted in my favour, but I was wrong. He was blinkered. Just as some French people could not reconcile English with racing cyclist, so he could not reconcile racing cyclist with intellect. Prejudice cemented both concepts into far opposing camps.

That might have been that. But cycling setbacks had toughened me to the world of hard knocks and taught me to be dogged.

Recalling reculer pour mieux sauter, I accepted the offer of a place at a college of education where my maturity, broad experience and self-motivation were indeed welcome. Three years later, after qualifying with distinction, I received backing from the college principal to reapply to university. This time I was accepted to read for an honours degree in English, on a shortened two years' course that took account of my unusual background.

I have never regretted my decision to stop racing when I did. The rigours of the professional sport demanded too much of my inherited constitution. It made no sense each year having to battle to pay off an overdraft of ill health before I could bank any fitness or indeed money. Despite giving of my best, I sensed I had reached a plateau of achievement by 1960 and my morale was in serious decline. I could have carried on for several years, but to what purpose? I was a good rider and capable of a top twenty place in any big stage race, given experience and fortune's fair wind. But I was not, and never would become, an ace. And the permanent role of domestique did not appeal. Driven to succeed at any price, I would undoubtedly have slipped into the drugs culture just like the rest. One had to be realistic. It was time for me to hitch a ride on another star.

But I have much to thank cycling for and am glad I took up the sport in my teens. It was not time wasted, delaying a career in a 'proper job', but an important part of my pre-university education, filling gaps in the obsessively academic grammar school curriculum. Cycling with my brother; I visited museums, old churches, battlefields and sites of historical and archaeological interest. History was brought to life and my curiosity stimulated. I acquired self-sufficiency and the ability to weigh risk against advantage. My cycling inheritance includes a blessed cussedness, useful in facing down bullies, snobs, zealots, the righteous and hubristic. I measure off their arrogant display against their real worth and often think to myself, 'I'd love to see you on the start line of a bike race, mate!'

In later life I have been fortunate to enjoy much better health. At seventy-two I still follow sport obsessively and, though I rarely cycle nowadays, have become a competitive runner over every sort of terrain and every distance up to and including the marathon. I shall continue to run for as long as I can, or until I drop.

The author at the finish of the London marathon, 2000.